Sɪᴍᴏɴ Pᴇᴀʀsᴏɴ's first-class Oxford degree led to an M.Litt. on D.H. Lawrence and the Apocalypse. He is now the head of English at a tutorial college in London.

Other titles in this series

A BRIEF HISTORY OF

THE END OF THE WORLD

SIMON PEARSON

CARROLL & GRAF PUBLISHERS
New York

Carroll & Graf Publishers
An imprint of Avalon Publishing Group, Inc.
245 W. 17th Street
11th Floor
New York NY 10011–5300
www.carrollandgraf.com

AVALON
publishing group incorporated

First published in the UK by Robinson,
an imprint of Constable & Robinson Ltd, 2006

First Carroll & Graf edition, 2006

ISBN-13: 978 0 78671 825 2
ISBN-10: 0 7867 1825 0

Printed and bound in the EU

In loving memory of Cynthia Pearson (1927–2006).
For whom there will be no end to our love.

PERMISSIONS

CONTENTS

ACKNOWLEDGEMENTS

This book would not have been written had it not been for the inspiration provided by Norman Cohn's wonderful work over the years. Anyone writing about such a subject is always walking in the shadow of this giant. A big thank you to Becky Hardie, an exacting editor but always a right one; to Saul David who liked the idea and gave invaluable advice and encouragement; to David Wyatt whose voluminous library on obscure theological issues I regularly raided; to Alasdair Brown for being a stimulating and generous-hearted colleague; to Tom Callaghan whose expertise on Hitler I regularly picked. Finally, a big debt of gratitude to Khadija, Eddy and Luca – for all the holidays, family outings and housework I missed.

INTRODUCTION

Apocalypse, Armageddon, *dies irae*, doomsday, or simply the End: there are a number of ways of referring to the end of the world just as there are many ways of reacting to just such a prospect. For some, it will involve a gigantic fireball as predicted in the *Book of Revelation*. For others, an asteroid, an alien-invasion or an ecological disaster will deal the killer blow. Whatever the means of destruction – metaphysical, interplanetary, man-made or biological – the prospect of global annihilation has been a constant in western consciousness down through the centuries. Sectarians and cult members, prophets and visionaries, oddballs and eccentrics: all of them have been predicting the end of the world since time immemorial. There seems to be no end to prophecies about the End of the World.

From a biblical perspective the End of the World is associated particularly with the *Book of Revelation* in the New Testament and the earlier *Book of Daniel* in the Hebrew Bible.

These two books form the mainstay of an apocalyptic tradition which has inspired and terrified in equal measure. The destruction of the world is also a part of the glorious consummation of God's plans – the total and utter transformation of the existing order of things. In its original biblical sense an apocalypse has this dual character; it is both destructive and consummating. God finally destroys the world only to replace it with a heavenly world which is infinitely superior to the former earthly one. Etymologically the word 'apocalypse' is derived from the Greek *apokalypsis*, from the verb 'to lift the lid off something', whence comes its secondary, more poetic meaning 'the lifting of a veil, a sudden revelation'. This was what the author of the *Book of Revelation* underwent on the Greek island of Patmos when he was exiled there sometime between AD 65 and 100. In one sudden instance, God lifted the lid to reveal the ultimate metaphysical reality – the supremacy of divine power over earthly. Strictly speaking, then, an apocalypse is a narrative which depicts how God grants his selected prophet or saint a vision or revelation of things that remain hidden to the rest of us. An angel or some such divine being is the bearer of the revelation; the prophet learns about *some* of the secrets of God's ultimate purpose, about how the world will end and how the dead will be judged.

Because of the violent connotations that apocalypse has many biblical scholars and theologians prefer the more sober, academic sounding term 'eschatology' (from Greek, *eskhatos*, 'last') when they refer to Jewish, Christian or Muslim beliefs about the final events and God's purpose concerning the whole of the created order. For some theologians and biblical scholars, 'apocalypse' and its derivative 'apocalyptic' have the smack of sectarian extremism about them. They conjure up visions of the old man with the placard informing us that the 'End of the World is Nigh'. Rather than denoting some divinely inspired revelatory experience, apocalypse is now a catchall word used to describe a particularly destructive event or process. However, I shall be using the term both in its biblical sense and also in its popular sense. After all, the term is now part of the currency of everyday discourse and has been thoroughly secularized. It can be used to describe wars, massacres, the destruction of the biosphere and the AIDS pandemic.

In its biblical sense, apocalypse still exerts a powerful grip on the modern imagination. According to a 2002 *Time/CNN* poll, 59 per cent of Americans believe that the events prophesied in the *Book of Revelation* will occur in the future.[1] The majority of American citizens believe therefore that the destruction of the world is the glorious consummation of God's plans. For many Americans, there is no contradiction between pursuing happiness on earth and looking forward happily to earth's imminent destruction.

To suggest, however, that end-time myths are unique to the Jewish and Christian faiths would be wrong. Myths of many ancient cultures depict similarly cataclysmic events to those described in the *Book of Genesis* and the *Book of Revelation*. Legends about floods and fires, destructive earthquakes and storms abound in many different cultures and societies. Cosmic battles between fractious deities continually break out. Many of these myths and legends pre-date the Jewish and Christian apocalypse by many hundreds of years. The end of the world did not originate in the Bible. End-myths have been around since pre-history. Zoroastrianism, for example, is an ancient religion originating in Persia, often credited as being the first truly eschatological religion.[2]

In the Zoroastrian world-view, the world is destined to end in a fiery apocalypse which brings about a total transformation of the world rather than simply a renewal of it. When compared to the world-view of another ancient people, the Vedic Indians, it can be appreciated just what a radical departure this represents. In the ancient Hindu scriptures, the world does not come to an end. Instead, cycles of history play out against vast expanses of time. When the solar system disintegrates, it is only a temporary lull before a new cosmos arises, phoenix-like, from the ashes. For the Vedic Indians, the cosmos is a place racked by the brute power of nature – earthquakes, floods and torrential rain continually being unleashed on it. Terrible as these destructive forces might appear, however, the cosmic order will always prevail. Cosmos triumphs over chaos. This is the opposite of what happens in apocalyptic faiths. In the end-myths of the Zoroastrians, and then later in that of the Jews, Christians and Muslims, the world ends in an incandescent blaze of destruction. The old world disappears utterly only to be replaced by a totally transformed new order of things.

What can account for the pervasiveness of such destructive fantasies? As Mark Twain observed, 'History doesn't repeat itself, but it rhymes.' In other words, our ancestors' patterns of belief are never duplicated exactly but reformulated in sounds which approximate to each other. The evolutionary biologist Richard Dawkins would regard the recurrence of apocalyptic myths in human history as a 'virus' that humanity periodically catches and falls foul of. In such a view, an outbreak of apocalyptic-itis can lay low whole communities and nations. Dawkins sets about religious leaders, Christian or Muslim, because they peddle the myth of immortality for those who are prepared to die for their faith. The 9/11 suicide bombers allowed themselves to be turned into guided missiles because they had been duped into believing that a posthumous reward awaited them.[3]

Others have sought a less divisive explanation for the pervasiveness of religiously inspired beliefs about the end of the world. From a Jungian perspective, human beings throughout history have always dreamt of the same things – it is just the symbols by which those dreams are expressed that are different. Accounts of cataclysmic battles abound in the myths and beliefs of many different peoples: in Hindu and Buddhist scriptures, in Roman and Greek myths, second-century Chinese writings and in Norse mythology. These can be compared to the most famous apocalyptic battle of all – the *Book of Revelation's* Armageddon. Here a militant Christ rides into battle against the forces of evil. In the other great apocalyptic faith, Islam, an equally violent end awaits the enemies of God.

The flood symbol too is a common apocalyptic type. In *Genesis*, the original flood precedes Creation when 'the earth was without form and void: and darkness was upon the face of the deep'.[4] The first act of God's creation was to separate light from darkness, the second the separation of the land from the sea. Later, God sends a flood to destroy man and the animal kingdom, sparing only Noah and the other occupants of the ark. Although this is the most famous flood-myth in world religion, it is by no means the only one. In fact, floods abound in many ancient myths and belief systems. That God or the gods should get angry with man and want to destroy him with water is a common occurrence. There is a flood in the ancient Babylonian *Epic of Gilgamesh*; in classical myth Zeus attempts to destroy mankind with a flood. In Hinduism there is the deluge of Vishnu. Flood myths can also be found in the myths of Peru and in China, in the myths of the Australian Aboriginals as well as those of the Native Americans. These myths come from vastly different cultures and societies but a common theme can be discerned. The human world has become corrupted and contaminated. For the world to be cleansed it must be destroyed – in part or as a whole.

What historical, social and psychological complexities inform such destructive visions of the world? The end of the world has been theorized as a psychic state. Jung revealed how the flood image is common to diverse civilizations and existential conditions in time. For him, it is expressive of our collective desires and dreams, those universal and largely unchanging fantasies which influence our behaviour, both private and political. The process of psychological 'individuation' involves breaking down past attitudes and conceptions about existence and synthesizing and transforming them into new attitudes and conceptions. We readily embrace catastrophe in order to attain a new state of wholeness. In such a view, the radical images of Apocalypse – deluges and great balls of fire – are not literal prophecies but metaphors for a destructive and transformative process that will bring psychic health.[5]

Others have offered a more social and political explanation. Political revolutionaries have sought inspiration from *Revelation* because it admits of the possibility of a radical and total change for the better. It holds out the promise of an absolute rupture with the past and the coming into being of a completely transformed present. In the Jewish and Christian tradition, apocalyptic texts fortify the oppressed and the downtrodden with reassurances that their trials and tribulations will eventually be rewarded in a glorious consummation. In either some future millennial state on earth or in heaven, the blessed will be rewarded with a special position while their enemies languish for eternity in hell.

*

In secular ideologies such an end-time scenario can be reimagined in social and political terms. For Marx, apocalyptic faith was an attempt to remedy the injustices of society. For him, it was a pained but futile response to suffering. Nevertheless Judaeo-Christian apocalyptic belief imbues his theory of the historical process. Like in apocalyptic thought, Marx's conception of time is very linear and end-oriented. After a period of revolutionary upheaval, a new age will be ushered in. It was social revolutionaries, not Christ returning on clouds of glory, who would create a paradise on earth, an uncorrupted world of brotherly equality and love.

The influence of the apocalypse myth on secular literature is an important strand in modern literary criticism. There's a whole branch of literary study which credits the Bible as the most important element in shaping and structuring the imaginations of writers down through the ages. Literary critics like Frank Kermode have theorized about how the apocalypse myth has an archetypal significance in western consciousness, influencing our conceptions of time and the narratives we construct.[6] A writer like D.H. Lawrence does not just simply use biblical analogies in order to give his work a doomsday flavour. For him, the Bible is a constitutive and structural part of his mind. Reality is refracted through the often lurid and strange prism of apocalyptic texts, principal of which is the *Book of Revelation*. The great late Canadian critic, Northrop Frye, termed the Bible 'the Great Code', and regarded it as the pre-eminent western storehouse of types, images, language and narratives which inspired one great writer after another in the western canon.[7]

The *Book of Revelation* has also been a great storehouse of inspiration to visual artists for the last two thousand years. From Hieronymus Bosch's extraordinary creatures to Michelangelo's masterpiece *The Last Judgement* and William Blake's mystical paintings, apocalyptic imagery has been an important part of the western tradition in art. One of the most exciting and memorable art events of the millennial year was the exhibition *Apocalypse: Beauty and Horror in Contemporary Art* held at the Royal Academy, London. As we were poised at the threshold of a new millennium, Jake and Dino Chapman's *Hell* reminded us of the horrors that had taken place in the century that was just about to close.

It contains over five thousand figures, all painstakingly made and painted by hand, as well as nine different landscapes containing a range of buildings and vehicles. The rectangular landscapes are mounted on rickety wooden trestles arranged in the shape of a swastika . . . In the centre, a volcano spews out Nazis. The landscapes are killing fields where tortures and punishments . . . are meted out to Nazis by naked mutant figures. Body parts, skeletons and skulls are strewn everywhere.[8]

The horrors of twentieth-century history – the trenches, the Holocaust, the threat of nuclear destruction – inform such a vision. It is a modern-day equivalent to Bruegel's apocalyptic *The Triumph of Death* (c.1562) which graphically depicts the wholesale destruction of humanity at the hands of an army of skeletons. In the past, such demonic visions terrified people into submission. Religious authorities could point to such images and whip up the spectre of imminent apocalyptic destruction as a way of extracting obedience and submission from the laity. For many of us today, the agents of destruction are no longer metaphysical but man-made: weapons of mass destruction, 'dirty' bombs and biological weapons. Many believe these are the instruments by which mankind will finally destroy himself. Man's wrath, not God's, will put pay to the world. In such a secular scenario, there is the apocalypse but no millennium. In other words, the end of the world is purely destructive. No new golden age will come after.

In contrast, those who have faith see apocalypse as destructive-consummating. In a world racked by such uncertainties and insecurities, apocalyptic myths wrest order out of disorder, meaning out of the chaos. There is a predetermined grand finale to history. A beginning implies an end. As Frank Kermode contends, ends are comforting. They give meaning to what has gone before and what will come after, congruence and shape to the hurly-burly of history. In times of cultural crisis, they can act as the equivalent of comfort food, providing sustenance and solace in an age of desperation and turmoil. John's glimpse of the whole span of time, from Alpha, the beginning, to Omega, the end, gives shape and hope to what would otherwise be an undifferentiated jumble of chaotic events. The grand ending envisioned in the *Revelation* is also a reminder of our little ending, our own death – inevitable and unavoidable.

'All's well that ends', someone once said. Suffering is bearable if we know that the end of time is imminent. For believers, Jewish, Christian or Muslim, the end of the old world issues in the dawn of a new, golden age. In order to hasten the end, adherents of these faiths scour contemporary history for 'signs' in order to confirm that they are indeed living in the end-times. In traditional apocalyptic belief, these signs are wars, famines and plagues. Since there's never a shortage of these, a continual state of heightened expectancy becomes the norm. Things simply cannot get any worse, we fondly imagine. But they do and somehow we carry on despite this.

Like every age, we believe that our one is uniquely decadent and therefore ripe for apocalyptic destruction. End-time scenarios crowd out our collective imaginations. Perhaps what heightens our doom-laden mood is the new communication technology. Terrible images of the latest terrorist outrage can be filmed on a mobile phone one moment, distributed around the world via the Internet the next. Prophets of doom therefore can spread their messages quicker and further than ever before. Within hours of the planes slamming into the Twin Towers or Hurricane Katrina hitting New Orleans, the Jeremiahs and Cassandras were out in cyberspace, interpreting the unfolding events in apocalyptic terms. On the web, a North Carolina pastor quickly came to see the 2005 New Orleans flood disaster as God's vengeance for America's role in expelling Jews from Gaza.[9]

The single apocalyptic event is now increasingly being experienced as a series of endings. Each successive development in communications technology means a fresh bombardment of images and ideas. Our apocalyptic imaginations are fired like never before by twenty-four hour rolling news operations such as CNN, beaming the latest disaster into our homes. Bird flu is the current one: for several years the highly pathogenic strain known as H5N1 has spread across Asia. Now it has arrived in many countries in Europe, causing widespread alarm. Images of flu-infected chickens fill our screens. No wonder many of us feel unable to cope and take refuge in age-old beliefs that the End is in sight. Such a myth is enabling because it helps us to make sense of what would otherwise be a chaotic jumble of news, disasters and ideas that come hurtling towards us at unprecedented speed.

The ultimate irony is that the greater our scientific and technological achievements, the greater our potential for creating chaos and destroying the world. Nowhere is this better illustrated than in the demented scaremongering that surrounded the new millennium. Before 9/11 became the focus of all our fears and uncertainties, it was the prospect of a catastrophic failure of technology that fulfilled the role. Doom-mongers predicted that mainframes would crash around the world in succession as their date systems rolled 1999 over into 2000. Known as the 'millennium time bomb' or simply 'Y2K' (Year 2000), the millennium celebrations were shot through with fear and anxiety as experts predicted the crash of everything from cash dispensers to missile systems, causing a global economic, political and social catastrophe. In the event, planes did not fall from the sky; I did not even have to reset my VCR. That brief temporal moment, when 1999 turned into 2000, was heavily freighted with meaning. All our fears about technology failing us were focused and brought to the fore at that moment.

Although the time bomb failed to detonate, fears about computer-generated chaos are still pervasive. Ironically the latest and most complex communications technology is being used to propagate some of the oldest and most 'primitive' beliefs about the end of the world. Tap in 'Apocalypse' on Google and you get over two million hits. 'Armageddon' yields a similarly high number. Cyberspace is now the haven for UFO enthusiasts, eco-prophets, doomsday merchants, New Agers and millennial cult members. Any one can now set up their apocalyptic cult and begin to proselytize worldwide, all from the comfort of their own living room. The fact that any one can peddle anything on the Net makes it completely random, purposeless and utterly devoid of morality. It is an unregulated state of chaos in which the child pornographer rubs shoulders with the great writer; where you can learn how to study a Shakespeare sonnet or make a shoe bomb.

In previous generations fears about modern technology focused on the ever-expanding nuclear arsenals. In the Cold War era, the end of the world was envisaged as a mushrooming cloud ascending into the heavens. Atomic bombs and then hydrogen bombs of increasing megatonnage engendered a Cold War psychosis. The nuclear endgame was figured in the old apocalyptic terms. The biblical Armageddon was recast in order to denote the magnitude of the destructive potential of warfare between the superpowers. Such an eventuality was the ultimate irony. Conceived in the nineteenth century as the saviour of mankind, science and technology have now given us the capacity to destroy the world several times over. In this respect, Albert Einstein has become an iconic figure. It was his equation $e = mc^2$ which was the basis for the development of the atomic bomb.

With the collapse of the Berlin Wall in 1989 and the cessation of the nuclear arms race, new enemies emerged to threaten America and its western allies. A big word like apocalypse was again on everyone's lips to describe the events of 9/11.

Fireballs, toppling towers, and a terrorist network inspired by its own apocalyptic beliefs lent a metaphysical significance to the event. A watershed in world affairs had been reached. The event was a before and an after. The Christian Right in America and Islamists both see 9/11 as the opening salvo in a cosmic war which will run for generations. For both sides, the enemy is the absolute incarnation of evil. In such a religiously charged atmosphere apocalyptic beliefs do not simply represent acts of violence and extremism. They actually help to engender them.

George W. Bush's 'war on terror' has a new enemy within its sights – Iran's president, Mahmoud Ahmadinejad. Since being elected in June 2005, he has talked about how the country should prepare for judgement day and about his desire to wipe Israel off the face of the map. The Islamic republic's nuclear bomb ambitions raises the distinct prospect of Washington taking military action which would spark violence across the Middle East and reprisals in the West. The ante was truly upped in April 2006 when Ahmadinejad announced that Iran now had the capacity to produce enriched uranium. In other parts of the Muslim world, apocalyptic beliefs are proving to be just as potent. They might inspire the Palestinian suicide bomber to blow himself up in Israel, or al-Qaeda cells to do their worst in western cities or in Bali or Kenya.

Meanwhile, in America Christian militias stockpile weapons and supplies in the belief that a 'holy war' is about to break out in their own backyard. The enemy here is their own government. This link between violence and religious belief is encoded in the Bible itself. In *Revelation*, Christ returns wielding a sword, thus offering a paradigm for a militant version of Christianity that appeals to people with violent and destructive tendencies. Such individuals find it all to easy to see themselves as agents of this militant Messiah, toting their AK47s and stamping on the unbelievers like grapes in a winepress.

This link between apocalyptic faith and violence is particularly noticeable in popular contexts. In common parlance, the word 'apocalypse' is often used simply to denote a uniquely destructive event. The Russian President Putin described the school massacre at Beslan in 2004 as 'apocalyptic'. The popular press has also seen the commercial value of appropriating the rhetoric of apocalyptic. This is how the *Sun*, Britain's largest-selling daily newspaper, headlined a story about a hurricane hitting America's south coast in September 2004: 'Apocalypse', it screamed, 'Ivan could kill 50,000 Americans. New Orleans to be wiped off map. One million fleeing for their lives.' In the event, of course, not anything like 50,000 Americans were killed. New Orleans survived; or at least it did until the end of August 2005 when Hurricane Katrina struck and the levees broke, flooding the historic city and killing hundreds.

Maybe conurbations like New Orleans will become the Mayan cities of tomorrow – a testimony to lost worlds and vanished civilizations. Like the traveller in Shelley's 'Ozymandias', we are haunted by ruins because they expose the fragility and illusoriness of human power and pomp. Lost jungle cities, ancient temples and monuments to the 'King of Kings' – all these bear witness to the fact that all civilizations have a beginning and an end. Apocalyptic myth reminds us that maybe even our own tall towers of steel and glass might one day be the object of speculation and reflection by future generations.

Popular culture is an excellent gauge to the extent apocalyptic images and terms have permeated secular contexts. Apocalyptic-sounding films and computer games continue to proliferate. For those Americans who do not subscribe to evangelical notions about this being the end-time, there is always Hollywood's version of the end of the world. A quick survey of films and computer games reveals how pervasive a secularized apocalypse is. *Resident Evil: Apocalypse* was originally a video game before it was made into a film. Here biological disaster threatens human existence in the form of the T-virus, filling the streets of suburban America with the walking dead. The zombie fest also filled suburban multiplexes both sides of the Atlantic. The 1998 blockbuster, *Armageddon* starring Bruce Willis, recast the biblical battle as a conflict between a group of oil drillers and an asteroid the size of Texas which was on collision course with earth. Like the dinosaurs some 65 million years ago, human beings were about to be wiped out by a huge ECA – earth-crossing asteroid.

Such catastrophism has always done good business at the box office. In the 1980s, Steven Spielberg's extraterrestrial came to earth and taught an American family how to be better human beings. In the 1990s, the figure of the alien mutated into something far more threatening and apocalyptic. In the blockbuster *Independence Day*, an armada of alien spaceships threatens the world. In the end, human ingenuity and moral decency wins the day; the President of the United States even gets to help out by taking to the air. The alien as agent of destruction was reprised in Spielberg's 2005 sci-fi blockbuster, *War of the Worlds* based on H.G. Wells' novel.

In popular music too apocalyptic images and postures are very marketable. The shock-Goth antics of Marilyn Manson are inspired by a figure who will often appear in our story – that of the Antichrist. In 'Everyday is Like Sunday', Morrissey called on Armageddon and the nuclear bomb to alleviate existential boredom. Romantic melancholics like Morrissey have always struck apocalyptic attitudes and postures. At the kitsch end of the spectrum, Armageddon has been turned into a theme-park 'experience' at the Disney Studios, Disneyland Paris. This has to be the ultimate post-modern experience – the end of the world served up as children's entertainment.

Religiously inspired beliefs about the end of the world have also to compete with scientific based one. Sixty-six million years ago, dinosaurs ruled the roost, undisputed masters of the animal world. Sixty-four million years ago they were gone, after having dominated the earth for 150 million years or so. Since 1980, there has been the theory that it was a single catastrophic event that wiped the dinosaurs off the face of the earth – a major collision with an asteroid or comet. Mightn't humanity go the same way as the dinosaurs – mass extinction through some similar geophysical catastrophe? In the twentieth century, accounts in *Genesis* and *Revelation* about the beginning of the world and its end were also challenged by theoretical physics and mathematics. Since Edwin Hubble discovered that the universe was expanding, the notion of a beginning and a possible end to it has exercised some of the greatest scientific minds of our age. Theories about the Big Bang, Big Crunch and Big Rip et. al, have made theoretical physicists and mathematicians bestselling authors and media stars, a process which first began with Einstein at the turn of the twentieth century. Their cosmological speculations make them the latter-day equivalent of the apocalyptic prophets who attempted to uncover the mysteries of the universe.

Such a situation is ripe for satire. Several sci-fi authors and humorists have depicted the new cosmology satirically in their work. Douglas Adams' *The Restaurant at the End of the Universe*, the second work in the *Hitchhiker's Guide to the Galaxy* series, features a restaurant whose patrons can repeatedly watch the end of all things as part of an after-dinner show. In the British sci-fi TV series, *Doctor Who*, a bizarre assortment of extraterrestrials gather together in a corporate hospitality suite on a space station in order to witness the end of the earth five billion years hence. This is the day the sun will expand and consume the planet in fire.

The time horizon of the future envisaged by the theoretical physicists encourages such levity. Who needs to worry about the end of the world if it's going to happen a few billion years hence? In contrast, environmentalists warn us that an ecological catastrophe is staring us in the face. As rainforests fall to the chainsaw, more holes are punched in the ozone layer, populations rise and other species fall, we are faced with a not-too-distant Day of Doom. It is worth remembering here the fate envisioned by John for those who destroy the earth. When the seventh seal is opened in *Revelation* divine wrath is poured on the destroyers; it is God's prerogative, not man's, to end the world. In ecological end-time myths, the destroyers are the polluters and the multinationals, who destroy our beautiful planet as though there is no tomorrow.

Rachel Carson's environmental classic *Silent Spring* struck an apocalyptic tone which makes reading it an unforgettable experience. 'Elixirs of death' is what she calls the pesticides which have been indiscriminately used and have rendered the spring silent.[10] Because of her conscious-raising legacy, eco-warriors are now the new Jeremiahs, prophesying environmental doom and catastrophe. In this end-time scenario, the world will not be suddenly engulfed in a fiery ball but will gradually come to the boil due to global warming. Hollywood caught the zeitgeist of impending ecological doom in the recent blockbuster *The Day After Tomorrow*.

In the opening chapters of *Revelation*, John repeatedly refers to those that have ears to listen. These are the elect. Similarly, God tells Daniel that only a few understand the import of the events which are about to occur: 'Many shall be purified, made white, and refined, but the wicked shall do wickedly; and none of the wicked shall understand, but the wise shall understand.'[11] At the time of the end, God intends that only those He calls 'the wise' will understand these prophecies. Many individuals have proclaimed themselves to be members of this select group. Throughout history, such figures have set dates for the End of the World only to see them pass without any eventuality. Despite the scoffers and the setbacks, however, prophets keep on coming forward to proclaim the hour is upon us. When the promised end fails to materialize on cue, what happens to the believers who invested so much hope and emotional energy in their beliefs? What happens when the prophet's predictions fail so publicly, so spectacularly?

Leon Festinger's *When Prophecy Fails* addresses these questions. It is the classic case study of how failed prophets cope with failure. Festinger's research team studied a flying-saucer cult. The cult's leader, a woman Festinger named 'Mrs Keech' living in a town he called Lake City, related how Sananda, a new incarnation of Christ, had paid her a visit in a flying saucer, having flown from the Planet Clarion. He told her that other forms called Guardians would come from Venus and usher in the Last Judgement. Lake City would soon be destroyed in a flood. Only an elect (i.e. those who listened to the messages) would be saved. When Mrs Keech's end-time prophecy failed to materialize, her blushes were spared with a simple explanation. It was only the members' prayers, it was claimed, which had averted a cataclysmic disaster.

So the failure of such a great prophecy – 'disconfirmation' is Festinger's term – was actually given a positive spin. In fact, rather than deterring cult members from the prophecy business, the failed prediction simply encouraged them to go out and recruit new members. Proselytizing was one way of squaring eager expectation with obdurate reality. Rather than giving up their beliefs, cult members simply believed even more strongly that the Guardians from Venus would be soon paying them a visit. The more people they could attract into their ranks the more likely their predictions would be to come true.

Festinger developed the famous 'cognitive dissonance theory' to account for this phenomenon – the psychological process whereby the gap between what is expected to happen and what in actual fact happens is bridged or at least minimized. When prophecies fail, then, the prophet often simply comes up with a new set of beliefs or explanations to account for the failure. Groups are reformed, doctrines changed, dates recalculated.[12] Festinger is particularly good on the psychological processes involved in such accommodation:

> . . . man's resourcefulness goes simply beyond protecting a belief. Suppose an individual believes something with his whole heart; suppose further that he has a commitment to this belief, that he has taken irrevocable actions because of it; finally, suppose that he is presented with evidence, unequivocal and undeniable evidence, that his belief is wrong: what will happen? The individual will frequently emerge, not only unshaken but even more convinced of the truth of his beliefs than ever before. Indeed, he may even show a new fervor about convincing and converting other people to his view.[13]

Festinger's comments provide a paradigm for analysing some of the figures you will be meeting in the following chapters – rapt charismatics and visionaries; self-aggrandizing religious leaders; fervent and idealistic social revolutionaries; enraptured mystics and disappointed utopianists; hell-fire apocalyptists and just the plain crazy. Our story will take in great works of art which have been inspired by the apocalypse myth and some of the darkest and most depraved deeds imaginable. Apocalyptic beliefs have inspired genocidal campaigns against the Jews and Muslims; they have also inspired campaigns for social justice and equality. It is a story in which man's violent propensities are on display as well as his capacity to remake the world in a better form. Destructive as well as consummating, the apocalyptic paradigm makes for extremes of both good and bad.

I

THE ORIGINS OF
APOCALYPTIC FAITH

Known as the *Book of Revelation*, the final book of the
Christian Bible has probably had more influence on history
and human behaviour generally than any other single piece of
writing. Rich in unforgettable and suggestive images, it has
variously terrified and inspired millions over the last two
thousand years. So protean are its images and symbols that
each age, in its own unique way, has been able to recast them to
suit their own particular needs, hopes and fears. So all pervasive
are these images in our culture that many might feel as though
they had read this strange and disturbing book even if they have
not actually done so. Contained in its pages is a phantasmagoria
of terrifying destruction and glorious renewal, involving bizarre
figures and surreal events. Hail, fire and blood are mixed
together and hurled down from heaven to earth; the four
horsemen of war, famine, death and destruction gallop across

the page; the great red dragon with ten horns and seven heads looms into view; the Whore of Babylon fornicates ferociously with the kings of the earth, drunk on the blood of the saints; stars fall to earth and a Beast arises from the sea; seas turn to glass or blood; a great battle in the sky wages, involving angels and demons. A whirlpool of destruction sucks in the whole of the created order as history runs its final course.

The horror and chaos, however, is simply a prelude to a glorious and miraculous transformation. After the battles and the cosmic upheavals, the New Jerusalem descends out of the heavens. For faithful Christians this is the end of the journey. It is here that they will live for all eternity – in a city that is both weightless and heavy with precious stones. Sapphires, emeralds, topaz, chrysoprase glimmer and glint radiantly. Here the alarums and horrors of history have finally resolved themselves. Plagues, famines and wars are now no more. Instead, people of all lands will walk together in harmony as they pass through the pearly gates of this city.

What were the historical events and cultural forces that helped shape such an extraordinary vision? A key to understanding some of the wilder imagery in *Revelation* lies in the fact that much of it is rooted deep in the past – in over six hundred years of Jewish history. During this period, the trials and tribulations of the Jewish people – famine, plague, military defeats, religious persecution and exile – fuelled and helped shape the apocalyptic images and symbols. But it is a story that goes back even further than that, to even more ancient times. Religious scholars are generally agreed that the origins of apocalyptic faith lie in the religion of the ancient Iranians. It is where the story of the end of the world begins – in the mists of pre-history.

In the west, the Persian prophet Zarathustra is better known under a later Greek form of his name Zoroaster. Most scholars believe that he lived some time between 1500 and 1200 BC and that the religion originated in the extreme eastern part of what is now Iran. Zoroaster began life as a 'zaotar', a fully qualified priest of an older religion, the traditional religion of the Iranians.

According to tradition, it was at the age of thirty that Zoroaster underwent a revelatory experience while drawing water on the banks of the Daitya river. An angelic figure appeared to him and led him into the presence of Ahura Mazda – a deity that is wholly wise, just and good. In the Zoroastrian faith, Ahura Mazda is the creator of *asha*, an all-embracing order. From the stars in the firmament, to the waters down below, to the separation of light and dark, to sons being respectful towards their fathers: all these are manifestations of this divine order. However, Ahura Mazda has an evil twin, the 'Hostile Spirit', Angra Mainyu. The two brothers are locked in permanent conflict as they battle for supremacy. This bad case of sibling rivalry will last until the end of time. Only then will there be an ultimate triumph of good over evil, Ahura Mazda over Angra Mainyu.

Zoroastrianism makes the distinction between unlimited time (eternity) and limited or bounded time (flawed earthly existence). Limited time is divided into two vast periods. First, Ahura Mazda created all things in a disembodied spiritual state; then he created all things in a corporeal state. In this last seven-fold creation Ahura Mazda brought the sky into being, the sea, the earth, plants, animals, humans and fire. This was done with the help of six lesser divinities, Amesha Spentas ('Holy Immortals'). The aim was to create allies in his battle against the forces of evil. This time is referred to simply as *Bundahisn* ('Creation').[1]

The second period within limited time is called *Gumezisn* ('Mixture'). This is when Angra Mainyu and his legions mount malicious assaults on creation in order to undo the good work. Through them death, destruction and disorder are brought into the world; immortality ceases for corporeal creatures. The sky is pierced, the water contaminated with salt, parts of the earth become desert, plants are destroyed along with animals and men; finally, fire, the purest element, is 'mingled with smoke and darkness in it'.[2] This is known as the 'time of Mixture'.

For Zoroaster, Angra Mainyu's attempts to counter-create must be thwarted at every turn. Such a view turns the world into a perpetual theatre of conflict. By exercising moral choice, individuals promote either the forces of goodness in the world or the forces of evil through their thoughts, words and deeds. Devout sacrifices and the strict observance of purification rites help to further the good creation and combat the forces of evil. Conversely, Angra Mainyu, the arch-antagonist, is always on the look out to swell his legions in his struggle with his twin. In the time of Mixture, good and evil spirits alike animate the material, physical world, imbuing it with a metaphysical and cosmic significance.

In this ancient combat myth, Ahura Mazda is destined to prevail over the forces of chaos during the time of Mixture. As its name implies, 'limited time' is a finite period and is destined to end. Then, the whole of the created order will be restored to its pure primal state – it will be both physical and pure, corporeal and eternal. This glorious moment is termed the 'Making Wonderful' and is a forerunner of the Christian concept of the millennium followed by an eternal heaven. Time is swallowed up in eternity; history ceases. Instead, the timeless and limitless vistas of eternity open up – uneventful and untroubled. This future state is designated the 'Third Time'; it is the time of 'Separation' when goodness is once-and-for-all separated from evil.

These beliefs about the end of the world mark an important moment in the history of world religion. In other ancient pagan beliefs the world was always seen as never ending. Like Zor-oastrianism, the ancient Babylonian religion arose in the Middle East. However, unlike its Persian counterpart, the Babylonian religion never saw the world as destined to end in some grand finale. Instead, there was an endless recurrence of events which made the world, in all its essentials, static and unchanging.

Similarly, Vedic Indians too saw the world as essentially unchanging. In their combat myths, these ancient forerunners of the Hindus saw the world as rent and riven by supernatural forces. And yet the world never actually came to an end. Wars, plagues, floods and droughts are part of a never-ending cycle of creation and destruction. Despite the world's imperfect state it was never bad enough for the ancients to want to completely destroy it. What made Zoroastrianism so different was the apocalyptic view it had of time. Rather than being a vast cycle, time was seen as linear. Time's trajectory was forward and purposive, a hurtling towards some divine consummation. By living a moral life, Zoroastrians could speed up time's journey towards its own extinction.

The urgency with which Zoroastrians waited for the end of 'limited time' is to do with the revolutionary nature of their beliefs about the afterlife. Before the end of time, when the righteous individual dies, his or her soul will ascend to para-dise and live in a bodiless condition. This spiritual resurrection is conceived of as being only half complete. The soul is in waiting for the time of Mixture to pass in order to be reunited with its body which will be resurrected after the universal Last Judgement. Rich man or poor man, master or slave, male or female: all would be judged by the same strict moral criteria. To be pure in thought, word and deed was the Zoroastrian mantra. This three-fold ethical principle was all important when the scales of justice would be brought out. If good thoughts, words and deeds tipped the scales downwards, then,

the soul would be waved across. For those found wanting in
the scales of justice another place awaited them – a filthy hell
of torment, a place of retributive punishment and suffering.

Such beliefs proved to be remarkably influential on the three
other great apocalyptic faiths: Judaism, Christianity and Islam.
Like God in *Revelation*, the Zoroastrian chief deity is both the
creator of the world and the destroyer of it. At the end of time,
there is an Armageddon-like struggle between the forces of
good and evil. Afterwards, all the vast hosts of the dead and
the living are gathered together at a great assembly where they
will be confronted with their deeds, both good and bad. The
34th chapter of the *Bundahisn* is the Zoroastrian equivalent of
the *Book of Revelation*. As in John's vision of the End, fire is
the apocalyptic element and is both destructive and regenera-
tive. A great ball of fire will melt all the metals and minerals in
the earth, producing a vast river of boiling metal, a great
deluge, which will engulf the world:

> Then they will cause all men to pass through that molten
> metal . . . And for him who is righteous, it will seem as if he
> is walking through warm milk; and for him who is wicked, it will
> seem as if he is walking in the flesh . . . through molten metal.[3]

Like Christ's Second Coming, Ahura Mazda 'will Himself
come to the world as a celebrating priest'. As for his great
adversary, Angra Mainyu, an altogether different fate awaits:
the Evil spirit, deprived of his power, will beat a hasty retreat
to the realm of darkness and the molten metal will flow into
hell and seal the gap through which he came.

In such teachings, the broad configurations of apocalyptic
faith can be discerned. The destruction of the world and the
'Making Wonderful', a combat myth involving angels and
demons, individual judgement, heaven and hell: later all these

elements would be adapted and developed in the eschatological teachings of the three monotheistic faiths – Judaism, Christianity and Islam.

The line of transmission was a complicated and winding one and is still being hotly contested by scholars. Empires have always been disseminators of religious beliefs and the ancient Persian Empire was to prove no exception. As Norman Cohn has observed, for some two centuries Judaea formed part of the vast Achaemenian Empire.[4] For generations there would have been a cross-fertilization between Zoroastrianism and Judaism. Like the Zoroastrians, the Jews regarded themselves as the righteous allies of God, the Chosen People, in the battle between good and evil. The Jews too had similar beliefs about the future life. The Jewish equivalent of Zoroastrianism's 'Making Wonderful' was the messianic age. During this time, the blessed would be lords of a fertile, prosperous and peaceful world, while their enemies would be cast down, never to rise again. In Christianity and Islam, the old world is destroyed in a similarly climactic apocalyptic event.

The Jewish apocalyptic genre grew out of an earlier prophetic tradition of the eighth to sixth centuries BC. Prophets such as Isaiah, Jeremiah and Ezekiel were preachers who called the people to task for falling short in their devotion to God and warned them of the dire consequences. Surrounded by warring and powerful enemies, the Jews sought consolation in such prophetic works due to their historical situation. Few in number and occupying a small country, the Jews sought power through their mythmaking. History was viewed in terms of conflict and collective struggle. If they repented of their sins and kept to the straight and narrow, then, they would eventually triumph over their godless neighbours and enemies. It was the great prophets who first articulated such a view. Later, the Jewish apocalyptists augmented the myths and gave them a cosmic rather than simply a national significance.

Both the Jewish prophetic and apocalyptic traditions arose out of the older beliefs of the ancient Israelites who lived in the land of Canaan. It's where the story of God's Chosen People begins. The emergence of a centralized Israelite state occurred around 1000 BC. Up to that point, the Israelites had been divided into two main groups or houses, the northern and the southern. Under King David and his son, Solomon, this united kingdom was ruled from their capital Jerusalem. It was not just a political centre but also a religious one. For the ancient Israelite, Mount Zion in Jerusalem was also the earthly abode of their patron god, Yahweh. It was he who helped the Israelites overcome their enemies and protected them from such other evils as drought, famine and plague. The royal capital was therefore imbued with a cosmic significance; the political and religious became one and the same. The fate of the city and the fate of the world were inextricably intertwined. If Mount Zion was preserved, then, so was the ordered world. When the First Temple was built on Mount Zion under Solomon it was a public proclamation of such beliefs. Here was an abode fit for God. It was also a good political move. The Temple's plans were supposed to have been revealed to David by God and were believed to correspond to that of the temple in heaven. The power of the Jerusalem monarchy was thus divinely underwrit.

Solomon's Temple still exerts an enormous power on to-day's world. A group of ultra orthodox Jews in Jerusalem want to rebuild the First Temple on its original site, currently occupied by the Islamic Dome of the Rock Shrine and al-Aqsa mosque. In building a Temple – the third one on that site – they will be helping to bring about the end of the world and the ultimate triumph of the Jews. In America today, some Christian Evangelicals are attempting to breed red heifers which will be sacrificed in the Third Temple and thus help to usher in the end of the world. Such eschatological beliefs have their origin in ancient Israelite beliefs concerning the significance of the first Temple.

A bastion of order in a disordered world, then, the Temple was sacrosanct to the ancient Israelites. In their cosmology, the forces of chaos, which God had defeated in his original creation, were amassing every day, threatening to engulf the whole of the created order. Like future apocalyptists, the Israelites were adept at identifying rival empires and powers as being cosmic monsters of misrule. History was thus imbued with a metaphysical sense of their own unique destiny. The Israelites' enemies were God's enemies. Such beliefs helped fortify them in times of national disaster such as when the ancient Assyrians invaded their lands in the eighth century BC. A once proud nation was reduced to a vassal state, its people carted off to Assyria to exile and enslavement. Such a historical disaster engendered a myth of loss and restoration. Out of defeat would come victory in the fullness of time. Through divine intervention, the exiles would finally be returned to their homeland. Today such myths about ingathering and restoration are central to the apocalyptic mythmaking of messianic Jews in Israel and Christian Evangelicals in America. For the end of the world to come about the Third Temple has to be rebuilt, the scattered tribes ingathered and the biblical lands restored.

It was in the sixth century BC that another national disaster was to have profound consequences on the world-view of the Israelites. Under the famous king, Nebuchadnezzar, the Babylonian army invaded Jerusalem in 586, razing its city walls and burning Solomon's Temple to the ground. Nebuchadnezzar's desire to humiliate his enemy knew no bounds. As if the invasion, destruction and plundering of the royal capital and Temple were not enough, Nebuchadnezzar then heaped another humiliation on the Israelites' head – that of captivity and exile. Although estimates vary greatly, a significant proportion of the Israelite people were deported to Babylon itself. They were forced to march 2,000 km (1,240 miles) across the northern edge of the Arabian Desert, down the Euphrates to Babylon.

In exile, the Jews were confronted at every turn by their enemy's power and might. The beauty and magnificence of Babylon was legendary. Perched on the banks of the Tigris and Euphrates, the city was protected by a vast double wall. Writing around the mid-fifth century, the Greek historian Herodotus claimed that the 'vast city [was] in the form of a square with sides nearly fourteen miles long and a circuit of some fifty-six miles'.[5] Even allowing for exaggeration, there's no doubt that the city was a mega-polis. On each side of the city walls were huge wooden doors, decorated with gold and bronze. So wide were the walls that chariot races could be held on them. Images of Marduk, the supreme Babylonian deity, and the other gods in the pantheon, were everywhere. Whereas the Jews were forbidden to portray God in paint or wood or marble, the Babylonian religion was unashamedly polytheistic and artists' imaginations were allowed free rein. At every turn, the exiles would have been confronted with images of dragons and winged beasts. Later, in Jewish apocalyptic writing, such images were to be recast as part of a demonic menagerie.

Babylonian buildings too would have exacerbated the suffering of the exilic Jews. A polychromatic riot of colours and images, the Temple of Marduk would have evoked painful reminders of the Jerusalem Temple their captors had destroyed. Later, in the *Book of Revelation*, Babylon would be recast as Babylon the Golden – the demonic anti-type to the heavenly New Jerusalem. It was during the exilic period, then, that the absolute duality between good and evil was conceived of as an urban polarity. The whorish opulence of the Babylonian temple and the palaces; the chaste restraint of Solomon's Temple in Jerusalem, later to be re-imagined as a sparkling bejewelled celestial city. Babylon equalled oppression and humiliation, Jerusalem freedom and triumph. Today, Babylon is still commonly used as a catchall phrase to denote absolute evil.

For many, the experience of exile resulted in a crisis of faith. Why had God allowed this to happen to God's Chosen People? Some came to the conclusion that God had simply abandoned them; others that the Babylonian gods must be more powerful than their own. A few sought an explanation closer to home. A small group of religious reformers looked not to God but to the Jewish people as the cause of their defeat and humiliation. Maybe, such a fate had befallen them because they had broken their side of the bargain with God. The Law was divinely sanctioned; by keeping to it Jews demonstrated their exclusive devotion to Yahweh. In the past, Yahweh had wreaked retribution on those who fell short. But what if they upheld to the letter each one of the 613 commandments of the Law? Surely, then, Yahweh might look favourably on them and return them to their homeland?

A new theology therefore arose out of the trauma of exile. Central to it was the belief in the conditional nature of the promise made between the Jews and God. This had far reaching consequences. It meant that the Jews were forced to rethink the whole of their history and identity. And because their history was transmitted through biblical texts, it meant that some of these had to be rewritten retrospectively in order to take account of what had just happened to them. So the redactors got to work – editing, re-interpreting and rewriting. Later we shall see how the prophetic books and the first true apocalypse in the Hebrew Bible, the *Book of Daniel*, exemplify this process of rethinking, revising and recasting.

And then something truly miraculous happened. Only some

fifty years since the Babylonians had destroyed the Temple and completely subjugated the small kingdom of Judah, they too were invaded and overrun. The Persian army swept in from the east beyond the Persian Gulf and occupied the Mesopotamian region. Led by Cyrus the Great, the first Persian emperor, the army stormed Babylon in October 539 BC. Faced with the city's vast impregnable walls, the Persians were obliged to use brains not brawn. The story goes that they dammed up the canals that hydrated the city and came in through the water channels. Having breached the city's defences, the Persians flung open those flashy bronze golden doors and massacred the inhabitants.

Such are the vicissitudes of history. One imperial civilization succumbs to another in a ceaseless cycle of conquest and downfall. For the exilic Jews, the only explanation for such a miraculous turn around was divine intervention. Babylon the Golden had been brought low, through the agency of Cyrus and his army, because God was working through history. In the past, Yahweh had been justly angry with the Jews for not being steadfast enough in their faith. When they had returned to the straight and narrow, however, God had rewarded them by overthrowing their enemies and releasing them from their captivity.

The ability to detect Yahweh's presence in the most unlikely of places is typified by Chapters 44 and 45 of *Isaiah*. Among biblical scholars, the consensus is that these passages belong to that portion of the great prophetic book written during the exile and was the work of a single prophet, 'Second Isaiah', who was active about 547–538 BC. The portions that he penned were added to the 'real' text of *Isaiah*, parts of which date back to the eighth century BC.

*

The Second Isaiah predicts the coming of King Cyrus who will liberate the Jews from their Babylonian exile and will bring them to the Promised Land. In these chapters, Cyrus the great is actually referred to as God's anointed one:

> That saith of Cyrus, He is my shepherd, and shall perform all
> my pleasure: even saying to Jerusalem, Thou shalt be built; and
> to the temple, Thy foundation shall be laid.

> Thus saith the LORD to his anointed, to Cyrus, whose right
> hand I have holden, to subdue nations before him.[6]

Although most probably a Zoroastrian, the Persian king is cast as an agent of Yahweh, working his will for the benefit of his people. Such a view is typical of the prophets generally. God shapes history; he could enter the human scene in order to rescue his people from national peril or he could use the enemies of his people (the Assyrians in the older sections of *Isaiah*) to punish them. To end the Babylonian captivity he had used Cyrus as the instrument of deliverance.

The Lord's anointed did not disappoint. Showing remarkable religious tolerance, Cyrus allowed the Jews to return to their homeland and worship their God. For the Jews, such a miraculous deliverance could be read only in one way. The Jews had been saved because they had remained steadfast in adversity and turned away from apostasy. Yahweh had been true to his word. Defeat had been turned into triumph. This sense of God working through history, overthrowing evil empires, dealing weal and dole, is an important element in the apocalyptic world-view. And it is here, after the fall of Babylon and the return of the exiles to their homeland, that such beliefs first began to be formulated.

In the apocalyptic paradigm darkness is the prelude to the dawn. The people are denounced for their waywardness; grim retribution is predicted if they don't repent and return to the straight and narrow. For those that do, a glorious deliverance

awaits. God will bestow boundless benefactions on the righteous and annihilate their enemies. The *Book of Ezekiel* con-
forms to this 'literature of crisis' formula. At the beginning of
the work, Ezekiel identifies himself as a priest exiled to
Babylon with King Jehoiachin and his court. His early, pre-
exilic oracles in Jerusalem are about the conquest of Judah and
the fall of Jerusalem. Sword, famine and pestilence, he predicts, will be visited on the Israelites for their polytheism and
idol-worshipping ways. Later, in exile, however, Ezekiel offers
the Israelites hope and solace. He foretells their eventual return
to their homeland and the violent destruction of their enemies.
A new age will be ushered in; God will cleanse the house of
Israel with the purifying waters of monotheism.[7] The new
covenant will fill the Israelites with a new spirit, a new heart
and restore the land of their forefathers to them. All the
dispersed Israelites – the deportees in Babylon, the Lost Tribes
from the northern kingdom lost to the Assyrians more than a
century before – will be rounded up and shepherded back to a
united Israel. The reassembled flock will be watched over by a
new David who, in turn, is watched over by God. Desolate
land and ruined cities will rise miraculously from the dust. A
new age will be instituted, watched over by the now wholly
benevolent figure of God:

> And I will make with them a covenant of peace, and will cause
> the evil beasts to cease out of the land: and they shall dwell
> safely in the wilderness, and sleep in the woods.
>
> And I will make them and the places round about my hill a
> blessing; and I will cause the shower to come down in his
> season; there shall be showers of blessing. And the tree of the
> field shall yield her fruit, and the earth shall yield her increase,
> and they shall be safe in their land, and shall know that I *am* the
> Lord, when I have broken the bands of their yoke, and

delivered them out of the hand of those that served themselves of them.[8]

Scholars have noted that *Ezekiel* contains an apocalyptic section found in Chapters 37 to 39. In Chapter 37, Ezekiel is carried out in the spirit of the Lord and set down in a valley of dry bones. These are the remains of all those who have died in invasions and famine. These are the children of Israel, hopeless, seemingly abandoned and scattered. A mass resurrection then takes place, described in terrifying detail: an army of the dead rises up, sinews, flesh and skin rapidly reconstituting as in some zombie movie. Such a miracle has, however, more of a political meaning than a metaphysical one. It symbolizes the rise once again of a united House of Israel. Understood in its original context, this episode denotes national and political renewal. The union of the two kingdoms of Judah and Israel will take place and a king of power and majesty will rule over the united nation: 'David my servant shall be king over them.'[9] In apocalyptic terms, the valley of dry bones is often seen as a prototype of the universal resurrection envisioned in the *Book of Revelation*: 'And the sea gave up the dead which were in it; and death and hell delivered up the dead which were in them: and they were judged every man according to their works.'[10]

Chapter 38 is where *Ezekiel* really gets interesting. It is here that we learn about the fate of heathens 'in the latter days'. If the earlier chapters of *Ezekiel* arose out of oppression and crisis, Chapters 38 and 39 are very much the literature-of-the-victorious. But it's not just the old enemies of Israel – hostile neighbouring countries – which threaten its national survival. A new enemy, mightier than the others, threatens to extinguish it entirely. God enjoins Ezekiel to prophesy against 'Gog, the land of Magog, chief prince of Meshech and Tubal'. This mysterious northern ruler is later to reappear in the *Book of Daniel*. Later still, in *Revelation*, Gog and Magog join Satan's final rebellion against God at the end of the millennium. In the *Book of Ezekiel*, Gog leads a vast coalition of heathens against Israel. Well armed and on horseback, this demonic army appears to be invincible – until that is God decides to intervene. He annihilates the enemy with a blizzard of hail and fire and then feeds the dead bodies to the birds and the beasts. What we see here is a kind of Armageddon-in-embryo. The forces of evil are ranged against the forces of good and in such a scenario – unlike in life – there can only be one outcome.

If Chapters 38 and 39 of *Ezekiel* can be regarded as a mini-apocalypse in the sense that they deal with the destruction of evil, then, the closing chapters of *Isaiah* can be seen as a foreshadowing of the millennium. Chapters 55 to 66 contain some of the most famous and celebrated passages in the Hebrew Bible. Many biblical scholars believe Second Isaiah did not author these prophecies but maintain, instead, that they belong to the half century or so after the end of the exile. The most famous prophetic passage depicts the messianic age – a perfect world which has been brought into sudden being through divine intervention. Unlike the time of 'Making Wonderful' in Zoroastrianism, this new order of things does not involve destroying the world first. It is the metaphysical equivalent of a surgical strike – the judicious use of specially directed destruction. Those neighbouring enemies such as Edom have the most to fear. On the day of reckoning, Yahweh will stand in a winepress stamping on his enemies, his garments splattered with their blood.

The *Book of Isaiah* finishes with a vision of the new age about to be ushered in. It is a passage of aching beauty and justly famous:

For, behold, I create new heavens and a new earth: and the
former shall not be remembered, nor come into mind . . . for,
behold, I create Jerusalem a rejoicing, and her people a joy . . .
and the voice of weeping shall be no more heard in her, nor the
voice of crying . . . The wolf and the lamb shall feed together,
and the lion shall eat straw like the bullock: and dust shall be
the serpent's meat. They shall not hurt nor destroy in all my
holy mountain, saith the Lord.[11]

From our present-day sorry state, God delivers us into this
perfect world in which predator and prey co-exist together in
harmony, in which the failings and frailties of the flesh are no
more. The messianic age is the great consummation in the
great Jewish prophecies, a forerunner of the heavenly Christian New Jerusalem. Unlike in a full-fledged apocalyptic faith
such as Zoroastrianism or Christianity, however, the old
world is not destroyed and replaced by a completely new
one. Instead, the great Jewish prophets pronounce that an ideal
king, a messiah (the 'anointed' one), would arrive and help to
usher in national restoration and the universal establishment
of God's kingdom, a messianic age. He will preside over a
golden age of social justice, figured in the miraculous transformation of the animal kingdom. The visions of exilic and
post-exilic prophets continue to exert a strong pull on the
imagination of artists, utopian visionaries and social revolutionaries – all those, in fact, who dream of a better, fairer, more
humane world than the one we currently occupy.

*

The *Book of Daniel* represents a major stage in the formation
of apocalyptic faith. Just as *Isaiah* and *Ezekiel* can only be
understood with reference to the history of the exilic period so
the *Book of Daniel* also reflects the social and political realities

of its time. Biblical literalists will argue that *Daniel* was written when it says it was written. The second half of the book names as author a certain Daniel who, according to Chapter 1, was exiled to Babylon. However, many biblical scholars date the work much later. Because its religious ideas do not belong to the sixth century BC, they date *Daniel* in the first half of the second century BC. At that time, it was not the Babylonians who were oppressing God's Chosen People, but the Greeks and their successor kingdoms.

Greek domination of the known world goes back to the fourth century BC. Alexander the Great's astonishing military conquests led to the formation of an empire, assembled in some ten to fifteen years, stretching from Greece to Egypt, Persia to North India. A man of vision, Alexander believed that all the different peoples of his empire should have common cultural links. This could be achieved through the internationalization and exportation of Greek culture, a process known as Hellenism.

After Alexander's death, the vast empire was divided into dynasties of Greek descent. One such successor dynasty was the Seleucid one, based in Syria. At the beginning of the second century it found itself controlling that part of ancient Palestine that was known as Judaea and which roughly corresponded to the former kingdom of Judah. An insignificant corner of a vast and glorious empire one might have been forgiven for thinking. Powerless, abandoned, under the heel of yet another imperial power: the Jews have always been most imaginatively invigorated when they have been least politically powerful. In the sixth century, during the exilic period, they had produced the great prophecies at a time when they had lost their monarch, their temple and their nation.

Now in the time of Syrian–Greek occupation in the second century the prophets were going to write another type of literature. This would be far more radical than the prophecies of Isaiah or Ezekiel. It would conjure up visions of undreamt heights of splendour and glory for the Chosen People. Conversely, it would cast down their enemies to ever lower depths of infamy and humiliation. Apocalypse was the name of this new type of literature. The crowning glory in this tradition of Jewish apocalypses is the *Book of Daniel*.

Like the exilic prophecies, *Daniel* arose out of a specific set of political and historical circumstances. Since 175 BC, the Seleucid king had been Antiochus Epiphanes IV. Under him the Syrian–Greek kingdom embarked on a particularly vicious repression of the Jews. His attempt to realize Alexander's vision of a Hellenistic world-empire involved ramming Greek culture down his subjects' throats. Riding roughshod over different faith, beliefs and customs was all done in the name of political unity. In 169 BC things came to a head when he attacked Jerusalem, defiled the Temple by erecting a statue of Zeus with his face on it and banned all Jewish religious practices wholesale. In biblical history this is known as the Antiochan persecution.

The Jewish backlash to Antiochus' tyrannical rule was not long in coming. A group of hardline Jews, known as the Maccabeans, led a revolt against him, fought a guerrilla-style war and prevailed against all odds. A small band of Maccabeans retook the Temple in 164 BC; surrounded by a vast Greek force, they were still able to repurify and rededicate it. To this day, Jews still celebrate this event with the Feast of Rededication or Hanukkah. Scholars believe that it was during this war between Antiochus and the Maccabeans that the *Book of Daniel* was composed. For those who believe in the literal truth of biblical prophecy, however, such a historical explanation is anathema. After the *Book of Revelation*, the *Book of Daniel* is the scripture most studied, pored over and interpreted by contemporary prophecy believers. For them, its author was the divinely inspired Daniel who penned the book bearing his name during the Babylonian exile.

The richness of *Daniel*, however, lies in the way it can be read both mythically and historically. As a child at Sunday school, I sat rapt listening to stories about Daniel's early life in Babylon. The story of how only Daniel could interpret King Nebuchadnezzar's dream about the metal Colossus knocked down with a stone like a skittle was a particular favourite. Then there were the miracles: the trial of Daniel's three friends in the blazing furnace and the writing on the wall and the fall of Belshazzar. Last and best of all was the story of Daniel's ordeal in the lions' den, vividly illustrated in our picture-book children's Bible. It is not hard to see why these stories appeal so much to children. The only writing on walls I had ever seen was graffiti. The only lions I had ever seen were the rather mangy ones at London Zoo. In contrast, here were lions whose slavering chops were clamped shut by angels because God loved Daniel so much he could not bear to see him killed in the den. At Sunday school we would sing the rousing child's hymn, 'Dare to be a Daniel' while being exhorted by our teacher 'to dare to stand alone'. Episodes from Daniel's life have always been given a homiletic spin. Our Sunday-school teacher recast the lions in the den as nasty playground bullies who had to be faced down. We all longed to be members of 'Daniel's band'. It sounded like a gang.

Not surprisingly, the apocalyptic second part of the *Book of Daniel* was never mentioned at Sunday school. This consists of visions and dreams in which God reveals to Daniel many things about his purpose and plan in world history and the everlasting kingdom to come.[12] This is hardcore apocalyptic prophecy, not the kind of thing to serve up to middle-class Anglican children. The *Book of Daniel* therefore tends to be dichotomized. There are those who stick to the picturesque

Sunday-school stories in the first half. Then there are the biblical prophecy believers who dwell obsessively on those disturbing visions of cosmic destruction in the second half. A more integrative reading would seem to be required. After all, Chapter 2 in the first half contains an apocalypse-in-embryo in which world history is divided up into four great periods.

This is how the story goes. One night Nebuchadnezzar dreamed a bad dream about a Colossus made of different metals: the head was made of gold, his breast and arms were silver, his belly and thighs brass, his legs iron, his feet iron mixed with clay. A large stone strikes the statue's feet of iron and clay and the whole thing comes crashing down to the ground. The various metals and the various body parts are blown away 'like the chaff of the summer threshing floors'.[13]

Only Daniel can solve the conundrum of the Colossus. He tells Nebuchadnezzar that the metals correspond to empires and their dominion: the gold head corresponds to the Babylonian Empire; the silver represents the Persian Empire; and the bronze the Greek. What really claims Daniel's attention, however, are the feet of iron and clay. Just as iron 'breaketh in pieces and subdueth' so will this iron empire break and subdue all other nations. This represents the extraordinary conquests of Alexander the Great. Nevertheless the successor states will be poorly bound together like iron and clay. The fall of Antiochus and the Seleucid dynasty is therefore being prophesied here. Such internal weaknesses will lead to fractures and fissures opening up, making it easy for the stone hewn by God to do its destructive work.

What will happen in the future to replace such clay-footed, grandiose empires? The author of *Daniel* tells us at length:

> And in the days of these kings shall the God of heaven set up a
> kingdom, which shall never be destroyed: and the kingdom

shall not be left to other people, but it shall break in pieces and consume all these kingdoms, and it shall stand for ever.[14]

A key apocalyptic theme is beginning to emerge which will resonate throughout our story. In the apocalyptic tradition, empires are often seen to be monuments to human vainglory, doomed to fall and shatter like the absurd Iron Man. After their fall, they will leave no trace, having been scattered like chaff to the four winds. The second-century Jewish apocalyptist that was the author of *Daniel* commends the one true empire – God's. This will be inaugurated after the fall of all the old earthly ones. It will be established in Israel. It will last forever.

The categorization of history into periods is an important element in apocalyptic faith. In the second part of the *Book of Daniel*, history is broken up into four successive world empires or 'kingdoms'. In his dream or nocturnal vision Daniel sees four beasts arise from a storm-tossed sea. They represent the same usual suspects. The first beast is a lion with eagle wings and has been associated with the Babylonian Empire (the winged lion was the royal symbol of the Babylonian Empire). It is brought to heel by having its wings plucked and being made to stand on two feet like a man. The second beast is a bear with three ribs in its mouth (Persian Empire); the third is a four-headed, four-winged leopard (Alexander the Great's speedily assembled Greek Empire hence the leopard). Finally the fourth beast, 'dreadful and terrible', arises more terrifying than the other three; it has huge iron teeth and nails of bronze, and devours and tramples in a most alarming way. Ten horns sit on its head. It is uniquely destructive: it 'shall devour the whole earth, and tread it down, and break it to pieces'.[15] Suddenly it sprouts a little horn which displaces three of the original ones. Grotesquely, this horn has eyes and the power of speech; it speaks self-important words. Such zoomorphic feats occur later in the *Book of Revelation*.

Unlike all the other beasts before it, this beast is uniquely and spectacularly awful and monstrous; it is not compared with any other animal. For those who believe in the *Book of Daniel* as a work of divinely inspired prophecy this last and most terrible of the beasts represents the Roman Empire. In other words, it is still more proof of the miraculously accurate way in which the Bible can predict the events of future world history. Most biblical scholars, however, have another explanation. For those who see *Daniel* not as the work of a divinely inspired prophet but as perhaps the work of a number of authors working in 169–165 BC, the monstrously horned creature represents another corrupt imperial power. The ten horns of the monster are the successor kings who come after Alexander the Great. The tenth horn is none other than Antiochus Epiphanes, the Hellenizer of the Jews, the desecrator of the Second Temple.

Such an imperial monster can only be stopped by divine intervention. This takes place with the emergence of the grotesque little horn. It is a sign that the consummation of history is at hand. God's appearance as the 'Ancient of days' is a spectacular *coup de théâtre* in this apocalyptic drama. Wearing garments white as snow and with a head of hair like pure wool, he sits on a throne of fire from which he dispenses justice, surrounded by a multitude of angels.[16] At the top of God's hit list is the fourth beast; it is hastily despatched and consumed in flames, the apocalyptic element *par excellence*. So ends the fourth and last empire. But as one empire ends a new one is inaugurated, a new king crowned. *Daniel* relates how 'one like the Son of Man came with the clouds of heaven' up to God enthroned. He is given everlasting dominion over a kingdom in which all the nations and people of the earth are united in serving him.[17] The other three remaining apocalyptic visions end in a similar fashion. The second one involves a ram and a goat, the third one is a vision of the seventy weeks and the last one is the wholly extraordinary vision of the time of the end. Although the symbolism may be different in each one, all four prophecies end in similar ways – with God swiftly vanquishing a seemingly invincible corrupt earthly power.

In *Daniel*, then, contemporary events are presented as though they have been divinely prophesied from the distant past. It is prophecy told retrospectively. By creating the character from the exilic period, the author or authors of *Daniel* are presenting their prophecies as though they have been divinely underwritten. Look, we are asked to believe, the overthrow of this Greek despot has been prophesied hundreds of years ago by the exilic sage. Later, with the *Book of Revelation*, we shall see how apocalyptic literature generally is a very effective way of consoling and fortifying an oppressed and suffering people. In such a view, the political and the metaphysical are inextricably bound up with each other. For the author or authors of *Daniel*, the Maccabeans are not simply political revolutionaries but the 'saints of God' locked in unceasing conflict with the forces of darkness. Antiochus is therefore not just another cruel and corrupt monarch. He is simply the latest incarnation of absolute evil, a kind of proto-Antichrist.

The prophecies which predate the *Book of Daniel* contain apocalyptic elements but are not in themselves apocalypses. What distinguishes *Daniel*'s prophecy from previous ones is the emphasis it places on a total and utter transformation of the created order: corrupt earthly empires are destroyed and replaced, once and for all, by a totally new order to things. Rather than it being a narrowly nationalistic celebration of Israel's future glory, *Daniel*'s vision has a truly cosmic dimension to it, raising it up to an apocalyptic level. Biblical scholars are generally agreed that it is the first true apocalypse in the Hebrew Bible. The imminence of salvation for the righteous and destruction for the ungodly is a two-fold process that has become the paradigm in apocalyptic religious literature. Later, the *Book of Revelation* at the end of the New Testament will develop this still further.

What further distinguishes *Daniel* from the earlier prophecies is 'The Vision of the Time of the End' which appears in the tenth chapter. It is an extraordinary climax to an extraordinary book, a step-by-step account of what will actually happen at the end of the world. Troop movements, the clash of arms, dynastic struggle and the fall of great empires: all are depicted in astonishing and unforgettable detail. These are the 'signs' of the end-times. Along with the symbols and images of *Revelation*, they will resonate profoundly in the visions and prophecies of future apocalyptic visionaries and prophets. The Jewish and Christian apocalypses will provide them with a conspectus of images, symbols and language with which to describe the end of the world.

On the question of the actual date of deliverance, *Daniel*, however, remains cryptic: 'it shall be for a time, times, and a half'.[18] Despite such asseverations, the final outcome is never in doubt. The end-time upheavals are followed by the reign of God in which the faithful, through a resurrection of the just, will be released from suffering and rewarded: 'And many of them that sleep in the dust of the earth shall awake, some to everlasting life, and some to shame and everlasting contempt.'[19]

For those who had thrown their lot in with Antiochus and his corrupt regime an eternity of contempt and public humiliation awaits them. The martyrs, on the other hand, will be resurrected to enjoy a corporeal life on this earth in ageless and perfected bodies. Scholarly opinion differs widely on the fate of the 'wise leaders', those that have been especially holy and steadfast in the struggle against Antiochus. Presumably the author of *Daniel* regards himself as one such figure: 'And they that be wise shall shine as the brightness of the firmament; and they that turn many to righteousness as the stars for ever and ever.' After this verse the angel who has been interpreting his vision enjoins Daniel to seal the book 'to the time of the end'.[20] The message is clear. God will not give up all his secrets until the End. Then and only then will all the secrets of heaven and earth be finally uncovered.

The last chapter of the *Book of Daniel* is full of such gaps and omissions that have tantalized biblical commentators for many generations. Apocalyptic sects home in on such passages and build their entire belief system around them. Self-styled apocalyptic prophets like David Koresh and the Branch Davidians have attempted to 'unseal' that book, along with the *Book of Revelation*, and predict the end of the world and what will happen to their particular group when it does. For such sects, the *Book of Daniel* contains all the answers; it is just a question of being 'wise' enough to be able to interpret it correctly. The rest of us, not vouchsafed such knowledge, will have to be content in asking questions rather than supplying answers. More than two thousand years on the *Book of Daniel* still continues to provoke many questions and supply few answers. It steadfastly refuses to give up all its secrets.

*

The *Book of Enoch* is another very important example of Second Temple Jewish literature. It is presented as though it were the single work of Enoch mentioned briefly in *Genesis*. In fact, biblical scholars incline to the belief that it was a collection of texts composed between the third century BC and the first century AD. Written by anonymous Jewish authors, they wrote under the pseudonym 'Enoch' in order to give their writing biblical authority and canonicity. Enoch was supposed to have lived before the Flood – his great grandson was Noah – and superhuman powers were ascribed to him. In *Genesis* 5:24, for example, we learn how Enoch 'walked with God' and how 'God took him' before he actually died. Around these bare bones, the authors of *Enoch* wrote a collection of five books that flesh out Enoch's adventures in the afterlife and in doing so give us an extraordinary insight into a whole host of Jewish beliefs in the centuries that preceded the Christian era. Biblical scholars know this composite text as *1 Enoch*.

Although it occupies a central position in the Jewish apocalyptic tradition, *I Enoch* has been relegated to the *Pseudepigrapha*, a Greek word which means 'false writing'. This term denotes a corpus of works that imitate the books of the Hebrew Bible and which were inspired by them but were not included in either the Hebrew or most Christian biblical canons. Despite its unofficial status, however, *1 Enoch* represents an important stage in the development of apocalyptic faith. During its time of composition, there was an extraordinary cross-cultural fusion between Jewish and Hellenic elements in ancient Palestine. The Enochian authors take images of Hades from Greek mythology and recast them as the Jewish hell – a vital component in the apocalyptic tradition. A wide variety of opinions, speculations and beliefs flourished in Judaism during Second Temple times and these are reflected in the adventures of Enoch. His celestial tour takes in the fall of angels, demons and the nature of hell, the coming of a messiah and a messianic kingdom, the end of the world and the Final Judgement. In fact, what we have here are all the components of what we later come to think of as Jewish and Christian apocalyptic beliefs.

The opening chapters of *1 Enoch* (1–5) dwell at length on Enoch's vision of the end of time. The magnificent opening, 'Prooimium', describes how at some unspecified time in the future God will descend from heaven, accompanied by his ten thousand angels, set foot on Mount Sinai, and execute judgement:

The great Holy One shall come forth from his dwelling,

(4) And the eternal God shall tread upon the earth upon Mount
   Sinai,

And he shall appear from his camp,

And reveal himself in the power of his might from the highest
   heaven.

(5) And all shall be afraid, and the watchers [evil angels] shall quake,

And *they shall seek to hide themselves* in all the corners of the
   earth.

And all the ends of the earth shall be shaken.

And great fear and trembling shall seize them to the ends of the
   earth,

(6) And the lofty mountains shall be shaken;

they shall fall and be disintegrated;

And the high places shall be laid low so that the hills are
   dissolved;

They shall melt like wax before the fiery flame.

(7) And the earth shall be rent in sunder, and all that is upon the
   earth shall perish,

And there shall be a universal judgement.

In this Last Judgement, the fate which awaits the righteous and
the ungodly is absolute:

(8) But with the righteous he will make peace, and he will
protect the elect, and mercy shall be upon them,

And they shall all belong to God.

And he shall show them favour and bless them all, and he will
   assist all and help us;

And light shall appear upon them, and he will make peace with
   them.

(9) Behold! he comes with ten thousand holy ones to execute
   judgement upon all,

> And he will destroy all the ungodly and convict all flesh of all
> the
> works of their ungodliness
> Which they have ungodly committed, and of all the arrogant
> and
> hard words which sinners have uttered against him.[21]

What angers God especially are apostates and blasphemers, those that 'have not been steadfast nor done according to his commandments but . . . have transgressed against him, and spoken proud and hard words with . . . impure mouths against his majesty'.[22] Such a failure brings disorder into God's divinely created universe.

The origin of disorder particularly exercises the authors of this apocalypse. Parts of 1 Enoch were written at a time when the Jews were suffering from Syrian and Roman oppression. It is not surprising therefore that it is deeply concerned with problem of the origin of evil. Why had God abandoned Israel and allowed evil to rule the world in their time? Chapters 6 to 16 of 1 Enoch, known as the Book of Watchers, provides us with an answer to such a question. It provides us with an origin myth about how the demons came into existence and, for a time at least, ruled the earth. When Enoch is taken on an inspection tour of Sheol, the shadowy underworld place of the dead, he sees angels in a fallen state and learns that these angels came down to earth, took on human form and had carnal relations with the 'daughters of men'. In doing so the angels forfeited their special spiritual quality God had endowed them with and became polluted. To make matters worse, these libidinous angels and their earthly consorts produced progeny – a race of giants whose appetites were so voracious that they set about devouring everything on earth, including human beings and one another.

The source for this material in the *Book of Watchers* is the first four verses of *Genesis* 6. There we can read about 'the sons of God' who are so enamoured by the 'daughters of men' that they marry them and produce 'mighty men . . . men of renown'.[23] Much academic ink has flowed in attempts to identify who the 'sons of God' are; this is a question which has exercised biblical commentators and scholars since the time of the Church Fathers (there are nine or more interpretations as to their identity). One interpretation is that the sons of God are the line of Seth, the third son of Adam.

For the *Enoch* author, however, there is no doubt about the identity of the sons of god. They are the angels who descended from heaven because they lusted after human women. By casting the sons of God in *Genesis* as fallen angels and elaborating on their story, the *Enoch* author has accounted for the presence of absolute evil in a God created world. These Watcher angels had a leader who went by the name of Semhazah. During this period, this was merely one name in a number of names that was being used to identify the supremely Evil One. This figure encapsulated the absolute essence of evil. Satan is course the name most people know him by.

In *Genesis* God is quick to respond to the threat posed by the giants. Straight after their introduction, God repents that he had created man and the beasts and sets about destroying the vast majority of them with the flood: 'And God saw that the wickedness of man was great in the earth, and that every imagination of the thoughts of his heart was only evil continually.'[24] In the *Book of Watchers* the precise nature of the world's sinfulness is itemized prior to the flood. In Chapter 7, man can no longer sustain the huge appetites of the giants and end up being devoured by them: 'They began to do violence to and attack all the birds and beasts of the earth and reptiles . . .

and the fish in the sea; and they began to devour their [men's] flesh, and they were drinking the blood.'[25]

Such a scenario is the stuff of nightmares and horror films. But the forces of evil just keep on coming. When the fallen angel, Asael, comes to the fore evil takes on a more recognizably human form; he teaches men how to make 'swords of iron and breastplates of bronze and every weapon for war'.[26] He then imparts the secrets of gold and silver jewellery, fashion and make-up to men, thereby corrupting future generations of women. In Chapter 8, other angels impart the secrets of the black arts of sorcery and astrology. In the hands of humans, such 'eternal mysteries' become evil, leading to an increase in impiety and fornication. As a result, war quickly ensues; blood spills across the face of the earth and the cries of the murdered ascend to the gates of heaven where they are heard by the archangels who request God's intervention. He accedes to their demand and sends the Flood, only sparing Noah and his offspring. The Deluge here is conceived as the 'First Great Judgement', not simply a precursor of the Last Judgement, the 'Great Judgement'. These two events are seen as twin events and form the overarching theme of this disparate collection of texts.[27]

God's retribution is swift in coming. Responsible for bringing warfare into the world, Asael meets a suitably violent end: blindfolded, bound hand and foot, he is cast into the depths of the earth, and covered with jagged rocks for all time. At the end of the world, he will be cast into the blazing fire. Semhazah and the other fallen angels are to be bound for 'seventy generations in valleys of the earth' until the Day of Judgement.[28] But first they will have to witness their sons destroy each other. God commissions Gabriel with the task of provoking the giants into an orgy of mutual slaughter until they are all dead. At the 'time of the end' they shall then be 'dragged off to the fiery abyss in torment' where they shall be incarcerated forever and ever.[29] Biblical scholars have pointed out that the fallen angels' subterranean fate owes a great deal to the Greek myth of Hades – one more instance of the extraordinary legacy of cultural cross-fertilization that took place in the centuries following Alexander the Great.

With the fallen angels held captive inside the earth and the giants heaped up into mounds of putrefying flesh, one might be forgiven for believing that evil had finally been eradicated from the world. Not a bit of it. In Chapter 15 God explains to Enoch how the giants' spirits will still haunt earth, creating evil wherever they go: 'But the *vicious* spirits (issuing) from the giants, Nephilim – they inflict harm, they destroy, they attack, they wrestle and dash to the ground . . . these spirits will rise against the sons of men and women.'[30] This myth of malevolent spirits stalking the earth explains the present-day condition of the Jews under Greek domination. Led astray, the present-day condition of the Jews is their just punishment.

In the apocalyptic world-view, the worse things get, the nearer we are to some glorious consummation when all injustice and suffering will be ended. God will descend from heaven with the angelic host, a time of tribulation will ensue in which the elect will be spared, leaving the unrighteous to be judged and punished. The precise nature of that punishment is described in great imaginative detail from Chapter 17 onwards. An archangel conducts Enoch to an extraordinary place: 'a deep abyss of the earth with pillars of heavenly fire' where he sees 'pillars of fire descending which were immeasurable in either height or depth'.

Beyond this abyss Enoch sees a 'place which had no firmament of heaven above, nor foundation of earth beneath it; there was no water in it and no birds, but it was a waste and horrible place'.[31] This fiery desert prison house is the place of punishment for the fallen angels and for the stars which failed to appear when they should have done. On the day of judge-ment, the fallen angels themselves will be brought from their subterranean prisons on earth to be cast into that fiery abyss. There they will be tormented for all eternity as punishment for having brought chaos and moral disorder into the world.

For the elect, an entirely different fate awaits them. In Chapters 24 and 25 we learn about how they will inherit a renewed earth, purged of the evil of former times. They will be uniquely blessed: their lives will be filled with peace, prosperity and joy. A tree will stand in their midst. It will scent the air with a wonderful aroma, sprout leaves that will never wither and die and bear abundant fruit. Smelling its fragrance will confer long life on the elect, a life so very different from the ones the Jews were living at present. It will be a life free of suffering and toil. It will be a life lived in perfect fellowship with God. The Almighty's presence will suffuse this paradise for he will come down from his transcendental realm and reside on a high mountain. This will be his throne. The elect will bask in his divine effulgence.

For Karl Marx, such a vision is an understandable but misguided reaction to earthly suffering. It is pie-in-the-sky stuff. For many, however, Enoch, Daniel and later John's visions of God punishing wrongdoers and rewarding the righteous fill a very large hole in the human heart. We need a vision of how things should be rather than how they might actually be. Rather than being an illusion, then, such a myth is enabling – it enables us to accept suffering, carry on and look to the future. Down-trodden, persecuted and oppressed, the Jews were the great creators of apocalypses because of their historical plight. Later, Christianity, an offshoot of Judaism, assimilated the Jewish apocalyptic tradition into its fantasies, visions and prophecies about the end of the world.

2

THE BIRTH OF APOCALYPTIC FAITH

In the three great apocalyptic faiths – Judaism, Christianity and Islam – the desert symbolizes the forces of chaos and disorder which threaten a divinely created order. Like the waters that forever lap at the shores of the created world, the desert is always there in the background, encroaching on the borders of order and civilization. In the myths of ancient Arabia, the desert is the abode of chaos-monsters, forever menacing cosmos and creation. In the Hebrew Bible too the desert is the domain of the demonic; the triumph of good over evil is often symbolized by the transformation of the desert into an oasis of fertility and order. Yahweh creates a highway along which God's Chosen People travel to freedom.

But the barren wilderness can also be a theatre of apocalyptic struggle. Down through the ages, visionaries and prophets have turned their back on the comforts of the city and gone to the desert in search of spiritual enlightenment. John

the Baptist found his prophetic powers in the Judaean wilderness, southeast of Jerusalem. The word of God came to him,
Luke confirms, in this desolate wilderness. There he expected a
Messiah, quoting *Isaiah* 'the voice of him that crieth in the
wilderness, Prepare ye the way of the Lord, make straight in
the desert a highway for our God'.[1] Muhammad too received
his great revelation in a desert. On the Night of Power, he
received the Koran in a cave on Mount Hira when an angel in
the form of a man appeared and instructed him to 'recite'.
Jesus himself spent forty days and forty nights in the wilderness and was then tempted by the devil.

No surprise, then, that the Essenes made the desert their
retreat when they sought a purer, holier life than the one
currently on offer in Jerusalem. It was on the northwest shore
of the Dead Sea that this important but obscure Jewish sect set
up their community. Sandwiched between the saline lake and
steep cliffs, the narrow coastal plain where they made their
home is the lowest dry point on earth. The surrounding cliffs
are pockmarked with thousands of caves like giant honey-
combs. It was in one such cave that the greatest archaeological
discovery of the twentieth century took place. In 1947 Bedouin
shepherds, attempting to rescue an errant goat, discovered
stone jars containing three manuscripts, two of them wrapped
in linen cloth. In succeeding years, remnants of about eight
hundred scrolls were found in a total of eleven caves at
Qumran in the Judaean desert. They are now known around
the world as the Dead Sea Scrolls.

Most scholarly opinion inclines to the belief that the texts at
Qumran were produced by the Essene sect which probably
came into existence in the early second century BC, during the
Antiochan crisis. Its end came in AD 68 during the first Jewish
war against Rome. Some time in the second century the more
observant and fanatical members of the sect, probably all men,

set up their own alternative to the Jerusalem temple, a monastery at Qumran, near the Dead Sea. Throughout Second Temple times the desert of Judaea was a locus for many breakaway religious groups and political dissidents. Like John the Baptist, the Qumran community saw their withdrawal to the wilderness as a religious mission; they too were making a highway for the Lord in the desert.

Although small in number – scholars believe that it can never have exceeded more than 200 – the community was absolutely convinced of its supreme spiritual power. The founder of the sect, a priest, known only as 'the Teacher of Righteousness', taught that the path of righteousness was an extremely narrow and exclusive one. Only the 'Teacher of Righteousness' and his successors possessed the secret knowledge that allowed them to interpret the Torah and other scriptures in the correct fashion. The community members, 'men of perfect holiness', constituted an elect, who strove with every fibre of their being to uphold to the letter all the commandments of the Law. This would ensure that one day the true Israel would emerge, triumphant and glorious.

By retreating to the desert, the sect was proclaiming its own unique identity. It was turning its back on what it considered to be the corrupt mainstream tradition of Judaism. Only sect members would be saved when God finally intervened in human affairs and brought to an end the 'age of wickedness'. Out there on the shores of the Dead Sea, the community was the sole locus of truth and divine favour in an ocean of darkness and wickedness. It was this sense of election that fortified the sect members in times of need and enabled them to embrace suffering with such indifference. In this respect, the Qumran community are the archetypal sectarians. They exulted in their apartness, glorified in their suffering and looked forward to the day when their enemies would be miraculously overthrown and cast down by their avenging God.

In such a world-view, suffering and sin – no less than happiness and goodness – is predetermined and must continue until the end. The *Community Rule* is a collection of rules and instructions for the communitarians; it also comments at length on the 'two spirits' which prevail on earth and in the cosmos. In this sharply delineated dualism, the world is divided between 'those born of truth' who 'spring from a fountain of light' and 'those born of falsehood' who 'spring from a source of darkness'. Although the 'Angel of Darkness' might succeed for a time in leading the 'children of right-eousness' astray – the Jerusalem priesthood were a case in point – the 'God of Knowledge' has foreordained this and will ultimately intervene to put final pay to the forces of evil.

As the source of both good and evil in the world, the Essenes' god certainly wielded enormous power. Through their secret knowledge of the true meaning of the Law, the sectaries of Qumran believed that they could tap some of that power. The elaborate purification rituals were a way of expunging the darkness in them and bringing themselves into the light.

To conceive of the rest of the world as an ocean of darkness was an effective way of defining and proclaiming their own holiness. The all-pervading darkness threw into sharp relief their own small and exclusive pool of light. Outside the community, the forces of darkness might hold sway – like the Romans who were painted in the darkest pitch. In times of crisis, when the forces of darkness threatened to completely extinguish the children of light, it was the library scrolls that fortified them. They contained visions of future glory. It was in such times that the Teacher of Righteousness played a crucial role. Divinely inspired, it was he who was able to decode the true import of the biblical prophecies, especially *Isaiah*. As a

result, he was able to reassure sect members that the countdown to the End had begun. When God finally intervened to
end the 'age of wickedness', a glorious future awaited the truly
righteous while absolute annihilation awaited the unrighteous.

The sect's brand of apocalyptic Judaism is given the clearest
expression in the *War Scroll*, one of the original seven scrolls
found in Cave One by Bedouin shepherds in 1947. It is also
known as the *War Rule* and *The War of the Sons of Light
against the Sons of Darkness*.[2] However you refer to it, there's
no doubt as to its content; the scroll provides the most
emphatic expression of the sect's apocalyptic faith. Here the
ultimate 'holy war' is conceived of lasting no fewer than forty
years. In this account, written at about the time of Jesus, the
Sons of Light (the elect of Israel) finally prevail forever over the
Sons of Darkness (the 'Kittim': Romans and other neighbouring powers). The angelic host swells the armies of the righteous
while the devil and his cohorts join forces with the Kittim.
When the Children of Light eventually overpower the forces of
darkness it heralds the final extinguishing of evil, clearing the
way for the God of Israel to rule eternally.

The forty–year-long conflict is only resolved on the very last
day of battle. There have been six bloody engagements; the
score stands at three all. In the seventh and final confrontation,
'the great hand of God shall be lifted up against Belial and all
the fo[rc]es of his dominion for an eternal slaughter'.[3] The
protracted nature of the battle illustrates an important theological point. While the eventual outcome is never in doubt –
God is all-powerful and preordains the victory of the Children
of Light – the fact that it appears to be a close-run thing
emphasizes the centrality of suffering in the lives of the righteous. To suffer was all part of God's plan. It was only at the
final hour, with things precariously poised, that God would
intervene in human affairs, ensuring the victory of good over

evil. This theology of suffering and rescue is eschatological drama at its most extreme. The apocalyptic imagination thrills to the victory snatched from the jaws of defeat. Such a scenario emphasizes God's providence and the special place the elect occupy in His plan.

The sect members expected divine intervention to whisk them out of the wilds of the Judaean desert, back to where they rightfully belonged – Jerusalem. There they would re-establish the correct type of Temple worship. What actually happened was somewhat different. In the summer of 68, the sect's archest enemies, the Romans, razed the settlement and snuffed out the Sons of Light. In the fate of this separatist Jewish sect we see the future fate of many such apocalyptic sects. What happened to the Qumran community represents the violent collision of prophetic belief and brute reality.

With the discovery of the Dead Sea Scrolls, a new dimension was added to our understanding of Christianity's Jewish origins. The parallels between first-century Judaism and Jesus' world-view have become ever more apparent since Albert Schweitzer's time. Geza Vermes, a world authority on the Dead Sea Scrolls, has written extensively on the Jewishness of Jesus. E.P. Sanders has also deepened our understanding of Jesus within the context of the Judaism of his time in such books as *Jesus and Judaism* and *The Historical Figure of Jesus*. What such scholars offer us is a very variegated view of the beliefs and expectations contained in that blanket term 'Judaism'. The Qumran sect reminds us that beliefs about the end of the world were alive and kicking when Jesus was starting his ministry. The urgency and sense of impending crisis would have been part of the atmosphere he would have breathed. It would have helped shape and infuse his apocalyptic sensibility.

*

The oldest gospel, *Mark*, portrays a Jesus who is obsessed by the imminent arrival of the Kingdom of God. In order to usher in this new age he has to do combat with the forces of evil that will attempt to thwart it. A stark dualism infuses such a world-view. As recorded by *Mark*, Jesus has an overpowering sense of cosmic war. *Mark* stresses the deeds, strength and determination of Jesus in doing combat with the forces of evil. He and his followers are convinced there are supernatural forces abroad in the world pitted against the forces of goodness. It would be only in the Last Days that these forces would be overthrown and defeated.

The eschatological drama begins with Jesus being baptized by John the Baptist in the river Jordan. John is a vociferous proclaimer that the Kingdom of God is nigh and that all must repent urgently. Contemporary scholars emphasize the importance of John the Baptist's influence over Jesus and his message. For example, in volume 2 of John Meier's towering work, *Jesus: A Marginal Jew*, the idea is developed that Jesus was probably part of the Baptist's early circle and that he was deeply imbued with his mentor's apocalyptic view of the Kingdom of God. In Meier's view, when Jesus left the circle of the Baptist to start his own ministry, he seems to have taken some of the Baptist's followers with him. As Meier's subtitle indicates, 'Mentor, message and miracles', John the Baptist's belief in the fast approaching End was central to Jesus' own message. Meier points to the Lord's Prayer, the Beatitudes and such passages as *Mark* 6:10 and *Matthew* 8:11–12 to develop his point.[4]

At Jesus' baptism the Holy Spirit descends. A divine force then impels him into the wilderness to do combat with Satan. Here he will be tempted for forty days. After he successfully withstands the blandishments of the devil, Jesus returns to Galilee where he proclaims the following: 'The time is fulfilled, and the Kingdom of God is at hand: repent ye, and believe the gospel.' Soon Satan attempts to rally his forces so that Jesus has to exorcize an evil spirit from a man in a synagogue. News travels fast that here is a great healer and miracle worker. Soon he has a whole city of devil-possessed citizens clamouring at his door: 'And he healed many that were sick of divers diseases, and cast out many devils; and suffered not the devils to speak, because they knew him.'[5] Just as the Qumran sectarians believed they were engaged in a holy war against the forces of evil, so Jesus and his early followers conceive of themselves as leading the assault on the demonic legions. Each act of exorcism Jesus performs is an act of cosmic significance. It reduces Satan's dominion and helps to usher in God's kingdom.

The return of Christ is the chief eschatological event. The Gospels, like the Essene writings and John the Baptist's teachings, view the coming of the Kingdom of God with great urgency:

> Verily I say unto you, there be some standing here, which shall not taste of death, till they see the Son of Man coming in his kingdom.

> But I tell you of a truth, there be some standing here, which shall not taste of death, till they see the kingdom of God.[6]

The authors of these prophetic verses have an acute sense of the lack of time available to repent and reform. As they relate it, Jesus' message contains a radically new conception of what it takes to enter the Kingdom of God. To abide by the letter of the Law was simply no longer sufficient; a new and deeper morality must come into being.

The imminence of divine intervention in human history will

bring about the Kingdom of God, following a bitter battle with the forces of evil. Clearly Jesus expects to return within the lifetime of his contemporaries. The Apostles too expected Jesus to return before the passing of their generation. The end of the world involves both destruction and consummation in a vexed and anguished interplay. Heaven awaits the righteous. As for the unrighteous – well, we are left in little doubt as to what their eventual fate will be:

> For whosoever shall be ashamed of me and of my words, of him shall the Son of Man be ashamed, when he shall come in his own glory, and in his Father's, and of the holy angels.

> There shall be weeping and gnashing of teeth, when ye shall see Abraham, and Isaac and Jacob, and all the prophets, in the kingdom of God, and you yourselves thrust out.

> The Son of Man shall send forth his angels, and they shall gather out of his kingdom all things that offend, and them which do iniquity; And shall cast them into a furnace of fire: there shall be wailing and gnashing of teeth.

> When the Son of Man shall come in his glory, and all the holy angels with him, then shall he sit upon the throne of his glory. And before him shall be gathered all the nations: and he shall separate them one from another, as a shepherd divideth his sheep from the goats.[7]

Jesus, as Son of Man, then will come to judge the whole world. All the nations will be gathered in a universal judgement. The homely image of the sheep and the goats cannot disguise the cosmic significance of the event.

In contrast, the resurrected male and female denizens of the kingdom become more than just human; in fact, they 'are as the angels which are in heaven' and will not marry. While the unrighteous burn in the furnaces of hell, the 'righteous shine forth as the sun in the kingdom of their Father'.[8]

Although Jesus' followers are told to expect the Kingdom in their own lives, they are also warned against apocalyptic prophecy. No one knows, Jesus warns them, when it is the end except for God. The disciples therefore have to remain ever vigilant in case their master returns and they are caught unawares. Expectation is powerfully mixed with ignorance: apocalyptic prophecy has always thrived off such contradiction and paradox. The lack of certainty about precisely when the end will come, combined with an equally powerful belief in its inevitability, has inspired prophetic predictions down through the centuries. The apocalyptist conceives of himself as one of the initiated who can fathom the mysteries of scripture and come up with a definitive time and date. When these predictions have been disconfirmed – as so many of them have been down through the ages – then it is simply a question of conjuring the numbers again.

At the beginning of his ministry, Jesus takes to the road and preaches throughout Galilee, casts out devils, heals the sick and calls sinners to repentance. He is beginning the work which will eventually lead to his martyrdom on the cross and the Atonement. He is carrying the fight to Satan, pushing back his dominion and bringing in the Kingdom of God. In order to widen his campaign against Satan he calls upon the twelve disciples to go forth and do the same. This will expedite the coming of the Kingdom. On the very first occasion when he sends out the disciples, he says to them: 'Ye shall not have gone over the cities of Israel before the Son of Man comes.'[9]

In Chapter 4 of *Mark*, Jesus' parable about the seeds falling on various types of ground emphasizes the continual vigilance the disciples must exercise in their apocalyptic combat with Satan. The word is sown but it is likely to fall on stony or thorny ground or sometimes those standing by the wayside have the seed plucked from their hearts by Satan before it can properly germinate. By sowing such divine seeds in the hearts of individuals Jesus and his disciples are bringing into being the Kingdom of God. The germinating seeds will miraculously become a field waiting to be harvested. In other words, they are replacing the lost terrestrial paradise of Adam and Eve and replacing it with a superior heavenly realm.

Mark is suffused with this sense of the imminence of total transformation. Despite all the healing, preaching and exorcism the Kingdom of God will be ushered in only after a terrible period of tribulation. The so-called Marcan Apocalypse predicts that when the end comes not one stone of the Temple shall be left standing. Preceding this are the Last Days, a period thronging with false pretenders to the title of Christ: 'For false Christs and false prophets shall rise, and shall shew signs and wonders, to seduce, if it were possible, even the elect.'[10] Nation will be pitted against nation, religious persecutions, famines and earthquakes will rack the world: cosmological disturbances will be the final sign that the End is about to be reached:

> the sun shall be darkened, and the moon shall not give her light,
> And the stars of heaven shall fall, and the powers that are in
>   heaven shall be shaken.
> And then shall they see the Son of Man coming in the clouds
>   with great power and glory.
> And then shall he send his angels, and shall gather together his
>   elect from the four winds, from the uttermost part of the
>   earth to the uttermost part of heaven.[11]

In the Hebrew Testament the prophets use the fig tree as a symbol of the nation of Israel.[12] In *Mark,* Jesus uses the sprouting fig tree metaphor as a way of figuring the imminent arrival of the Kingdom of God. Just as fig trees are harbingers of summer so must the disciples look out for signs of the End of the World. That Jesus clearly expected an early summer is made explicit in verse 30: 'Verily I say unto you, that this generation shall not pass, till all these things be done.' The same message is hammered home in *Matthew*: 'Verily I say unto you, there be some standing here, which shall not taste of death, till they see the Son of Man coming in his kingdom.'[13] Here the chief eschatological event, the Second Coming of Christ, is explicitly predicted to happen within the lifetime of some of the Apostles.

Unlike the Essenes, Jesus did not rely on armies of followers brandishing swords. Instead legions of angels would enable him to fulfil his messianic role. When he speaks of his Second Coming it is with angels and heavenly powers that he surrounds himself.[14] Then the nations of the world 'shall see the Son of Man coming in the clouds of heaven and great glory'. Earthly potentates will submit without striking a blow. When the angel's trumpet blasts they will range themselves with the resurrected dead and wait for judgement.

In a beautiful passage in *Romans*, Paul envisions the faithful putting on the spiritual armour of faith as they do battle with the forces of evil. The light and dark imagery recalls the Qumran *War Scroll*:

> And that, knowing the time, that now it is high time to awake out of sleep: for now is our salvation nearer than when we believed. The night is far spent, the day is at hand: let us therefore cast off the works of darkness, and let us put on the armour of light.[15]

Towards the end of the first century, however, Christians had to face the fact that Jesus had failed to reappear in apocalyptic splendour upon the clouds of heaven. These early Christians were beset with a problem that has vexed prophecy believers down through the ages – disconfirmation. Non-occurrence of the events foretold can lead to the discrediting of an apocalyptist's reputation. The early Christians were faced with a similar dilemma. What do you do when the time and the season fixed for the Second Coming has elapsed and Jesus still has failed to turn up? One solution is to make up a new date or come up with an explanation as to why the original calculation was flawed. Often this can involve intellectual sleights-of-hand. Certainly the author of 2 *Peter* is required to exercise quite a lot of mental agility to explain the non-appearance of Jesus to the early Christians. As a way of answering the scoffers, the author reconfigures our conceptions of time itself: 'But, beloved, be not ignorant of this one thing, that one day is with the Lord as a thousand years, and a thousand years as one day.'[16]

A thousand human years are in the sight of God just one day. If we overlook the fact that in the original promise the reckoning was by man's years not God's, then a very simple point is conveyed to the waiting Christians. They may have to wait some time before Jesus returns.

Nowadays, in our doom-laden times, Jesus the apocalyptic prophet is very much in the ascendant. Books about his end-of-worldism such as Bart Ehrman's *Jesus: Apocalyptic Prophet of the New Millennium* sell very nicely. It is a highly entertaining read but hardly an original thesis; Ehrman portrays Jesus as Albert Schweitzer did nearly a century before: as a first-century Jewish apocalyptist, one of many living in that era:

Jesus thought that the history of the world would come to a
screeching halt, that God would intervene in the affairs of this

planet, overthrow the forces of evil in a cosmic act of judgement, and establish his utopian Kingdom here on earth. And this was to happen within Jesus' own generation.[17]

In such a view, Christ the Messiah has been shrunk down to size to be replaced by the lowly Jesus of Nazareth, a prophet who believed (wrongly) that the end was nigh, if not within his lifetime, then, certainly within the lifetime of his followers. When the longed-for end failed to arrive on cue Christian copyists felt obliged to get to work on his original message, disguising its original apocalyptic flavour.

*

No one has ever tried to disguise the apocalyptic flavour of the *Book of Revelation*. The last book and only apocalypse in the New Testament, many have found it too flavoursome by half. Perhaps the most influential book ever written, the *Book of Revelation* very nearly never made it into the official canon. For centuries, it was in danger of being consigned to the margins like the earlier *Book of Enoch*. When eventually it was accepted as canonical, it established itself as the apocalyptic text *par excellence* – the ultimate end-time vision. Hence it is often referred as *the* Apocalypse, as if it were unique rather than being one among a number in this genre. How you view this book will of course depend very largely on your religious beliefs. For contemporary Christian prophecy believers, *Revelation* has been divinely authored like all the other books of the Bible. In such a view, John simply recorded what Jesus Christ revealed to him. Whereas Muhammad recited the word of God, John wrote it down.

In contrast, there are those secular-minded scholars and critics who do not see John as a prophet in his own right but simply as an author of religiously inspired literature which belongs to the genre of apocalyptic. Although *Revelation* is undoubtedly the most famous and most influential example of just such a piece of literature, it is nevertheless part of a wider body of writing. It is to be interpreted with reference to the *Book of Daniel* and the earlier Jewish prophecies. In such a view, the *Book of Revelation* has a paradigmatic quality to it. It is read as an individual's response to the age-old conflict between good and evil, a projection of the hopes of a persecuted minority. For such scholars, the work was probably written towards the end of the reign of the emperor Domitian, around AD 95–96. As Norman Cohn has noted, the author calls himself 'John', and traditionally he has been identified with the Apostle John, son of Zebedee. However, it is 'more likely that the John in question was an itinerant prophet', active in the churches of the Roman province of Asia, the western coast of what is today Turkey.[18]

The *Book of Revelation* begins with an ending: it is now 'the hour of fulfilment' and John receives a prophetic vision of what will happen directly from Jesus who in turn has received it from God. Unlike Daniel, John does not need the intercession of an angel. Unlike the author of the *Book of Enoch* he does not need to hide behind a pseudonym. He clearly identifies himself and explains in vivid detail how he received the visions and messages included in the book. 'I was in the Spirit on the Lord's Day', he records, 'and heard behind me a great voice, as of a trumpet, saying "I am Alpha and Omega, the first and the last: and, what thou seest, write it in a book, and send it unto the seven churches which are in Asia".'[19] The 'Lord's Day' mentioned here at the beginning of *Revelation* is not the Sabbath but the day in which the world will be destroyed. In other parts of the scripture it is referred to as 'the day of the Lord'. John has been miraculously transported into the future, not bodily but in the spirit, in order to give us a preview of what will happen on the last day of the world.

On the Lord's Day he is caught up by the spirit and granted a startlingly vivid vision of the risen Jesus:

I . . . heard behind me a great voice, as of a trumpet . . . And I turned to see the voice that spake with me. And being turned, I saw . . . one like unto the Son of Man, clothed with a garment down to the foot, and girt about the paps with a golden girdle. His head and his hairs were white like wool, as white as snow; and his eyes were as a flame of fire; And his feet like unto fine brass, as if they burned in a furnace; and his voice as the sound of many waters. And he had in his right hand seven stars: and out of his mouth went a sharp two-edged sword: and his countenance was as the sun shineth in his strength. And when I saw him, I fell at his feet as dead. And he laid his right hand upon me, saying unto me, Fear not; I am the first and the last: I am he that liveth, and was dead; and, behold, I am alive for evermore . . . and have the keys of hell and of death.[20]

Those who have kept the faith can expect a glorious future (they will walk with Jesus robed in white); they will be spared the time of tribulation, the period prior to the End of the World, that the rest of the world and its inhabitants will be subject to. The transcendent figure of Christ with a double-edged sword in his mouth is the arch dispenser of justice. For those who keep the faith unto the end absolute earthly power will be granted them:

And he that overcometh, and keepeth my works unto the end, to him will I give power over the nations: And he shall rule them with a rod of iron; as the vessels of a potter shall they be broken to shivers: even as I received of my Father.[21]

The dominant note of the book is struck early on: infinite rewards for the good, retributive punishment for the bad.

Those who are distastefully lukewarm in their faith will be spewed out. Like a thief in the night, Christ will return unexpectedly. Those who welcome him in will be rewarded, those who don't punished. Pot smashing, thieves in the night, invitations to supper: the imagery of the opening chapters is domestic, even vulgar.

A more exalted plane is reached in Chapter 4. John sees a door open up in heaven and a voice like a trumpet enjoins him to come and see what the future holds. He sees a vision of an enthroned figure overarched by a rainbow, jewel-like, surrounded by twenty-four elders with gold crowns. Before the throne is a sea of glass like crystal, and surrounding the throne are four beasts with six wings and multiple eyes. The enthroned carries in his right hand a book with seven seals which no man on earth is able to open. Only Christ can open the book and unseal the seals. Christ, who is now conceived of as a Lamb with eyes and seven horns, takes the book from God's hand to a musical accompaniment from the four beasts and twenty-four elders. Having shed his blood to save mankind, only Christ is capable of opening the seals.

The seven-sealed book here is an antitype to the one at the end of the *Book of Daniel*. In the earlier apocalypse, God closes up the book so that not all the secrets about the future of the world are revealed; the words are to be 'closed up and sealed till the time of the end'. In *Revelation*, however, Christ will finally open Daniel's book. In doing so he will be revealing the true meaning of human history. At that time, an angel specifically commands John 'seal not the sayings of the prophecy of this book: for the time is at hand'.[22] *Revelation* is therefore often regarded as a re-interpretation of *Daniel* from a Christian perspective as well as a kind of sequel to it. It will answer many of the questions *Daniel* left unanswered; it will develop the symbolism of the earlier apocalypse and elaborate upon it in an extensive and highly imaginative way. For example, the opening of the seven seals is a narrative device of extraordinary dramatic power. Whereas the seal and book metaphor is used in *Daniel* fleetingly to figure that secret knowledge which is tantalizing beyond Daniel's comprehension, in *Revelation* the central chapters are preoccupied with the unsealing of the book which occasion ever more bizarre and earth-shattering events.

In Chapter 6, when the Lamb looses the first four seals he reveals forces that God would use to bring judgement upon the oppressors of his people; the famous four riders on their different coloured horses – white, red, black and pale – are given power and authority by Christ. These four horses and their riders symbolize respectively military conquest, civil war, famine and death. In the Hebrew Bible, in the great prophetic books *Jeremiah*, *Ezekiel* and *Isaiah*, God had punished and judged his enemies and the unrighteous through these means. For example, in *Jeremiah* God used famine in His judgement upon Israel; in *Revelation* famine is associated with the black horse and its rider. With the opening of the fifth seal, we are told why God should bring such destructive judgements upon the world. John relates how he sees under the altar the souls of those Christian martyrs that were slain for their faith. They cry out for vengeance but are comforted with white robes, told to rest and be assured that when the time is right the judgements will begin.

The opening of the sixth seal unleashes a vortex that sucks up the whole of the created order. There's an earthquake. Then the sun turns nightmarishly black, the moon into a lurid shade of blood red. Stars fall to earth. The firmament is rolled up like a scroll and the mountains and islands move. Such disturbances engender extreme perturbation in the rich and powerful; they attempt to hide themselves from God's wrath in caves and dens. John regards such pathetic scenes with undisguised relish. This is payback day for the underdog. Later, such a reversal of the earthly social order appealed strongly to revolutionaries and political radicals.

All is not destruction, however. Between the sixth and the seventh seals, John sees two visions in an interlude which offers an important glimmer of hope. In the first vision, John sees four angels standing at the four corners of the earth, holding back the winds from blowing on the earth, sea, or on any tree. John then sees in the east an angel who has the seal of God; he cries out to the angels to desist from destruction until the faithful have been sealed in their foreheads. In total there will be 144,000 sealed on earth like this, 12,000 each from the twelve tribes of Israel. When God's wrath and judgement pours down on earth those sealed will be spared, although they will still have to withstand the time of tribulation. In the second vision, John envisions the future blessing in heaven that awaits those who withstand this tribulation on earth. He beholds an innumerable multitude in heaven, drawn from all nations standing before the throne and the Lamb, clothed in white robes and holding palms. These lucky souls have come out of the great tribulation with their robes washed and made white in the blood of the Lamb.

After this dramatic interlude, it's back to the destruction of the world. Chapter 8 opens with a half-hour of silence in heaven but this is only a lull before the storm. Seven angels with trumpets appear, heralding some pretty bad news for humanity. An orgy of destruction both earthly and cosmic ensues. Hail mixed with fire and blood rains down on the earth, destroying a third of the trees and grass. Next a great burning mountain is thrown into the sea, turning a third of it into blood, disastrous to marine life and shipping alike. This is swiftly followed with the great burning star Wormwood falling on a third of the rivers and springs of water, poisoning vast numbers of men. A third of the sun, moon and stars are darkened. Giant locusts with human faces, horses' heads and scorpion tails plague all those on earth who have not been sealed in the forehead. Horrors mount with the blowing of the sixth trumpet. Four angels from the east are loosed and promptly marshal an army of 'two hundred thousand thousand' riding lion-headed horses breathing fire and brimstone. A massacre of unimaginable proportions ensues – this supernatural force wipes out a third of mankind.

At last the seventh angel sounds. Voices in heaven proclaim the victory of Christ's kingdom over the earthly kingdoms; 'the temple of God was opened in heaven'; more thunderings, lightnings and earthquakes then ensue. Next, in Chapter 12, comes the dramatic entrance of the mysterious 'woman clothed in the sun', travailing in birth. A great dragon appears with seven heads on which are ten horns; with a swish of its mighty tail, the monstrous creature makes a third of the stars drop from the firmament. The dragon is determined to devour the child as soon as it is born but God gathers up the child and saves it, leaving the mother to flee into the wilderness. The angel Michael and his hosts then take on the dragon, now identified as Satan, and cast him out of heaven on to the earth. Woe has now come to those on earth because Satan is among them. Having failed to destroy the woman clothed in the sun, he vents his wrath on the faithful.

We have now reached midway in the apocalypse and an even more dramatic entrance occurs. In Chapter 13, a seven-headed and ten-horned Beast rises from the sea. The zoomorphic form of this creature – it combines the characteristics of a leopard, a bear and a lion – clearly owes a great deal to the *Book of Daniel*. John is vouchsafing the authenticity of his vision by drawing on the earlier Jewish apocalypse. A second beast, later called the 'false prophet', arises from the earth and assists the first one in forty-two months of tyrannical rule. During this time, the second beast from the land blasphemes, performs miracles, and erects a speaking statue of the first beast from the sea. Many are won over. Those that aren't are persecuted mercilessly. In order to buy or sell, everyone is required to be marked with the figure 666, a demonic parody of God sealing the faithful in the forehead.

Only a heroic and militant Christ can defeat such a world power. For those who accept the mark of the Beast, they will have to reckon with one 'like unto the Son of Man' and an angel, both brandishing sharp sickles. The kingdom of the Beast is reaped, those that are guilty are mowed down like ripe grapes, thrown into a winepress and crushed until their blood rises to the height of a horse bridle. But, just when we think things cannot get worse they do. In Chapter 15, seven angels appear with seven vials and quickly pour out on sinful humanity a series of plagues. The Beast's followers are now afflicted with sores, particularly in their mouths; rivers and seas are turned to blood once again and the sun scorches them. Darkness engulfs the Beast's kingdom. The Euphrates river is dried up, the great cities of the world collapse in an earthquake; islands and mountains disappear; gigantic hailstones pound the earth. Bathetically, the Beast and the false prophet, once so plausible, can only croak frog-like words. When the sixth angel pours his vial, the stage is set for Armageddon – the kings of the earth will be gathered together in one final but doomed attempt to defeat the forces of goodness.

In the next chapter, one of the great apocalyptic types appears – the demonic city of Babylon. It is represented allegorically as a great whore who fornicates with the kings of the earth. Decked out in gaudy clothes and bejewelled to an inch of her life, this shameless lady rides a scarlet-coloured beast which has the usual attributes – seven heads and ten horns. She is drunk on the blood of the saints. An angel explains to John the significance of this figure. The seven heads and the horns represent kingdoms that have existed and ones which have not yet come into existence. Whether kings past or to come their fate is the same – they will be crushed by the 'Lord of lords, and King of kings'. Babylon is fated to burn with fire, along with the merchants who traded with her and the kings who consorted with her. The vision of Babylon the Golden laid low is a richly haunting one. The city is abandoned and desolate. No music sounds in the streets. No candle will burn there. Babylon's destruction is the archetypal fall of the rich and the powerful.

As the smoke settles over Babylon the Fallen, we enter the final phase of the apocalypse. Now the great protagonist of the *Book of Revelation* makes his final and triumphant entry in the great apocalyptic drama. Christ appears on a white horse out of heaven, leading an angelic army on similar mounts. His eyes are like flames; he wears a bloody vestment; on his head are many crowns. No longer a lowly Nazarene, Jesus is now a militant Christ. Both judge and warrior, he is a fear-inspiring and all-powerful figure; from his mouth issues a sharp sword to do down nations that oppose his rule.

No matter that the Beast has found plenty of human allies in his war with God. Christ scythes down them down with the sword in his mouth, leaving their remains for the vultures to pick over. The Beast and the false prophet are captured and thrown alive into a lake of fire. Satan himself is chained by an angel and thrown into the bottomless pit which is shut and sealed. Here he will reside for a thousand years after which 'he must be let loose for a short while'. This is the original millennium, a thousand-year period in which the Christian martyrs are resurrected and reign with Christ on earth.

After the millennium has run its course, Satan is released for a final battle, only to be defeated once and for all. Everyone who has ever lived will then be resurrected and consigned either to heaven or hell. With the Last Judgement, time ends. History segues into eternity. The old earth and heaven is replaced by a new heaven and earth. The descent of the New Jerusalem is a fitting ending to the consummation of all time. Metaphorically, this city is like a bride decked up for her wedding, it is a dwelling for God among men. Like a father wiping away the tears of his children, God will banish death in his new realm; there will be an end to mourning, crying and pain for the old order has been entirely replaced. Heaven and earth, so often out of joint in the past, will dovetail perfectly, never to be sundered again. Human beings will commingle with angels. The celestial city is at once weightless and monumental, ethereal and intensely vivid. Sapphires, emeralds, amethyst, topaz, chrysoprase encrust the walls; a street is plated with pure gold like glass. Spangling, gleaming and glittering like a jeweller's shop window, the city's radiant light will not be dimmed. Here the elect will live forever in the light of the Lord, there being no longer the need for a sun or a moon. Here earthly kings and the rulers of nations, once at war with each other, will live in harmony, give over their wealth and pay homage to a higher power. Water, once the destructive element in *Genesis*, now becomes the river of life; next to it grows the Tree of Life which bears twelve types of fruit and yields every month.

After all the terror and the darkness of the preceding chapters, we are left then with a vision of dazzling light – the New Jerusalem coming out of the skies. For the faithful the End of the World is not a terminus but a radically new beginning, the start of a journey above and beyond to a realm of eternal peace, beauty and harmony. Such a vision held a special appeal in the last centuries of the Roman era, as the empire tottered, fragmented and finally disintegrated. The twelve pearly gates are always open to those of pure heart, closed to those 'unclean'. Christ assures John that he will come 'quickly', a word which recurs repeatedly, suffusing the whole narrative with a sense of crisis and feverish expectancy. As time speeds up to its final consummation, locality after locality passes before our eyes in phantasmagoric blur. This time–space compression induces a sense of delirium which is finally resolved in the vision of the celestial city descending from the clouds. Static, unchanging and tightly bounded, such a place reveals the Jewish–Christian desire to have a place called home in a world rent with conflict and persecution, injustice and suffering.

*

One of the first to be inspired by such a vision of an imminent and better future-life was Montanus in the second century. He led one of the very first millennial groups to spring up in the wake of the *Book of Revelation*. The binding of Satan for a thousand years leads to Christ's millennial reign on earth for that term as predicted in Chapter 20 of *Revelation*. During this thousand-year interval between the Second Coming and the conclusive battle between good and evil, Christ reigns over a 'heaven on earth' in which all suffering is banished and peace, justice and harmony prevails. Such beliefs have their roots in the idea of the more secular Jewish messianic kingdom as envisioned by the prophets in the Hebrew Bible. In *Revelation* 20 this is developed into Christ's earthly millennial reign.

For millennarians, only the faithful few are slated for salvation. Believing that the millennium is imminent, they look forward to a complete transformation of the terrestrial state of things through a supernatural agency. Certainly Montanus fits the millenarian paradigm. Declaring himself to be the incarnation of the Holy Ghost, he formed a movement in Phrygia, the western part of the Anatolian plateau in present-day Turkey. For Montanus and his *illuminati* ('the enlightened') this was to be where a miraculous event was about to occur in the very near future. Along with his two prophetesses, Priscilla (or Prisca) and Maximilia, Montanus claimed to be the voice of the Paraclete, an appellation of the Holy Ghost which occurs in John.[23]

Christ was about to return to earth and it was here on Phrygian soil that the New Jerusalem would descend. The little town of Pepuza, not Jerusalem, would be the apocalyptic city. Epiphanius, a fourth-century writer on heretics, is a major source on Montanus' teachings, although hardly an unbiased one. Through his reports we learn how this revelation came about. While sleeping, Priscilla was visited by Christ who came to her and slept with her 'in the likeness of a woman, clad in a bright robe, and he planted wisdom in me and revealed that his place (Pepuza), is holy, and that here Jerusalem comes down from heaven'.[24] The Montanists were to be dogged with accusations of sexual immorality by their detractors despite their fulsome avowals of chastity. Maybe it was Priscilla and Maximilia who had abandoned their husbands to take up the mantle of divinely inspired prophetesses that inspired such prurient interest in commentators.

But what really bothered Epiphanius and other commentators were the claims sect members made about the origin of their ecstatic visions and utterances. They were judged to be quite unlike the utterances of Old Testament and New Testament prophets. Epiphanius draws the distinction between Old and New Testament prophets and Montanists. Even when they were 'in the spirit', biblical prophets were always aware of what they were saying. In contrast, the Montanists fell into a rapt, trance-like state of total and utter possession. Such ecstasies were deemed dangerously heretical because the Montanists evidently regarded them as divinely inspired. It was not just a question of having an unseemly or extravagant prophetic style; it was the fact that Montanists regarded themselves as the authentic voice of the spirit of God that was the challenge to orthodox belief.

In order to help usher in the new dispensation, Montanists were urged to embrace an arduous asceticism and undergo severe penitential disciplines. They were hunkering down for the final countdown. Route one on the road to salvation was martyrdom. Marriage was deemed a detour. When the time came the *illuminati* were to gather together in one place – Pepuza – and await the descent of the celestial city from the heavens as predicted in Chapter 21 of *Revelation*. The failure of such a prophecy to materialize was spectacularly public. Whole Christian communities abandoned their homes in pursuit of a millennium only to have to return to their homes empty handed. What was to be done, the *illuminati*, must have cried? If not now, then when? True to the Festinger's paradigm of failed prophecies, their inner light was not dimmed but shone out ever brighter. When it came to failed prophecies, the Montanists did what countless sects have done down through the centuries – reconcile mundane reality with glorious prophecy beliefs by devising new dates and revising the old one. They even stepped up their efforts at proselytizing new members.

The primitive Christian Church was aseethe with such fervent millennial expectation. In this respect, Montanus was wholly typical of the age, just more extreme than most. In the ensuing centuries, Montanism was to spread across Asia Minor, Africa, Rome and Gaul. It survived until the ninth century. The alarm with which the Church viewed such a phenomenon is wholly typical of the way in which hierarchically organized Christianity has always reacted to individuals and movements which claim to be uniquely inspired. When Montanism claimed Tertullian of Carthage in the third century as its latest convert, the Church was deeply shocked because it put the seal of approval on a movement it had tried to discredit. After all, Priscilla and Maximilia had both transgressed boundaries laid down by traditional patriarchal religious authority. Fancy having women in such positions of authority! Remember the ecstasies, the frenzied trances, the rapturous utterances! To cap it all, now one of the famous theologians in the West had turned his back on orthodoxy and embraced sectarian extremism. Under Tertullian's leadership Montanism flourished in Carthage in the third century and spread through North Africa. His writings are one of the few primary sources for Montanist teaching.[25]

The spread of Montanism reflects the fervid religious climate of the times. The early Christian movement had miraculously sprung up in the shadow of the End. When Christ had failed to return as expected many were on the lookout for charismatic prophets who could offer an explanation as to why this had not happened or when it would indeed happen. End-time predictions then filled a massive emotional vacuum. The prevalence of apocalypticism among the early Christians contrasts strikingly with the situation with mainstream Judaism. The failure of the second Jewish revolt against Rome in AD 135 had not only very political repercussions but also resulted in an important doctrinal shift. Once the apocalyptic genre had been the mainstay of the Chosen People who longed to do down their enemies and exalt themselves; now Jewish leaders condemned it as futile and dangerous. Texts like the *Book of Daniel* still retained their popularity; but rabbis began to interpret them less on a literal and predictive level and more on a symbolic and allegorical one. Literal biblical prophecy gave way to a form of devotional worship centred on interpreting and following the Torah.

In contrast, the radical and insurrectionary nature of much millenarianism was an important factor in its spread. Such a belief empowers the lowly, endowing them with a spiritual glory over and above their earthly masters. For Montanus, the world was one vast theatre in which the drama of the Last Days was being acted out. In the lead role was the Holy Ghost, pouring out prophecies and visions to believers which challenged the ecclesiastical authority of the day – the Catholic Church. Who needed a bishop or intercessionary priests when you could be visited directly by the Holy Ghost? Frantic and frenzied outpourings of religious energy were also just as likely to attract as to repel. For the early Church Fathers, Montanism was the writing on the wall – it warned them about the dangers posed by apocalyptic expectations. It is here in the second century that we see the age-old clash between institutionalized religion and those self-proclaimed apocalyptic agents of God.

*

We have seen so far how the birth of apocalyptic faith has been a long and protracted one. If Zoroastrianism represents the inception, then the great Jewish prophecies were the gestation from which issued finally the first fully fledged Jewish apocalypse in one book, the *Book of Daniel*. In the post-natal period, as it were, the *Book of Revelation* represents maturation. Its offspring are multiple and varied including radical and mystical millenarians like Montanus in the second century and the latest televangelists and Internet prophets of today's world. There is, however, another important family member. Often overlooked by western, biblically inclined religious scholars, Islam has contributed greatly to apocalyptic faith and its worldwide spread.

Along with Judaism and Christianity, Islam is the third and youngest member of the so-called Abrahamic family of monotheistic faiths. Abraham bulks so large in the Koran because, it is believed, Allah revealed through him the truth of monotheism. Viewed from a koranic perspective, there is continuity between the three great faiths. For Muslims, their God is not different from the one worshipped by Jews and Christians; he is the same figure but with an Arab name, Allah. Muhammad's Jewish and Christian predecessors were Abraham, Moses and Jesus, regarded as revered messengers of the one supreme and almighty God. These figures introduced important revelations at particular stages in God's unfolding plan. As a result, the Koran refers respectfully to Christians and Jews as 'People of the Book' ('Book' means here divine scripture, i.e. the Bible and the Torah).

Nevertheless, the Jewish and Christian revelations are still regarded merely as the prelude to the greatest revelation of them all – when Muhammad started to receive the Koran in seventh-century Arabia. Meaning 'recitation', the Koran is regarded quite literally as the speech of God. When God spoke to Muhammad in the cave on Mount Hira it was from all eternity and it was to the whole of humankind. He was now the bringer of God's message to the whole world. For the next twenty-three years he received a series of revelations that were eventually written down and became the 'created' Koran. This was the earthly version of the 'uncreated' Koran, a transcendent and timeless book containing God's words, infallible and final.

Those portions of the Koran dealing with the end of the world are supplemented by the Hadith, the official sayings of the prophet which were collected during his lifetime and written down by scribes. In the majority branch of the faith, Sunni Islam, the events preceding the end of the world bear a striking resemblance to a Christian end-time scenario. Moral and social breakdown, natural and cosmic disasters and social and political upheaval: all these are read as 'signs' that we have entered the end-time. In the Christian apocalyptic tradition, the Antichrist presides over this explosion of evil; in Islamic eschatology the equivalent figure is the Dajjal, the arch tempter or deceiver, who will lead the world astray when he appears. Only those true Muslims who have willingly submitted their will to God's will are able to resist this one-eyed evil man. Everyone else will be subject to a time of tribulation. Just before Dajjal succeeds in annihilating the Muslims, Jesus will come down from the heavens and kill him. There then will follow a messianic age, led by either Jesus or another messianic figure called the Mahdi. He will institute a new world order in which everyone has been converted to Islam. After the time of the Mahdi, then the forces of evil (Gog and Magog) will invade the world and set about destroying it. It is at that point that Allah will bring about the end of the world.

On the Day of Judgement, Allah will mete out divine justice with infallible firmness, fairness and rigour. As in the *Book of Revelation*, the events preceding this grand assize are rendered with great dramatic and poetic force:

> When the sun shall be darkened,
> when the stars shall be thrown down,
> when the mountains shall be set moving,
> when the pregnant camel shall be neglected,
> when the savage beasts shall be mustered,
> when the seas shall be set boiling,
> when the souls shall be coupled,
> when the buried infant shall be asked for what sin she was
>   slain,
> when the scrolls shall be unrolled,
> when heaven shall be stripped off,

when Hell shall be set blazing,
when Paradise shall be brought nigh,
then shall a soul know what it has produced.[26]

The righteous are rewarded with the pleasures of *Jannah* (heaven) while the unrighteous are punished in *Jahannam* (hell). The sensual nature of the Islamic heaven or *Jannah* has been an endless source of interest for westerners, much of it prurient. In *surah 55*, heaven is described as a well-shaded, cool and well-watered garden. There will be fruit aplenty, couches lined with brocade and willing virgins (*houris*), 'lovely as rubies, beautiful as coral', cloistered in cool pavilions.[27] In *surah 47* the blessed are treated to rivers of milk, honey and wine – 'a delight to the drinkers' – and a cornucopia of rich and exotic fruit.[28] For Richard Dawkins, writing shortly after 9/11, such a vision of heavenly reward feeds the dangerous fantasies of the suicide bomber: 'Testosterone-sodden young men too unattractive to get a woman in this world might be desperate enough to go for 72 private virgins in the next.'[29]

An altogether different fate awaits those found wanting. At the moment of death, disbelievers are chastised and humiliated as a prelude to being sent to hell – the angels beat their faces and their backs before snatching their souls. In *surah 69* the righteous and the unrighteous are each given a book on judgement day, in the right hand and in the left hand respectively. The endless torments of the damned are like something from the worst Boschean nightmare. The instruments of torture include maces of iron, burning clothes and molten drinks. In this metaphysical torture chamber, skin is burned off bodies only for it to grow back again so it can be seared off again. In *surah 47* the unrighteous are forced to drink boiling water that bursts their bowels apart. Extremes of heat and cold are applied to the body.

In the Koran, time is not organized along a linear axis. The Hour of Judgement is not reached at the end of the book as it is in the Bible; it can break out at any time. Each moment of every day is alive with apocalyptic possibilities:

> To God belongs the unseen in the Heavens
> and in the earth.
> And the matter of the Hour is as a twinkling of
> the eye, or nearer.[30]

The koranic Last Judgement itself sounds very similar to the biblical one: boundless benefactions for the blessed, endless torments for the damned. What is radically different, and one which will come as a surprise to most readers, is the role reserved for Jesus in the Last Days. According to the majority Islamic view Jesus (Isa in Arabic) was not the Son of God, but simply a prophet like Muhammad, but less so. It is believed that Jesus/Isa never died when he was crucified; instead, he was raised into heaven still physically alive, where he lives now. In the Hadith, 'Book of the Battles', it speaks of Jesus/Isa with a lance in his hand with which he will kill the Antichrist (Dajjal).[31] We see here elements of *Revelation* 19 which describes the destruction of the Antichrist.

But things then take an unexpected turn. This messiah-figure behaves in a most unchristian way: he kills pigs, breaks the cross, demolishes oratories and churches and kills Christians except those who believe in him (i.e. not as the Son of God but as a mere prophet). In other words he is now fighting a holy war for Islam. The violence is deemed necessary for it is cleansing and will bring about a peaceful millennial rule lasting all of forty years. He will then die and Muslims will offer the funeral prayer for him. From a Christian perspective, this 'changing' of the biblical accounts to uphold a Muslim world-view is typical of the Koran generally. For Muslims, of course, the koranic versions of the stories about Noah, Abraham, Moses, Jesus and the other biblical figures are the true ones and they are being changed back to their true meaning, i.e. an Islamic way of thinking.

So far we have considered the Sunni majority view about the end of the world. The other great view in Islam is the Shiite one. Both branches of Islam have different apocalyptic scenarios because of their fundamentally different conceptions of what an imam is. Among the Sunnis the term refers to the leader in the Friday prayer at the mosque; any pious Muslim may function as an imam. For Shiites, on the other hand, the imam is not just a religious authority but also a figure endowed with apocalyptic significance. According to such beliefs, the First Imam was Ali, Muhammad's son-in-law and the Prophet's closest male descendant. With such a bloodline, Shiites believe Ali should have directly succeeded him as the leader or *caliph* of the Muslims after the prophet's death. In the event, he was passed over three times. Shiites regard these first three *caliphs* as nothing more than Ali's usurpers (Sunnis believe in their legitimacy, terming them 'the rightly guided').

Eventually Ali did become the *caliph* but he ended up being assassinated – a fate which ensured him mythical martyr status. Because he is regarded by Shiites as the first true *caliph* and as the divinely inspired First Imam, Ali's bloodline takes on great dogmatic significance. The Shiite doctrine of the Twelve Imams holds that only Ali, his sons Hasan and Husain and nine other direct linear descendants of Husain can be regarded as Imams. When the Eleventh Imam died in 874, it was said that he left behind a young son, who God had miraculously hidden ('occultation') in order to save his life. The Last Imam is known as al-Mahdi (the rightly guided one). For so-called 'Twelver Shiis', he will return one day towards the end of the world as a messiah-like figure and inaugurate an era of justice.

*

We live in a world now supposedly polarized between Christian West and Islamic East. The three great apocalyptic faiths appear to be at war with each other like never before. In the Middle East, Israelis and Palestinians are locked into a murderous and bloody conflict which shows little sign of being resolved in the immediate future. On either side are extremists – Zionists and Islamists – who fuel the conflict. In an America dominated by Christian Evangelicals, Muslims are the next great enemy, having replaced the Soviets. For their part, many Muslims return the compliment by casting America as the latest western crusader, intent on humiliating and subjugating the Arab world. With fifty million viewers, the Al-Jazeera news channel is one of the world's most influential broadcasters. When it beams the latest images from Abu Ghraib or video footage of British soldiers beating up Iraqi teenagers, al-Qaeda's recruitment goes up. In such a climate, it is worth remembering that Judaism, Christianity and Islam share a common heritage – the great patriarch Abraham.

3

VISIONS OF THE END IN EUROPE: PART ONE

In the early years of the Christian Church, the world was very much divided up between optimists and pessimists. The early Christian Church looked optimistically to the future; it would help to bring God's Kingdom into being through its ministry on earth. Doom-mongering apocalyptic prophets, on the other hand, wanted the end to come as quickly and as violently as possible in order to usher in the heavenly kingdom. The world was deemed to be such a hopelessly corrupt place that only God's miraculous intervention could save it. Human efforts at ameliorating the mess were doomed to failure. The medieval historian Richard Landes has characterized this conflict in terms of an apocalyptic bestiary.

Roosters crow about the imminent dawn. Apocalyptic prophets, messianic pretenders, chronologists calculating an imminent doomsday – they all want to rouse the courtyard, stir the other animals into action, shatter the quiet complacency of a sleeping community. Owls are night-animals; they dislike both noise and light; they want to hush the roosters, insisting that it is still night, that the dawn is far away, that the roosters are not only incorrect, but dangerous – the foxes are still about and the master asleep. In some sense, the history of eschatology is the history of the conflict of these two birds; and the documentation naturally favors that one who has been and will be correct as long as history is written – the owls.[1]

The battle between roosters and owls was one which was to exercise the minds of some of the greatest figures in early Church history. As a full-throated rooster, trumpeting the millennium, Montanus was viewed with dismay by the owlish Catholic Church. Their hootings got ever louder and strident. Finally, in AD 431 at the Council of Ephesus, Montanus was branded a heretic and millennialism was condemned as a dangerous superstition.

Despite these official condemnations, history has recorded the tendency of Christians to predict Christ's coming in every generation. If you believe history is irrevocably deteriorating as we advance unstoppably towards a period of terrible suffering called the tribulation, then your desire for Jesus' return and his thousand-year rule becomes ever more urgent. These are the roosters in Landes' apocalyptic scenario. Known by theologians as premillennialists, they hoot ever more loudly in times of trouble and upheaval. For them, Holy Scripture represented a road map through which they could plot the course of future world events. For prophecy believers, dates, calendars and numbers are signs and portents invested with mystical and magical secrets only the initiated and the wise can penetrate.

When Christians were being fed to Roman lions then the roosters were very much in the ascendant. When the Roman government decided to mark the thousandth anniversary of Rome by stepping up its persecution of the Christians, then a frenzy of apocalyptic speculation ensued. Such a response is wholly understandable and predictable. Generally, apocalyptic faith can be seen as the strongest possible protest against human cruelty and barbarity. In such a view, it is better to end the world now than let such atrocities occur.

But what would happen to the Christian faithful when they went from being a persecuted minority to becoming the religious mainstream? Miraculously, such a situation was to prevail in 313 when the Roman Emperor Constantine ended the persecution of the Christians. Before his death in 337 he himself was baptized. Almost overnight, Christians went from being a marginalized and persecuted sect to becoming the adherents of the only legal religion in the Roman Empire. Not surprisingly many detected God's hand in such an extraordinary turn around. The challenge now facing the early Church was how to exercise earthly power. This necessitated a new orientation in their faith. Before the great inspirational text had been *Revelation* 20 which detailed the imminent arrival of Christ's visible one thousand-year reign on earth. This was now read in a new way in order to accommodate the Church's new-found power and prestige. Why would you want the world to end, now that you were in a position to shape and transform it according to your more most cherished and firmly held beliefs?

A problem which exercised the early Christians was precisely when the promised millennium would begin. For prophets like Montanus it was literally next week. Such literal predictions, however, had foundered spectacularly on the hard rock of fact – 'cognitive dissonance' is what Festinger termed it. Evidently a less literal and a more allegorical approach to numbers and dates were required. For many scholars and divines, Chapter 3 in the *Second Epistle of Peter* in the New Testament held the key. In this letter to the faithful about the non-appearance of the apocalypse at the appointed time Peter sets out the difference between divine time and human time: 'a day is with the Lord as a thousand years and a thousand years as a day'.[2]

Such a conception of time was the basis of the 'Cosmic Week' theory. The theory goes something like this. God had created the world in six days and put his feet up on the seventh. The six days of work and the day of rest, the Sabbath, were interpreted as representing the future seven ages, each of which would last a thousand years. God's six-day working week was effortful; likewise the six ages of one thousand years each would be years of work and endurance. However, the seventh day of creation was the day of rest. This was interpreted as the seventh age of a thousand years and was none other than Christ's millennial kingdom on earth.

According to this calculation, then, human history would last six thousand years. It would then be followed by the thousand-year millennial reign. Then the Last Trump would sound and God would destroy the world, once and for all. Such a theory answered the question about the world's duration. But in order to answer when precisely the world would end required a fixed starting point. At what point did the six thousand years start from? And this was where things got muddled. Generally, opinion agreed about the six-thousand-year duration of earthly time, followed by a thousand years of millennial bliss. But a great deal of theological ink was spilled as to when exactly time began. As a result, a consensus was never reached, allowing an assortment of prophets to put forward their own cosmic chronology.

Writing in the early third century, the Roman official and Christian scholar Sextus Julius Africanus made use of the Cosmic Week theory in his calculations as to when time would end. In his *Chronographiai* of 221, he calculated that Jesus was born in the 5,500th year since creation. According to such a timescale, this meant that he would return in AD 500 in order to inaugurate his millennial kingdom. For Africanus' early third-century readers, the date was too far off in the future to excite much interest.[3] The owls might have asked why exercise yourself about a far-off future event when your own life will have ended long before?

The roosters, however, got increasingly restive as the countdown to the millennium neared its appointed time. By AD 400, the time was sufficiently near for it to stir up fervent anticipation and terror. Other prophets sought to assuage the situation by simply putting off the day and projecting it further off into the future. Paradise was to be postponed. An alternative calculation predicted that the millennium would take place in 800 or 801. In the event, it was the coronation of Charlemagne and not the inauguration of Christ's kingdom on earth that was the key event of that year.

But it was not only canonical scripture which could inspire such end-time speculation. Written after the death of Constantine in 337, the Christian Sibylline Oracles constitute a body of apocalyptic writings which were enormously influential in popular messianic movements. These prophecies grew out of the earlier Jewish Sibyllines which were supposed to be the inspired words of prophetesses and whose function was to convert pagans to Judaism. In the Christian Sibyllines the figure of Christ the warrior-saviour was augmented with that of the figure of the Roman Emperor. Constantine was the first to be given a messianic makeover; after his death the Sibyllines continued to endow the figure of the Roman Emperor with eschatological significance. He became the Emperor of the Last Days, making his first appearance in the oldest of the Sibyllines known to medieval Europe, the *Tiburtina*, which in its Christian form dates from the middle of the fourth century. With dynastic struggle engulfing the Roman Empire, it tells of a 'time of sorrows', when Rome will be captured and tyrants will oppress the poor and innocent and protect the guilty. But then an emperor will arise who unites the eastern and western halves of the empire under his rule. Later, in the late eleventh century at the time of the First Crusade, Charlemagne was recast in this explicitly eschatological mould. Sibylline prophecies cross-fertilized with popular folklore to ensure that the first Carolingian should wear the mantle of the Emperor of the Last Days.[4]

Augustine came on to the scene at the end of the fourth century. It was a time seething with apocalyptic speculation. The roosters, cock-a-doodling the end of the world, were well and truly in the ascendant. For the owlish Church authorities a great theologian was required who could effect a paradigm shift away from a too literal interpretation of *Revelation* 20. Completed in 426, Augustine's *The City of God* did just that. Central to literalist beliefs were the apocalyptic numbers which attempted to superimpose a timeline on God's redemptive plan for humanity. For Augustine, a 1,000 years or 42 months or the 144,000 who are sealed in *Revelation* could be interpreted in any number of different ways. In other words, they were allegorical in nature rather than literal markers of time and quantities. According to his allegorical reading of *Revelation* 20, the number 1,000 did not denote the thousand-year millennial rule of Christ on earth – the seventh age. In Book Twenty of *The City of God* Augustine explains that the number 1,000 can be interpreted in two ways:

It may indicate that this event happens in the last thousand years, that is, in the sixth millennium, the sixth day, as it were, of which the latter stretches are now passing, and a Sabbath is to follow that has no evening, the rest, that is to say, of the saints, which has no end. Thus our author used the term 'a thousand years' to denote the last part of the millennium – or 'day' – which remained before the end of the world, employing the figure of speech by which the whole stands for the part. Alternatively, he may have intended the thousand years to stand for the whole period of this world's history, signifying the entirety of time by a perfect number.[5]

Augustine saw himself in the midst of the sixth age of earthly history, stretching from the first advent of Christ to the Second Coming. This was the Church Age which would be followed by the seventh age which lies outside the temporal realm: it is the eternal state in heaven.[6]

In Augustine's ecclesiological interpretation of *Revelation* 20, then, the institutional Catholic Church itself is identified with the Kingdom of God. Through the Church the heavenly reign of Christ manifested itself on earth and thus into the individual soul. So the millennium, conceived originally as an imminent future event – a 'not yet' – was deemed to be an immanent 'already'. In such a reading, the *Book of Revelation* became less a literal prophecy about the consummation of the cosmos and more a symbolic account of the struggle each individual has with evil, death and eventual judgement before God. The 'millennium' therefore became transposed from being a literal thousand-year reign on earth to a heavenly reign with the saints in heaven. The technical turn for this is amillennialism which literally means 'no millennium'.

Why did Augustine set his face so firmly against a literal millennium on earth, especially when he admits that he too once believed in premillennialism?[7] What bothered Augustine was how the seven-day Sabbath of a thousand years had been turned into a bacchanalian banquet – Augustine speaks of 'unrestrained material feasts'. Like a lot of former debauchees – one thinks of Tolstoy – Augustine embraced a rigorous asceticism after his conversion. The body, with all it fleshy importunities, was roundly rejected in favour of the imprisoned but immortal soul. In the Augustinian new moral order, there was to be an absolute separation of the fallen, terrestrial city and the heavenly divine one. There were to be no grand feasts of celebration as there were to be in the Jewish messianic kingdom, no superabundance of food and drink.

His allegorical interpretation of *Revelation* 20 in *The City of God* led directly to the rejection of millennialism at the Council of Ephesus in 431.[8] The Augustinian view that Christ's ultimate triumph is a purely transcendental affair and not a sublunary one is a doctrine espoused not only by the Catholic Church but also by the Lutheran and Reformed Churches. Amillennialism generally holds that the millennium is present now in a spiritual form rather than being held out as a future earthly state. Both good and evil will continue in the world until the end of the current Church Age when Christ will return on the Last Day to manifest the perfect and eternal kingdom in heaven. In contrast to such a view, premillennialism holds that any time now a future golden age will be ushered in. We are now in the convulsive last days in which corruption is piled up on corruption, disaster on disaster until something has to give.

In the medieval world, the great motifs of most people's lives were plagues, wars and famines. Often these catastrophes were read as though they were the signs that the end was nigh. Little surprise, then, that people should have lived in a permanent ferment of millennial expectation. To read into adversity some sort of supernatural message must have comforted the afflicted. It gave meaning to what would otherwise have been a meaningless obscenity. With suffering and evil making carnival, the apocalyptic figure of Antichrist takes centre stage. He becomes a symbolic projection of all peoples' fears, a tangible embodiment of metaphysical evil.

Viewed apocalyptically, an incompetent or despotic leader could easily be recast as Antichrist. Like pinning the tail on the donkey, Antichrist's identity has been assigned to a whole host of historical figures. For the earliest Christians, the Roman emperor Nero was a natural candidate. During the Middle Ages, the Antichrist changed ethnicity; some churchmen identified him with Saladin, the conqueror of the crusaders, others with a Jew. In his multifarious mutations, the Antichrist has donned papal purple (particularly popular during the Reformation), military uniforms (Napoleon, Hitler, Stalin) or has been associated with particular political institutions (the EEC, British Parliament) as well as modern political leaders such as JFK and a former Israeli prime minister. More sinisterly, in 1999 the evangelical Reverend Jerry Falwell whipped up a great deal of controversy when he claimed that the Antichrist was still living and was probably a Jewish male. Antichrist has even been identified as computer technology and with those associated with its development. Tap in 'Bill Gates and Antichrist' in Google and many sites come up, providing a new take on the phrase the 'gates of hell'.[9]

The enduring appeal of the Antichrist is that he can be all things to all people. If you believe abortion to be evil, then he could be recast as a private clinic owner. In modern America, Christian fundamentalists might draw on the Antichrist myth in order to express their rage at all things modern. Timothy LaHaye, a bestselling novelist and stalwart of the Christian Right, spoke on a talk show about being engaged in a 'religious war' against the exponents of 'secular humanism [who] are filled with the devil'.[10] In the Muslim world, the Antichrist might be identified with George W. Bush or Ariel Sharon. Identifying your enemy as Antichrist himself or his followers, Gog and Magog, is to paint your political enemies in the darkest pitch possible.

One of the most famous works on the Antichrist is Adso of Montier-En-Der's *Letter on the Origin and Time of the Antichrist*, written around 950. This was the most complete treatise on the Antichrist to date. It's a sort of demonic version of the lives of the saints, an anti-hagiographic work written in a suitably sensational and racy style. The French monk's description of the Antichrist was widely translated and disseminated throughout Europe and would cast its peculiar spell on the imaginations of the apocalyptically minded for centuries to come. Adso begins by identifying Antichrist's 'ministers of malice' – historical figures such as Antiochus, Nero and Domitian. He then goes on to give the figure a wider applicability. Anyone who lives 'contrary to justice and attacks the rule of his way of life and blasphemes what is good . . . is an Antichrist, the minister of Satan'.[11]

Of particular importance is Antichrist's ancestry and conception. Adso relates how he would come from the Jewish tribe of Dan, a tradition that goes back to second- and third-century theologians and would guarantee centuries of murderous anti-Semitism. Adso layers this myth with his own sinister imprimatur: Antichrist's mother is impregnated by the devil in a demonic parody of the Immaculate Conception. Antichrist has now gone from being a human figure to being the absolute essence of metaphysical evil, the 'son of perdition', the demonic counterpart of Christ. Association implicates the Jews in his dark, demonic deeds. Antichrist has sprung from their race. Nurture then compounds his innate evil. Growing up in Babylon, the demonic city of biblical apocalyptic, Antichrist will be reared by magicians and sorcerers who will instruct him in their dark arts. He will then come to Jerusalem, slay all the Christians he cannot convert to his cause, rebuild Solomon's temple, be enthroned and there masquerade as Christ.

His career as Christ's demonic double involves duping kings and the people, dispatching missionaries throughout the world and performing great miracles – fire will be made to fall from the sky, trees blossom and wither, the dead will be resurrected. Those he cannot seduce with prodigies he will torture and kill. This initiates the period of Tribulation when faithful Christians either turn apostate or become martyrs. As in all good morality plays, however, hubris is quickly followed by nemesis. At the end of a Greek tragedy, often a god descends from the heavens courtesy of stage machinery and sorts out the human mess. In the Christian apocalyptic drama, Christ's Second Advent serves a similar function. Antichrist's comeuppance has been divinely ordained:

> Since we have spoken about his beginning, let us say what end he will have. This Antichrist, the devil's son and the worst master of evil, as has been said, will plague the whole world with great persecution and torture the whole people of God with various torments for three and a half years. After he has killed Elijah and Enoch and crowned with martyrdom the others who persevere in the faith, at last God's judgment will come upon him, as Saint Paul writes when he says, 'The Lord Jesus will kill him with the breath of his mouth' (2 *Thess.*: 2:8). Whether the Lord Jesus will slay him by the power of his own might, or whether the Archangel Michael will slay him, he will be killed through the power of Our Lord Jesus Christ and not through the power of any angel or archangel. The teachers say that Antichrist will be killed on the Mount of Olives in his tent and upon his throne, in the place opposite to where the Lord ascended to heaven.[12]

Adso's gloss on the myth of the 'Last World Emperor' was one of the most influential things in the treatise. Before the coming of Antichrist, he argues, a Frankish king must reign. This king would triumph over all the enemies of Christendom and rule a peaceful, Christian world. He would then go to Jerusalem, lay down the imperial crown and robes at Golgotha which is then followed by the appearance of Antichrist and the final 'time of troubles'. To be regarded as the Last Emperor was a great honour. Many kings and warlords had messianic pretensions and believed themselves to be just such a figure.

Written about the time of the First Crusade, the oldest extant epic in French, *The Song of Roland* (c.1098–1100) depicted Charlemagne in such terms even though he had died some three hundred years earlier. He had united Christianity against the conquering armies of Islam and either converted or annihilated Muslims, Jews and non-believers. His feats of military prowess take on an apocalyptic importance: 'There will be none like him until the Day of Judgement.'[13] At one point, he prays to God to prolong the day so he can go in pursuit of the 'pagans'; his request is duly granted.[14] When Saragossa falls to him, the Franks smash up synagogues and mosques in the city. Then they take the pagans up to the baptistery; if any of them resist baptism they are 'hanged or burned or put to death'.[15] Later, we shall see how this myth of the Last Emperor, popularized by Adso and such literary epics as *The Song*, fed the exterminatory zeal of the First Crusade.

The timing of Adso's work, around 950, is also important in our story. Written about fifty years or so before the end of the first Christian millennium, it has often been cited as an expression of a collective millennial hysteria that was supposed to have seized western Europe. Historians have long argued over this. At one end of the historical spectrum there is Hillel Schwartz's *Century's End* which is a virtual denial that anything especially noteworthy took place around this date. At the other end, there is Richard Erdoes' *AD 1000* which gives us the full-blown 'panic terrors' treatment. Schwartz begins with a compelling account of what was popularly believed to have happened in AD 1000 only to pull the carpet completely from beneath the reader's feet:

> None of this is true. Not the suicides, not the flaming swords, not the whips. Not the absolution, nor the parole, nor the forgiveness of debts. Not the mass hysteria, the fatalism, the nightmare. Not the families abandoned (or swept up) by an army of pilgrims, not the wealth divested (or spent on saddle-bag supplies) by pilgrim knights. No, not the buildings left to decay. Not even the panic itself, unless all accounts of general consternation have been suppressed. And no mechanical clocks to strike the midnight hour at millennium's end, no hallelujah choruses at a minute past twelve.
>
> None of it – at least according to the last hundred years of scholarship.[16]

One obvious flaw in the millennial-year-madness scenario is the question of medieval timekeeping. The later tenth century did not share or have the means to indulge in the peculiar modern obsession with time keeping. For general millennial madness to break out a sufficiently large number of people need to be agreed about what precisely the date and the time is so they can calculate when the last minute of the last year of the century will roll over into a new millennium. Then they can gather together at a particular place at a particular time and see out the old millennium and see in the new, all in a suitably frenzied and hysterical state. For different people living in different parts of Europe, however, there were different ways of calculating the date. This lack of uniformity and precision meant that the end of the world was not reduced to a precise moment in time, as in our 2000–year celebrations, but was spread over a period of approximately five years. We can speak therefore of a series of ends of the world as isolated communities scattered across Europe used their own calendars to predict the millennial dates. It was not so much a Big Bang, then, as a series of minor local explosions.

If the level of fear and mayhem surrounding the year 1000 has been exaggerated, what does this say about how we recast the past in order for it to conform to our apocalyptic fantasies? What sensationalist accounts of AD 1000 perhaps reveal is our need to freight nice round numbers like 1,000 with a metaphysical significance and symbolism. Perhaps we want to believe that the passing of AD 1000 was a truly earth-shattering event because we too have passed a millennium milestone. That our ancestors reacted in a certain way to the first millennium legitimates our own desire to make our own second millennium a truly earth-shattering event. Apocalypse Then becomes our Apocalypse Now. An element of this crept into the London millennium celebrations. The highlight was supposed to be the 'River of Fire' spectacle: the Thames was to be engulfed in a conflagration. In the event, the River of Fire turned out to be a bit of a damp squib.

For those who want to believe the end-of-the world scenario in AD 1000 there is always Raoul Glaber. A Burgundian monk, he wrote a five-volume history of his times which chronicles in great detail how people reacted to the first millennium. In the run-up to 1000, Glaber gathered reports of a terrifying comet, now known as Halley's Comet, that crossed the sky in AD 989 and must be a portent of the end. Great forest fires sweeping across Italy and Gaul, the death of famous men and an outbreak of heresy in Sardinia added to the apocalyptic ferment. For Glaber, these were incontrovertible signs that time was about to be swallowed up by eternity. When no such thing occurred, Glaber and other apocalyptic prophets did what they have always done when prophecy fails – came up with a new date. Apocalyptic speculation duly shifted to the year 1033; strictly speaking the reign of Christ on earth did not begin until the death and resurrection of the Saviour, which occurred, according to the New Testament, when Jesus was thirty-three years old. So might not this be the year when the events prophesied in *Revelation* come true? It was a case, then, not of Apocalypse Now but of Apocalypse Later.[17]

While tenth-century Christian Europe was or was not in a ferment of apocalyptic speculation, depending on whom you read, the first of two key Icelandic texts was being written, giving an insight into ancient pagan beliefs about the end of the world. The tenth-century epic poem *Völuspá*, also known as the *Poetic Edda* or the *Elder Edda*, spans the whole arc of time, from the beginning to the end, all in sixty-five stanzas. Composed early in the thirteenth century, the *Prose Edda* or the *Younger Edda* by Snorri Sturluson, describes in detail the events leading up to, during and after Ragnarok, the Last Battle which ushers in the end of the world.[18]

In the Nordic world-view, there are always forces afoot threatening the ordered cosmos. Yggdrasil, the World-Tree, the tree of fate, is the pillar of the entire universe, the nourisher and provider of the spiritual and physical world. Nevertheless, a serpent gnaws constantly away at the roots of Yggdrasil, symbolizing the ever-present nature of the internal threat. Meanwhile, outside, there are legions of giants forever on the boundaries of the ordered world, forever wanting to destroy it. The frost-giants are a particular bugbear – as they must have been for the real-life inhabitants of the Scandinavian world. Other agents of chaos also include wild beasts, mischievous trolls and evil spirits who lurk in the forests. On sea, strange and terrible monsters were always liable to come out of the dark fathomless depths and sink Norse boats. These are the Nordic equivalent of the monstrous dragons and beasts in Judaeo-Christian apocalyptic literature. They are the quintessence of nothingness, chaos and death.

Such cosmic forces of destruction need a suitably heroic figure to combat them. In the Nordic pantheon, the hammer-wielding Thor is just such a figure. He fights and kills his arch-antagonist the frost-giant Hrungnir, and so saves the world of the gods. Time and again, he saves humanity from a similar fate. Nevertheless, the end of the world cannot always be averted. Portents of the coming end are vivid and unforgettable. There is a succession of terrible winters, none of which is relieved by summer. In the *Eddas*, the freak weather conditions lead to a moral and social breakdown; internecine strife and incest flourish unchecked. The darkness is therefore both moral and physical. Cosmic disorder reflects the breakdown of society. The sun and moon are devoured and the stars are hurled from the heavens, plunging the world into ever-deeper depths of darkness. An earthquake uproots trees from the earth, mountains totter and then fall. Every chain, manacle and fetter is snapped and shattered. The god of misrule and anarchy, Lowki, is released from his captivity along with his son, Fenrir, a gigantic wolf. When this beast gapes, his lower jaw hits the ground, his upper one the sky. Rivers of drool drop from his chops and his 'eyes and nostrils . . . blaze with fire'.[19] Such a terrifying apparition is in the best traditions of apocalyptic bestiary. Fenrir could have come straight out of the more lurid chapters of *Daniel* and *Revelation*.

The Nordic equivalent of Armageddon is truly impressive and justly famous. Drawn from the four corners of the earth, fire giants and monsters gather to do battle with the gods. This vast-monster force rolls remorselessly on to Vigrid, the great plain on which the final battle will be fought. A watchman on the Rainbow Bridge, which links the home of the gods and mankind, signals the monster-army's arrival with a trumpet blast. Ragnarok has now begun. As in *Revelation*, where trumpet-blowing angels signal the destruction of the physical world, the trumpet blast is also the sound of doom in the Nordic myth.

On this doomsday, Odin leads the way in his gold helmet and shining corselet. Odin places himself against the wolf Fenrir; Thor stands by his side, but can render him no assistance, having his hands filled with the Midgard Serpent. Thor gains great renown for killing the monster but in the process loses his life. The dying serpent's last act is to drench him in deadly poison. Eventually, Odin succumbs to the wolf and is eaten. But the beast's victory is short lived; one of Odin's sons takes revenge by ripping its throat out. Loki and Heimdall, the trumpet-blower, are engaged in such an evenly matched contest that they end up killing each other: 'Thereupon Surt will fling fire over the earth and burn up the whole world.'[20]

It is not only the gods who meet their end on the Vigrid battlefield. The leader of the fire-giants, Surt, unleashes a great fireball which consumes the cosmos. Heaven and earth, gods and humans are annihilated alike. As in the *Book of Revelation*, however, the destruction is also a form of consummation. New abodes will come into existence, some good and some bad. The best place of all will be Gimli, a building fairer than the sun, roofed with gold, in heaven. There, the gods will live at peace with themselves and each other. There will be other halls too – one overflowing with good drink, another made wholly of red gold. The souls of the good and virtuous will live in these halls. The unrighteous, on the other hand, can expect halls with walls made out of serpents, wattled together. The serpents spew forth their venom through which the damned have to wade.

Crucially the earth survives but is completely transformed. The old earth disappears into the sea. According to Chapter 67 of the *Prose Edda*, 'The Renovation of the Universe', however, another earth will arise out of the depths. It will be lovely, verdant and miraculously fertile. Asgard, the realm of the gods, may have been destroyed but a meadow has been spared. A tiny human remnant has also survived Surt's firestorm; they will be the progenitors of a new race of men. Odin's son Balder will repair here from the abode of death (Hel), along with the sons of other gods, where they will sit around and recount stories of Fenrir and the Midgard Serpent. As in Jewish and Christian apocalyptic, destruction and upheaval is followed by transformation and reward.

Ragnarok is the pagan equivalent of the Christian Armageddon. It is a mythical climactic battle in which the forces of good eventually prevail over evil. Endowed with apocalyptic significance, war becomes the ultimate heroic act – through acts of military valour the warrior can actually save the world from the forces of chaos that threaten it. The great combat myth of ancient Zoroastrianism therefore finds its equivalent in the combat myths of Christianity and Nordic mythology. It is when mythmaking turns into the making of history that such beliefs become dangerous and can have potentially catastrophic results. During the time of the Crusades in the eleventh century, Armageddon was not projected into some mythical future but enacted out in the historical present. Rather than imaginary monsters, real human beings were put to the sword.

*

In November 1095, Pope Urban II delivered a famous sermon at the Council of Clermont in which he called for Christians to unite and recapture the sacred city of Jerusalem which had been under Muslim rule for some four and a half centuries. His

main object was to assist Byzantium so that it could drive the
Seldjuk Turks from Asia Minor; in return he hoped the Eastern
Church would rally behind Rome, thus restoring the unity of
Christendom. But there was also a pressing political agenda in
the papal summons. The nobility in Europe needed to be given
something to do other than simply knock chunks out of each
other on the battlefield. France in particular was racked by
short, bloody and incessant local conflicts. Certainly Urban
envisaged a band of knightly crusaders, crossing continents in
order to save the Byzantine Christians; those who were motivated by such pious concerns would earn remission of their
sins. But there was also the prospect of giving the warrior-class
something to do. To win their support, material as well as
spiritual rewards had to be held out. In the long trek south-
wards, lands and booty would be aplenty.

It is questionable, then, whether Urban's call to the Crusade
was inspired by apocalyptic beliefs. One of the accounts of
Pope Urban's speech does contain apocalyptic motifs but that
particular version of his speech was written well after it was
delivered.[21] The different accounts all emphasize different
things because the listeners who wrote down their versions
of it later responded to it according to their own concerns and
interests. Robert the Monk, for example, emphasized the
apocalyptic role the Franks would play in expelling the pagans
and extending Christianity in the Middle East like their
illustrious forebear, Charlemagne. In his version of Urban's
speech, the Franks are the Chosen People, God having con-
ferred great glory in arms on them. They are exhorted to 'enter
upon the road to the Holy Sepulchre; wrest that land from the
wicked race, and subject it to yourselves'.[22]

In fact, the prospect of recapturing Jerusalem seems to have
played little part in Urban's original plan. But when prophets
and visionaries gave their own version of the papal speech to

the laity the Holy City was to play centre stage. This was the city that had been burned by the Babylonians and destroyed by the Romans. In medieval times, Jerusalem was at the heart of apocalyptic fantasies and fervent belief. The mass pilgrimages to the Holy Sepulchre in 1033 and 1064 were noteworthy not only because of their size but also because of their social makeup – the poor and the dispossessed swelled their numbers. In 1095, they had everything to gain from a pilgrimage to the Holy Land – spiritual and earthly rewards – and very little to lose.

As Norman Cohn has noted, it was just not the nobles, properly booted and suited, who answered Urban's clarion call for a Crusade.[23] The people who formed an alternative 'army', whipped up by the preachings of self-styled prophets and messiahs, saw themselves as a cross between holy warrior and pilgrim, militant and martyr. The chroniclers called them the *pauperes*; men, women and children – whole families in fact – who stitched the Cross on to filthy sackcloth and armed themselves not with lances and swords but with clubs, knives, staves and agricultural implements. This was the so-called People's Crusade, and its members were motivated by far more apocalyptic concerns than their noble counterparts in the advanced guard. For this rag-tag 'army', the recapturing of Jerusalem offered prodigious hope; the earthly city was a symbol of the bejewelled heavenly city in the *Book of Revelation*. In the simple minds of the *pauperes*, the earthly Jerusalem would lead them to a realm of infinite riches, both spiritual and material.

The First Crusade, the most successful of all the Crusades, was thus constituted. At the head were the soldiers of Christ, led by men of royal blood like Robert, the eldest son of William the Conqueror, and Hugh of Vermandois, the brother of Philip I, the ruling King of France. At the rear, were the pilgrims, religious fanatics and mountebanks, assorted adventurers and whole families in carts loaded with their chattels. The eschatological nature of their beliefs persuaded many of them that they were being lead by the Emperor of the Last Days. Men like Godfrey of Bouillon, Duke of Lower Lorraine, and Raymond of Saint-Gilles, Count of Toulouse, were seen in eschatological terms, thus fulfilling the Sibylline prophecies. In the imaginations of the *pauperes*, the Emperor of the Last Days would annihilate the enemies of Christ and raise up the lowly and the downtrodden and usher in the age of bliss.

The enemies in the east, the Muslims, were of course the number one enemy but they were as yet out of reach. As they made their way across Europe, the People's Crusade found a foe, and a defenceless one at that, very much closer to home – the Jews. It was in the Rhineland that the most vicious pogroms were to take place. As a major trade route, the Rhine valley was a magnet for Jewish merchants who had settled there for centuries and prospered. The belief that killing Jews was a necessary preliminary to the Second Coming was not the official Church doctrine. The Church contented itself with the general conversion of all Jews to Christianity before the Second Coming. However, some theologians adopted a more hardline attitude. They argued that the Jews would not be converted; at the Last Judgement they would be sent packing to hell along with Antichrist. In such a view, the Jew became the archest-enemy of God, the essence of metaphysical evil. To kill him was to deprive Antichrist of his allies in the Last Days. In killing him, you could well be determining your eternal destiny.

In the spring and summer of 1096, Rhineland cities witnessed the consequences of such genocidal beliefs. When the Popular Crusade arrived at a city like Worms, synagogues were sacked, houses looted and Jewish communities murdered, all because the Jewish inhabitants did not accept baptism. Other cities like Mainz witnessed similar atrocities.

Later, it was deemed to be more cost-effective to simply murder them rather than attempt baptism. It has been estimated that between four and eight thousand Jews were murdered between May and June 1096.[24] Count Emich of Leisingen, a leader of the First Crusade, massacred Jews who refused to convert, secure in the knowledge that God had divinely elected him the Last World Emperor. Genocide was the ultimate act in the eschatological drama.

The First Crusade, then, was not only a war against Islam but also a war on the Jews, a start of a tradition of religious intolerance and racial hatred which was to play out across the centuries and whose bitter legacy we are still reaping to this very day. Both Jew and Muslim were recast in the popular imagination as demons, agents of Antichrist that had to be eliminated in order for the one true faith to prevail. The position of the Jews was particularly perilous; they were very much the enemy within. They were the more ancient enemies of Christendom and had been assigned an important eschatological role for centuries. With the collapse of the Jewish state in Palestine in the second century, Jews were scattered throughout Europe and yet they existed still very much as an identifiable cultural and religious entity due to their unwillingness to assimilate. In the popular imagination, then, Antichrist or his ministers could be living next door. They were the Other, the slayers of Christ, Satan-worshippers who sacrificed young male virgins in their rituals, Herod-like child-killers, foul black demons in human form. Such views resurface again and again in popular lore. Chaucer explores the blood-libel in 'The Prioress's Tale' from *The Canterbury Tales* which features a little boy who is brutally murdered by usurious Jews. This is a fictional representation of a widespread and firmly held belief in the medieval period – that Jews killed helpless and innocent Christian children.

Muslims fared little better. In 1122, Peter the Venerable,

Abbot of Cluny, established a centre at his monastery for the translation and refutation of Muslim writings. This scholarly work was soon perverted into gross distortions of the life of Muhammad. 'Mahomet' is portrayed as a false prophet, a sensualist, a warmonger and a drunk. Mahomet became a stock character on the medieval stage in the mystery plays and romances and was joined by the figure of the Saracen. He is the god, patron or saint or even relative of various villains who pray to him or swear by him.

It is against this background of racist stereotyping and religious intolerance that the First Crusade should be seen. If you believed the Jews or Muslims were agents of Antichrist, then, the logical conclusion was that they should be annihilated in order to usher in the Last Days and the Kingdom of the Saints. The perpetrators were wholly convinced they were good Christians, purifying the world of foul and demonic elements in order to make it fit for the New Jerusalem. This interplay between militarism and religious fanaticism is aptly illustrated by what happened when the crusaders arrived eventually at the fortified walls of the earthly Jerusalem. On 7 June 1099, they got down on their knees in an act of collective worship. Having crossed continents, lost thousands on their way and suffered appalling deprivations, Christ's soldiers were convinced that their safe arrival must have been divinely ordained. Now it was payback day – they were attacking and destroying a people they associated with the demonic host.

The storming of the city began a month or so later at night. Contemporary accounts make it sound like Boschean hell, a vision of the End. Huge siege towers were parked up against the sides of the walls, great balls of fire dropped from the battlements; arrows and pitch poured down; men, women and children scrambled desperately about in the dark, filling the city moat with rubble and debris in order to build a causeway. When the crusaders eventually breached the city's formidable defences, two days of butchery ensued in which Jews and Muslims alike perished. The chroniclers tell of rivers of blood in the streets, the crusaders knee deep in gore. Despite the horror, the western sources are brisk and matter-of-fact in their descriptions of the carnage; they appear as unmoved describing the atrocities, as were the perpetrators who committed them. When it was over the Crusade leaders went to the Church of the Holy Sepulchre to give thanks to God.

But the Muslim world would never forget or forgive the looting of sacred shrines in the holy city and the wholesale slaughter. In their eyes, the crusaders were little more than savage barbarians, hell-bent on rape and pillage. To this day, Osama bin Laden and the *jihadis* invoke the term 'crusade' in order to denote aggressive western imperialism. For their part, westerners have pilloried and crudely stereotyped Muslims for centuries. Ever since the ninth century, when Christendom witnessed the seemingly unstoppable advance of Islam, theologians and commentators had deemed Muhammad to be a precursor of a Saracen Antichrist. When the First Crusade got under way the Muslim was portrayed in popular epics as a devil that had no right to live. To recapture Jerusalem therefore from the Muslims would be to defeat Antichrist and his ministers. Although today they are often in conflict, Jews and Muslims shared a common fate in medieval times – both were on the receiving end of Christian apocalyptic fantasies.

Later, in the twelfth century, Muslims were to find their own equivalent of the Emperor of the Last Days in the great general Saladin. It was he who was to seize back Jerusalem from the Christian 'infidels' in 1187. As a counter-response, Pope Gregory VIII launched the Third Crusade, spearheaded by England's very own Richard the Lionhearted. Viewed from different perspectives, the Christians were either infidels or warrior-pilgrims. Likewise the Muslims were either ministers of Antichrist or *jihadis*. The rhetoric of apocalyptic often involves simple, antithetical configurations like these. Post-9/11, these have become rife: 'holy war', 'war on terror', 'the axis of evil', beacons of democratic light in a wilderness of despotic darkness. Little surprise, then, that George W. Bush's war on al-Qaeda and Iraq has been dubbed the 'Last Crusade'. Much of the discourse surrounding the conflict can be traced back to the original Crusades of the medieval age.[25]

*

In the history of apocalyptic thought Joachim of Fiore (c.1132–1202) holds an important place. His ideas, and versions of them, have been remarkably influential both in the eschatological and prophetic strain in Western European thought and in secular contexts down to comparatively recent times. He saw history as consisting of an ascent through three successive stages, each of which was presided over by a particular member of the Trinity: the Age of the Father/Law; the Age of the Son/Gospel; and the Age of the Spirit/Holy Ghost. The first phase or *status*, presided over by the Father, spanned the whole period from Adam to Christ. The second phase was under the jurisdiction of the Son and was said to have commenced with the Incarnation. This Age of the Son, the Abbot believed, was now drawing to a close. The third age, assigned to the third member of the Trinity, the Holy Ghost, was proclaimed as the final dispensation which was about to be instituted in human history.

Whereas traditional notions about the millennium conceived of it as the Kingdom of the Saints on earth which would then be replaced by the Kingdom of God in heaven, Joachim taught that the third age on earth was of unknown duration. This had profound implications. As a result, it took on less the aspect of an interim state and more the character of the ultimate consummation of things. Such theories flew in the face of Augustinian teachings about the millennium. As we saw earlier, Augustine banished the millennium with his notions about the Church Age and perfection only being attainable in a posthumous, supra-temporal realm.

In contrast, Joachim's third and final age (predicted between 1200 and 1260) would see the Church wither away, leaving behind it a ruling race of celibate monks who would live by direct inspiration from the Holy Ghost. They had been marked by the revelation of a new and final dispensation, the *evangelium aeternum*. Marjorie Reeves has demonstrated just how extraordinarily influential this triadic division of history has been.[26] Refracted through a prism, the myth of the 'Eternal Evangel' was passed down from one generation of prophets and visionaries to another, often taking on the ideological colouration of their particular age. A generally pervading Joachitism infused many of the apocalyptic sects that sprang up during the English Civil War era. The left-wing historian, Christopher Hill, made these prophets and visionaries famous after years of academic neglect. For their part, literary critics have detected Joachite ideas about the Trinity in the work of the Romantic poet, William Blake and in modern prophetic writers such as Huysmans, D.H. Lawrence and W.B. Yeats.

One of the great appeals of Joachim's ideas is the way in which the final dispensation, that of the Holy Ghost, supersedes the former two ages. Such a theory could become heterodox because it implies that there will be a transcendence of historical Christianity. The new dispensation will supersede the two former ones. In the new age, all the existing rules and institutions are abolished in favour of direct revelation from the Holy Ghost. This concept of the 'Inner Light' appealed particularly to the apocalyptic sects that sprang up during the English Civil War. Their political radicalism was often underpinned by their belief that they were an elect, acting under the promptings of the Inner Light. Very often the *illuminati* succumbed to the heresy of antinomianism – the belief that for the pure all things were pure. The normal moral and social laws could be flouted because the elect could not fall from grace.

Joachim would have been appalled to see his theories and speculations perverted in this way. Heterodox excess was certainly not his style. He thought of himself not as a divinely inspired figure but as biblical exegete, safely within the fold of the Catholic Church. To be sure he had helped revive the prophetic tradition based on scripture after Augustine had stymied it. But there were very real and pressing reasons why he should have done this. What lent urgency to his creation of a new end-time scenario was the considerable threat posed by Islam. He became an apocalyptic adviser to Richard the Lionhearted when he visited the Abbot at Messina on his way to the Third Crusade during the winter of 1190–1. Joachim prophesied that it was the English monarch's divine destiny to drive Saladin from Jerusalem. In the event, it was the great prophecy interpreter who was destined to see his prophecy fail. In 1192, Richard returned to Europe with Saladin still in residence in the Holy City.

In one of Joachim's most important works of prophecy, the *Book of Figures*, written towards the end of his life, he interprets Saladin's triumph over Christians in the east as a sign that the second age was about to run its course – there were no more than two generations left – and that this was the reign of the persecuting Antichrist. The Antichrist himself will be a false teacher from the west who will ally himself with the Saracens, and that together they will attempt to 'wipe the name of Christ from the earth'. But Christ himself will conquer

Antichrist and his supporters, and the Jews and the pagans will be converted, and the great seven-headed dragon (the persecutions of the Church in the past, present and future) will be crushed and imprisoned in the abyss. Gog, the second and final Antichrist – yes there will be two Antichrists not just one – will be defeated in the Final Battle.

The events of the Apocalypse were thus read into current historical events; they become the signs that had been predicted in *Revelation* and were now being fulfilled. As for the future, it was seen very much in terms of a Christian–Muslim conflict.[27] Such anti-Islamic prophecies particularly proliferated after the fall of Jerusalem in 1187. Later prophecies would cast the Ottoman Empire in the Antichrist role.[28] By incorporating Muslims into a Christian eschatological scenario, one normally occupied by the Jews, Joachim and his like were attempting to account for why God had allowed the infidel to become such a religious and military threat. Such beliefs have an all too familiar ring to them in today's world. In the heartlands of Christian Evangelical America, the Islamic world is readily cast as a demonic force whose annihilation, predicted in scripture, will usher in the Last Days.

It is not just the threat posed by other religions which have fuelled apocalyptic speculation. Natural disasters too have loomed large in the history of the end of the world. Earthquakes, tsunamis, plagues and epidemics: all of these, past and present, have fanned the apocalyptic flames. A world expert on geo-hazards has identified four natural catastrophes lying in wait for the human race: a volcanic blast, a giant wave, a cataclysmic earthquake and an asteroid impact.[29] Added to the geophysical threat there is also a biological one. The Spanish flu epidemic after the First World War killed millions across the European continent. AIDS is doing the same in sub-Saharan Africa. The great biological disaster in medieval times

was the Black Death. When the plague reached Western
Europe in 1348, it was the greatest calamity amidst a series
of calamities which were to befall Western Europe in the
fourteenth century, making it probably the most calamitous
century there has ever been. The Hundred Years War, widespread famine, the collapse of the medieval Church, the rise of
revolutionary movements and heresies, mass exterminations
of Jews: all of these convulsions pale into insignificance beside
the 'Black Death', 'the Pestilence', 'the Great Mortality'.

The magnitude of the disaster is mind-boggling. In terms of
the numbers who died we are talking far more than the two
world wars of the twentieth century combined. In Western
Europe, about a third of the population are thought to have
perished in the *annus horriblis*, 1348–9. It has been estimated
that 40 per cent of England's priests were wiped out along with
vast swathes of the peasant labour force, leading to a labour
shortage and massive rates of inflation. By the end of 1350, the
Black Death had subsided, only to recur in fresh outbreaks for
the next several hundred years.

The medieval reaction to the epidemic was depressingly
predictable. As ever, historical events were refracted through
the distorting prism of the *Book of Revelation*. So rather than
being ascribed to the bacteria carried in the blood of wild black
rats and the fleas that lived off them, the disease was thought
to have a metaphysical origin. The fist-sized swellings, first red
then black (hence the 'Black Death'), the gouts of blood
vomited up when the infection enters the lungs were seen
not as medical symptoms but as signs of the coming end. The
disease was deemed to be a divine punishment meted out to a
sinful world. Mass flagellant processions sprang up, criss-
crossing the continent, in an attempt to assuage an angry
God. The flagellant would engage in frenzied bouts of penitential self-whipping with a leather scourge, studded with iron

spikes, in an attempt to drive out the devils lurking within the collective body. Others vented their fear and loathing not on themselves but on that perennial scapegoat, the Jew. It was he and his satanic cohorts who must have poisoned the wells and spread contagion. The misery of the Black Death was therefore accompanied by the most vicious and sustained assault on European Jewry prior to that of the Nazis. The summer of 1349 in Germany was abuzz with stories about well-poisoning Jews, leading to a series of terrible pogroms in major German cities. Those who carried out the killings, like the members of the People's Crusade earlier, could easily convince themselves that they were wielding the warrior-saviour's sword of justice. Through killing Jews they were pushing back the frontiers of Antichrist's plague-ridden kingdom.

The seismic social shifts, in part caused by the Black Death, led to the first-ever mass popular uprising in England. The Peasants' Revolt of 1381 so shook the foundations of English medieval society that some thought they were the divinely appointed convulsions of the Last Days. In the next chapter, we shall see how political radicalism, utopian fantasizing and apocalyptic speculation were to fuse together in a similar fashion during the English Civil War years. So the millennium, once the object of selfish desires for unlimited material and sensual indulgence, now becomes the 'Egalitarian Millennium'. In early socialist myth-making, the ringleaders of the revolt – John Ball, Wat Tyler and Jack Straw – were cast as proto-socialists and anarchists building a New Jerusalem under an English sky.

*

The waning of the Middle Ages did not see any abatement in the history of apocalyptic thought. Chaucer, the father of English literature, died in 1400; he had chronicled the habits, morals and beliefs of the old medieval world as well as bringing into being a recognizably modern consciousness. In 'The Pardoner's Tale', he had lampooned the religious superstitions and gross abuses of medieval Catholicism. However, Chaucer is the brilliant exception rather than the rule; for most people living in the 1400s the ancient apocalyptic beliefs still exerted an enormous pull on their collective imaginations. Antichrist continued to stalk the highways and byways of the Christian mind; his evil presence was detected wherever calamity fell. The periodic outbreaks of plague which erupted throughout the first half of the fifteenth century only served to confirm that he and his ministers were still alive and kicking.

But new ideas were also afoot which were eventually to come to fruition in the next century. In the past, apocalyptic beliefs had demonized the Jews and Muslims; now it was the turn of the Catholic Church itself to be on the receiving end of them. The Taborite rebellion of 1419 to 1434 was directed not against some external foe but on the official Catholic Church itself. The Taborites stripped the sacraments down to communion and baptism, denied the Real Presence and were virulently iconoclastic: in their places of worship the veneration of saints and holy images was banished. Hand-in-hand with such religious radicalism was a political agenda which sought to overthrow the feudal system and establish an anarchist millennial kingdom on earth. The blueprint for this would be the utopian community established around Mount Tabor, a mountain they had renamed south of Prague. Here Christ would return to rule the new millennial kingdom. In the fourteenth century, such radicalism, both political and religious, proved fatal; the mainstream Hussite movement closed ranks with the Catholic Church and eradicated the sect. Nevertheless, the Taborites had challenged the legitimacy of the Catholic Church and their rebellion indicated which way the wind was going to blow in the next century.

The last decades of the fifteenth century were ones permeated and dominated by apocalyptic preoccupations. One of the most famous medieval historians has written about a 'general feeling of impending calamity [which] hangs over Europe, a sombre melancholy weighs on people's souls'.[30] All strata of European society were affected. Columbus' first voyage to the New World in 1492 was initially inspired and then sustained by apocalyptic beliefs. As every schoolboy knows, the man who 'discovered' America did so by accident – when he set out he thought he was going to arrive in India. Perhaps what is less well known is Columbus' sense of his own millennial purpose. He had discovered a continent only to turn it into a millennial kingdom. Reading Christopher Columbus' diaries leave us in no doubt that he assumed a messianic mantle. He was quite convinced that he had been divinely appointed to open up the Americas and bring Christianity to the Indians. Towards the end of his life, he wrote 'God made me the messenger of the new heaven and the new earth of which He spoke in the Apocalypse of St John . . . and he showed me the spot where to find it.'[31]

Columbus' paymasters, Ferdinand and Isabella of Spain, also capped that year through the reconquest of Granada and the expulsion of the Moors, marking the end of the long Christian holy war against the Muslims. And the Jews, the original creators of apocalyptic literature, once again became the victim of yet another Christian end-time scenario. The year 1492 was the one in which the Spanish Inquisition whipped up a frenzy of anti-Semitism in Spain, leading to the mass expulsion of Jews from the country.

As the century drew to a close, an apocalyptic sensibility was still all-pervasive. Hope for Adso's 'Last World Emperor' continued up until the Reformation. It was in this climate that the French King Charles VIII led an army into Italy in 1494 to pursue

French claims to the south. Amidst this turmoil, emerged the great apocalyptic prophet of the age – the Dominican friar Girolamo Savonarola. After the overthrow of the Medici in 1494, he was able to put into practical effect his brand of apocalyptic as he became the sole leader of the city. He railed against the rich and powerful, the clergy and the corrupt Pope Alexander VI (he returned the compliment by excommunicating him). Instead of the old corrupt order, Florence was to become a new democratic republic, a seedbed from whence would spring the moral and spiritual regeneration of the whole of Italy.

This utopian visionary even managed to cast the money-minded Florentines as the saving remnant, God's elect, who would play a glorious role in the new moral order. This would only be accomplished, however, if Florence submitted peacefully to the invading Charles VIII of France who was now cast as the Last World Emperor. Unfortunately, Charles VIII failed to live up to his messianic billing; his defeat spelled the end for Savonarola. The social revolution he had attempted to institute literally went up in smoke. The Dominican apocalyptic firebrand was burned at the stake.

*

In pursuit of the apocalyptic in Italy, we travel from Savonarola's Florence to the Umbrian town of Orvieto. There we can join the tourist trail to the cathedral. Passing through a warren of medieval alleys, the visitor is suddenly stopped in his tracks by the looming facade of the cathedral. It's a fanfare of Byzantine Gothic; life-sized sculpted figures look out from Gothic niches, in the midst of which there is a delicately carved rose window. But inside there is an even greater wonder to behold. It is here, in the Chapel of San Brizio, that we find Luca Signorelli's seven large frescoes depicting the Last Days, the resurrection of the dead, heaven and hell. Painted between

1499 and 1502, these dramatic scenes on the side walls of the chapel are introduced with a kind of pictorial prologue; the frescoes on the large arch spanning the entrance to the chapel make an emphatic statement of apocalyptic intent.

Signorelli did not have much space into which to pack the events of the Last Days; he had to make do with the narrow spaces on either side of the entrance door to the chapel. This required him to divide the scene into two narrative sections. The lower right part of the fresco depicts the signs of the end. In the foreground King David and the Sibyl act as witnesses to the end-times, signs of which include the usual cosmological phenomena: a red moon, a black sun, stars going pale etc. On earth, fires and earthquake sweep the earth, murder and mayhem run riot. In the upper left section of the fresco bat-like demons soar through the blackening sky, bombarding earth with flaming arrows. Below, in the lower left, the last survivors on earth fall over each other as they attempt to shield themselves from the demonic onslaught. Art historians have read the turmoil of these scenes as reflecting the wider turmoil within the Papal States. Apocalyptic speculation was rife due to a series of natural disasters, fear of the perennial bogeyman the 'Turk', and outbreaks of anti-Semitism.[32]

The scene is set for the main act in the eschatological drama. Passing through the archway into the chapel itself, the power and magnitude of Signorelli's apocalyptic imaginings become evident. We see scenes of angels, in a golden effluence, placing crowns on the heads of the blessed who have been chosen to ascend into heaven. The upper part of the scene shows angels playing and gazing at the Blessed, some of whom kneel whiles others prepare to take off in flight to assume their rightful position in heaven. The counterpart of this scene is the extra-ordinary 'Damned consigned to Hell'. Armoured archangels guard heaven while devils with grotesque bat-like wings carry off the damned to their new abode. On the left two devils hurl the bodies of the damned on the crowd below who form a scrum of writhing and tormented flesh. Howls of anguish and protestation go up as specific torments are inflicted on the damned. In the centre a devil takes a young woman on his shoulders. Another one is borne aloft, piggyback style. In the foreground a woman lies on her belly while a devil, with one foot on her head, pulls her toes apart. Ouch! Ears are ripped off, flesh clawed and fanged. A wild and violent mood is engendered through the colours and tones. The tan and white flesh tones of the mortals are jarringly juxtaposed to the orange, lavender and green of the devils' skin.

Another scene is a revealing indicator of the apocalyptic obsessions and paranoia gripping the larger society at the time. It is a scene depicting events which are almost unknown anywhere else in Italian art. Approaching the wall behind the altar, a figure homes into view preaching outdoors in front of a crowd. He stands on a pedestal. From a distance he appears Jesus-like in his garments, hair and beard. He could be Jesus' twin in fact. On closer inspection, however, it emerges that he has dark skin and exaggerated facial features, physiognomic signs of the corruption that lies within. One then notices the demon at his shoulder, whispering words into his ear and which then come out of his mouth. It's that great impostor himself, the Prince of Evil, the Antichrist. Around him are gathered a crowd of the rich and famous, many of whom are portraits (the apocalyptic visionary Dante is recognizable in the second row to our right). In the back is the Temple, a vast Renaissance pile, in the porches of which soldiers plunder treasure and pile it up in front of Antichrist. Another group of soldiers behead a man.

On the left, followers of Antichrist are murdering more Christian martyrs. But the end of his reign is predicted. Above the scenes of carnage, an angel casts him down in a shower of gold. In Christian terms, the frescoes run the whole gamut of human experience: the sacred and the profane, the physical and the spiritual, the divine and the demonic. Their purpose is simple – to remind worshippers about their place in the great cosmic scheme of things. Wedged between two vast eternities, heaven and hell, the individual is forced to choose which side he is on and thereby determine his eternal destiny. The walls become a stage, a *theatrum mundi*, on which a master scenographer orchestrates the action of a great eschatological drama. Either we can stand with Christ and suffer or we can tumble headlong to hell with Antichrist and his ministers.

Contemporaneous with Signorelli's frescoes are Albrecht Dürer's famous woodcut prints illustrating the Apocalypse (1498). Considered as the greatest artist of the German Renaissance, these extraordinary works nevertheless retain a more Gothic, northern flavour than the rest of his work, befitting to the violent and dynamic events that are depicted. Michelangelo too caught the apocalyptic mood of the age: beginning work on the Sistine Chapel in 1508, he created scenes involving devils and writhing forms in his *Last Judgement* which clearly reveal the influence of Signorelli.

Such visual images are an important part in the history of the end of the world. What might have been abstract and ethereal was made real and concrete to ordinary people. The Church was their theatre; paintings depicting the end of the world were part of an elaborate backdrop which helped them to grasp the magnitude of the prophesied events. The three-part drama of trial, suffering and eventual deliverance could throw up stunning images which still compel our attention today. In the next century there would be new wars, plagues and famines to add grist to the apocalyptic imagination. History would not short change the next generation of artists of raw materials for their apocalyptic imaginings.

4

VISIONS OF THE END IN EUROPE: PART TWO

In the sixteenth century, militant millenarianism was once more on the march and was to prove just as deadly as it had been before. The radical Taborite tradition was maintained in the millenarian myths and movements which emerged in the first half of the new century. In this febrile atmosphere, a figure emerged who was to exert an important influence on the communist revolutionaries of the nineteenth century and whose fame and notoriety still endure to this day. Thomas Münzter's story provides a useful paradigm of what can happen when apocalyptic faith and radical politics coalesce. As so often in our story, the combination proved explosive.

Born in Thuringia, Germany in 1488, Münzter seemed more destined for the library or cloister than the battlefield. He read Hebrew and Greek and was steeped in the patristic and scholastic theology of the day. A few years younger than

Luther, Münzter was at first a follower of the great reformer and then a fierce and formidable enemy. Between 1517 and 1520 Luther's actions provided Münzter with an alternative to the Catholic Church of the day. When he nailed his theses against the sale of indulgences on to the church door at Wittenberg, disputed in public the infallibility and supremacy of the Pope and wrote and published the three treatises which led to his excommunication, he was leading the way for priests like Münzter. At first, he was content to follow where the Doctor led – away from the orthodoxy of the medieval Catholic Church towards the reformed faith. Later, however, he was to reject the new Lutheran creed just as he had abandoned the 'old religion'.

For one thing, Luther's key doctrine of justification by faith alone had little appeal to Münzter. In his apocalyptic scenario, what mattered was predicting when the world would end, an event which was imminent and looked forward to with feverish anticipation. Luther too believed he was living amidst the Last Days but believed that it was impossible to predict when the end would come. That it would come – and to be prepared spiritually – was what mattered. To do this, the true word of God had to be spread through the channels of the world. For Luther, the great obstacle to this was the false religion masquerading as Christianity. In his apocalyptic scenario, therefore, the Pope himself, God's representative on earth, was the Antichrist and the Whore of Babylon the Catholic Church and all its misbelievers. In contrast, Münzter preached a bloody and militant apocalyptic faith which had wide-ranging social and political implications rather than just simply religious and theological ones. Not since the time of the Taborites had such revolutionary and radical beliefs been expounded.

The *Book of Revelation* proved decisive in Münzter's political awakening. Convinced that the Last Days were at hand

and that he was part of the Elect who had received the Holy Spirit, Münzter came to see himself as a Last Days Warrior. It was his job to exterminate the godless so that the Second Coming could take place and the millennium ushered in. Whatever retarded this event quite simply had to be annihilated. As part of an elect body, prompted by the living Christ within, the Last Days Warrior was absolved of the normal prohibitions and laws which govern the rest of us. If this indwelling spirit prompts you to kill for the sake of a future millennial kingdom, then you do so in the certainty that you are one of the Elect, divinely sanctioned to murder and maim.[1]

It was in such terms that Münzter thought of himself. Like the warrior-Christ in *Revelation*, he too would be the wielder of the double-edged sword of divine justice. It was the force of such beliefs which turned Münzter from being an obscure scholar into a soldier in God's battle against the forces of evil. So closely did Münzter identify himself with the living Christ within that he became virtually indistinguishable from God. It was the Almighty who told him to convert and win recruits among the poor and downtrodden in the area close to the Bohemian border. When he was forced eventually out of there, he moved on to Bohemia itself in the hope of finding a saving remnant of the earlier Taborite movement.

Here he revivified that old eschatological parable of the wheat and tares which Jesus had preached in order to figure the events of the Last Days. He was now God's scythe, ruthlessly cutting down his enemies in an apocalyptic harvest-time. He would wield the scythe, the peasant's weapon, not the sword, the chosen instrument of the corrupt rulers. In his end-time scenario, the elected wheat would be separated from the demonic tares, which parasitically fed off the fruits of the earth. The prodigious violence recalls that envisioned in *Revelation* in which the stars fall like ripe figs and the harvest of the earth is cast 'into the great winepress of the wrath of God'.[2] Münzter conceived of violence in similarly cleansing terms. The Fall had alienated humanity from God; the rich and the powerful had exacerbated the situation still further. To restore human contact with God and thus bring in the golden age on earth, human being would be pitted against human being. Münzter's sharpened his scythe for the coming show-down.

In the event, the apocalyptic harvest failed to materialize. The messianic wielder of the scythe was unceremoniously booted out of Bohemia. Münzter was now baseless, and spent the next couple of years wandering around Germany like some medieval *propheta*. In 1523, a new chapter in the Münzter story opened when he moved into the small town of Allstedt in Thuringia. It was here among the miners, peasants and arti-sans of the region that he was to create a militant messianic movement that was to challenge the authority of the clergy and the secular rulers and lords. Allstedt was to become for Münzter what Wittenberg had become for Luther – a power-base from which to launch a Reformation. Unlike Luther's Reformation, however, Münzter's religious pro-gramme was going to be total and final and would help usher in the end of the world. He would have no truck with the secular ruling authorities ('red poppies and blue cornflowers'), recognizing only the authority of the living God that was sharpening his scythe within him.

During this period of revolutionary ferment, the *Book of Daniel* loomed large in Münzter's sermons and preachings. It was re-interpreted in order to give it an urgent contemporary spin. In Münzter's theory of history, the last of the four world-empires is nearing its end; the world is now in the grip of the Prince of Evil whose ministers – the secular rulers and clergy – attempt to extend his dominion. This division of history into four great phases of history baulks large in German thought, even resurfacing in such avowedly secular thinkers as Marx. In such a desperate situation only a radical and violent response from the saving remnant will deliver the world from their evil. In a 1524 sermon, Münzter articulates an apocalyptic vision full of exterminatory zeal and violent imagery:

> The sword is necessary to exterminate them. And so that it shall be done honestly and properly, our dear fathers the princes must do it, who confess Christ with us. But if they don't do it, the sword shall be taken from them . . . If they resist, let them be slaughtered without mercy . . . At the harvest-time one must pluck the weeds out of God's vineyard . . . But the angels who are sharpening their sickles for that work are no other than the earnest servants of God . . . For the ungodly have no right to live, save what the Elect choose to allow them.[3]

We see here a kind of theocratic fascism, the survival of the fittest not in biological terms but in spiritual ones. The old biblical metaphors – sifting the wheat from the tares and tearing weeds from the vineyard – hide but cannot completely disguise the murderous intent behind Münzter's apocalyptic fantasies.

Like the leaders of the English Peasants' Revolt and the Taborites, Münzter assigns a special role for the poor and the downtrodden in the great universal drama that was about to be enacted. Only they would be sufficiently pure to cleanse the world of ungodly elements and usher in an egalitarian millennium. For Münzter, any one who thwarted this should be summarily wiped off the face of the earth. Included in this last category was Luther. Once Münzter's mentor, Luther was now his deadly enemy. He was associated with the Beast of the Apocalypse and the Whore of Babylon because of the accommodation he had made with secular rulers like the two princes of Saxony, the Elector Frederick the Wise and his brother Duke John.

For his part, Luther saw Münzter as a dangerous insurrectionary, who would spoil the pact he had made with the secular powers for the sake of the Reformation. In 1525, when the Peasants' War was shaking the very bedrock of German society, he raged against the peasant prophet. For Luther, the real enemies were not the princes of Saxony but the Pope and the papal authorities. He identified them with the Antichrist, the ultimate purveyor and peddler of false religious beliefs. The revolution envisaged by Luther would be a spiritual and theological revolution, not an earthly and political one. Through disseminating the unalloyed truth of the Gospels, Luther conceived of purifying the world of its ungodly elements in preparation for the Second Coming. Then Christ would return, bringing with him divine justice, the only justice that truly mattered because it involved the fate of the eternal soul rather than that of the transitory body. Social revolution was not on Luther's eschatological agenda. In his view, the world was soon going to end in any case; what mattered was the fate of the individual soul in the hereafter not the body politic in the here-and-now.

In Luther, Münzter had made a powerful and dangerous enemy. Spurred on by Luther, the princes of central Germany joined forces with those of the south and west to oppose the Peasants' War. On 15 May 1525, the princes' army confronted the peasant one in a very one-sided conflict. One army was trained, had a great deal of artillery and a large cavalry. The other one had very little artillery and was mostly armed with scythes and farmyard implements. But such a mismatch did not deter Münzter; the divine scythe-wielder after all believed in firepower of a more spiritual kind. According to one

account, Münzter made a passionate speech in front of the
peasant army under a rainbow banner. In it he affirmed his
status as a man marked out by destiny. God, he declared, had
spoken to him, assuring the peasants victory over their better-
armed and trained enemy. Münzter himself would catch the
feared cannon balls in the sleeves of his cloak. When hostilities
commenced, the peasant army soon broke ranks and fled in
panic. The enemy cavalry then scythed hundreds of them
down. For his part, the cannon-ball catching leader escaped
from the battlefield only to suffer the indignity of being caught.
He was later tortured and then beheaded in the camp of his
archest enemies – the princes.

The Anabaptist movement, which spread far and wide
during the years following the Peasants' War, cherished the
memory of Münzter, despite the fact that he never called
himself an Anabaptist. This name was actually given to a
movement by its enemies (from Greek *ana*, 'again'). It was a
blanket term, covering a movement which consisted of some
forty independent sects, each grouped around a leader who
claimed to be a divinely inspired figure. Central to their beliefs
were the precepts which they thought they found in the New
Testament; these were interpreted in the light of the direct
inspiration which they believed they received from God. Their
doctrines about rebaptism were noteworthy: infant baptism
was repudiated as a blasphemous act; adult baptism was
thought to be the only proper one. Anabaptists therefore
rejected the name given to them because for them they had
only been baptized once, as adults.

But it was in their social habits, rather than their tenets
about baptism, which most distinctly marked them as a sect
apart. Private property was eschewed in favour of a community of goods ideal. Among these sectarians a hard line
separatist mentality prevailed. The state and the established

order were seen to be so corrupt that they were regarded as manifestations of Antichrist. Catholics and Lutherans were thus tarred with the same brush. Such subversive views were not calculated to appeal to anyone in power and authority and a backlash was not long in coming. When it came, Anabaptists were adept in turning their own isolation and persecution into an important part of their own self-mythologizing. The onslaughts and persecution directed at them were seen as apocalyptic in nature. They were the rebaptized Saints and those forces ranged against them were the Antichrist and his followers. Soon, however, his reign would draw to a close. Then the Elect would arise, overthrow corrupt rulers and establish an egalitarian millennium on earth for themselves.

In the late 1520s, flare-ups of revolutionary Anabaptism occurred in the towns of southern Germany. Prophets like Hans Hut, an itinerant bookbinder, kept Münzter's legacy alive, fulminating against the rich and the powerful and prophesying how he and the rebaptized Saints would lay low the rich and the powerful when Christ returned to earth. For all the violence of their rhetoric, however, such messianic pretenders could easily be snuffed out by the authorities. Like Münzter, Hut met a violent death. He was captured and imprisoned in 1527 and was never seen alive again.

When the right social and economic conditions prevailed, however, the result could be entirely different. In Münster in northwest Germany, powerful guilds were locked in conflict with the clergy and the nobility. Heavy taxation, outbreaks of the plague and rocketing inflation produced a powder-keg situation. In times of such social upheaval, the poorer classes became politically radicalized and outbreaks of such militant millenarianism were common place. In 1533, followers of

Melchior Hoffmann, a celebrated German mystic and lay preacher, flooded into the town of Münster in northwest Germany. Many of them were Anabaptists from the Netherlands and brought with them radical politics and violent theology.

In Hoffman's eschatological teachings the *annus mirabilis* would be 1533 because 1,500 years had elapsed since the death of Christ. The site of the millennial kingdom would be Strasbourg, with he himself riding into the city with Christ in the clouds. Followers were enjoined to wait patiently for the dawning of the new age, secure in the knowledge that they were the elect who Christ would reward on his return.

Hoffman's emphasis on waiting represented a quietist strain in Anabaptism. When Hoffman fell foul of the authorities and ended up in prison, new leaders emerged, Dutch Anabaptists, who proclaimed loudly the need for violent insurrection as an essential precondition for ushering in the millennium. These new leaders in Münster wanted instant revolution in order to institute a radically new social order. In fact, the anarcho-communist order they envisioned was not new but was based on the social and political order which was supposed to have prevailed in the days of the primitive Church. In order to achieve this the godless had to be wiped off the face of the earth before the ideal could be achieved.

The corollary of such beliefs was the glorification of suffering – a characteristic of sectarians down to the present age. Anabaptists identified their suffering with that of the martyrs of the first three centuries of the Christian era. Believers modelled themselves on the apostles, travelling to the various scattered Anabaptist communities, 'dipping' adults as they went, all done in the certitude that they were living at the end of time. One of these self-styled apostles was Jan Bockelson, who was later to find fame and notoriety as John of

Leyden. Under his rule, Anabaptists in Münster were infused with a ferocious militancy and revolutionary fervour.

February 1534 saw the first Anabaptists armed rising which involved occupying the town hall, and winning from the Lutheran majority the right to legally practise their faith. Many Lutherans viewed this victory for the Anabaptists as the writing on the wall and took the first opportunity to hotfoot it out of the town. Such a course of action proved prescient. Buoyed by their earlier victory, Anabaptist preachers whipped up a frenzy of collective millennial madness. The focus now for supernatural expectation was Münster itself; Anabaptists from far and wide were urged to come to the town in preparation for the End of the World which would surely happen before Easter. Presided over by the community of the righteous, Münster would be the ark in the coming deluge, the saving remnant, the New Jerusalem. In the new theocratic state, only the pure and the Elect could remain, the others (Lutherans or Catholics) were either sent packing or were rebaptized publicly. Once the persecuted, the Anabaptists were now the persecutors.

The Roman Catholic authorities viewed the Anabaptist seizure of power in Münster with dismay and immediately set about laying siege to the city. Neighbouring towns and principalities rallied round the prince-bishop and contributed arms and supplies. Under Jan Matthys, the Dutch 'prophet' who had converted and baptized John of Leyden, a reign of terror soon descended on Münster, all in the name of the millennium. Along with his protégé, Mathys instituted a religiously inspired reign of terror. The private ownership of money was outlawed; giving up your hard earned cash was made a test of true Christianity. Those who demurred were executed. Life under such a theocratic government sounds similar to life in Pol Pot's Cambodia or Stalin's Soviet Union.

In sixteenth-century Münster, however, the state propaganda was biblical rather than secular. In the communal dining halls diners were regaled with morally uplifting passages from the Old Testament as they ate their cheerless meals. The true Christian believer would happily embrace communist doctrines about the abolition of private ownership and working for profit because they were in accordance with God's will. Go against the regime and you were effectively going against God. Opponents of the state were thus demonized and could expect no mercy.

In order to inculcate these new doctrines and ideas effectively the Anabaptist leaders wanted a clean and utter break with the past. Frenzied bouts of public book burning were meant to symbolize how the new social order was wiping the collective slate clean. Like the Nazis, the Anabaptists liked to think of themselves as 'primitive' in the sense that they had not been corrupted by too much book learning. In such totalitarian regimes simple brawn is always preferable to sophisticated brain. For the Nazis, knowledge was always a mystical experience derived from kinship and blood. For the Münster Anabaptists, knowledge and wisdom came directly from divine inspiration not from a text. The Children of God were encouraged not to think for themselves – leave that to their divinely inspired leaders. Those who were deemed the wisest were those through whom God communicated directly – namely Matthys, John of Leyden et al. It was their version of the truth that would be transmitted to the believers, not the rival truths contained in the library. The book burning therefore had a theological purpose. When Matthys banned all books save the Bible, he was quashing all theological speculation, enabling him to canalize his own doctrines and beliefs directly into the minds of the believers

Things, however, were soon to take a turn for the worse.

Matthys' theocratic fascism appears positively benign in comparison to what was to come after his untimely death in March 1534. John of Leyden emerged as his successor, God's latest representative on earth. Under his leadership, the Münster regime was going to strip away the very last vestige of human freedom – sexuality. Before, the Anabaptists were known for their sexual continence. Adultery and fornication were capital offences. In John of Leyden's millennial kingdom, however, a radical sexual revolution was about to take place. Polygamy was now the order of the day. It was incumbent on the long-suffering citizens of Münster to go forth and multiply. Apocalyptic groups and sects have always seen sex as a way of instituting a new millennial reign. Populating the world with the Children of God is one way of ushering in a new biological and metaphysical order. Good looking and charismatic, John of Leyden was no slouch when it came to populating the world with the Children of God. He had a personal harem of fifteen wives. A law was passed which made it a legal obligation for all women under a certain age to marry, whether they wanted to or not.

John of Leyden's reign of terror in Münster provides a salutary reminder of what happens when a social vision and millenarian beliefs are allied. Proclaiming himself to be the Messiah of the Last Days, he abrogated universal spiritual and temporal dominion. Under his rule, time was to begin again. The regime renamed streets and the days of the week in order to mark the uniqueness of John of Leyden's accession. Even new-born children were to be named by the king. A national emblem, an orb with two swords, was devised, symbolizing John of Leyden's claim to universal power. Divara, wife number one, was proclaimed queen and held court like her husband, lording it over the other wives from the purloined mansions near the cathedral.

The nightmarish dystopia conjured up by John of Leyden and his queen has an Orwellian flavour. In the new social order some were infinitely more equal than others. Any one who demonstrated an unwillingness to hand over their goods, or any other form of dissent, would be executed in front of the king. More often than not he would carry out the beheadings and the quarterings himself. When the blockade came in January 1535, famine soon came in its wake. John of Leyden simply requisitioned all the food. In the face of mass starvation and an incipient rebellion, he proclaimed that deliverance would come by Easter. When deliverance signally failed to materialize, he fell back on the usual back-pedalling – he had only meant that they were to be spiritually saved.

Besieged, starving and ruled by a monster, the Anabaptists of Münster were finally put out of their misery when the siege was lifted in June 1535. All the Anabaptist leaders perished. As for John of Leyden, he was paraded around for a few months in public on a chain, like some grotesque for the delectation of the Catholic Church. Then in January 1536, he was brought back to his New Jerusalem, otherwise known as Münster, and publicly executed with red-hot irons along with two of his accomplices. Their mutilated bodies were used to deter any other would-be messiahs; they were publicly exhibited in iron cages, hanging from the Gothic steeple of St Lambert's Church. Such was the inglorious end of the reign of the Anabaptists' 'king'. Nowadays the cages have become a tourist attraction and can be seen in the tower.

In seventeenth-century England, rebellion against a centralized religious authority often took on a similarly apocalyptic form as it did in sixteenth-century Münster. During the tumultuous years of the English Civil War and the Commonwealth, congeries of apocalyptic sects and groups sprung up. One of the most famous was the Fifth Monarchy Men. They took their name from the prophetic dream of Nebuchadnezzar in *Daniel* 2:44 in which a fifth monarchy would succeed the Assyrian, Persian, Greek and Roman monarchies/empires. In their eschatology, Fifth Monarchists viewed this period as the millennial reign of Christ on earth in very literal and physical terms, just like Christians had done prior to Augustine. The turbulent events of contemporary history were read therefore as part of a divine signifying system. The execution of Charles I in 1649 was seen as ushering in the Last Days; the final apocalyptic battle and the destruction of the Antichrist were to take place between 1655 and 1657. Then there would be the thousand-year reign of the Saints (i.e. themselves) on earth. Contemporary political figures were recast in typological terms. When Cromwell dissolved the Rump Parliament in April 1653, Fifth Monarchists hailed him as a second Moses leading God's chosen people to the Promised Land. The Nominated Assembly of 1653 represented the high-water mark of Fifth Monarchist influence; many of the delegates were from Fifth Monarchy congregations.

This sudden accession of power, however, was followed by an equally spectacular fall. The circumstances surrounding the abrupt dissolution of the Assembly and the establishment of a Protectorate were seen by them as a betrayal; Cromwell was appointed, not elected, Lord Protector, thus infringing personal, religious and political freedoms. Once allies of Cromwell, religious radicals now became his sworn enemies. As was their wont, the Fifth Monarchists and other dissident groups cast their former saviour as an apocalyptic type – the arch impostor, the demonic deceiver, the Antichrist. In order to usher in the millennial kingdom, this polluter of the political and spiritual wellsprings had to be removed. The 1650s were marked therefore by Fifth Monarchist agitation against the Protectorate, culminating in the uncovering of Thomas

Venner's 1657 plot to overthrow it. On that occasion, Venner was imprisoned and subsequently released in 1659 as an act of clemency by the new Protector, Cromwell's son Richard. When Venner attempted another coup after the restoration of the monarchy in 1660, the royalist authorities were less forgiving than their puritan counterparts. 'Venner's Rising' as it has become known was a desperate last-ditch attempt to realize the millennial reign of the saints. Four days of street fighting in January 1661, however, resulted not in the rule of the saints, but in the summary execution of the radical militant leaders, the imprisonment of some hundred Fifth Monarchy men and some four thousand Quaker supporters.

Puritan theology hinged on the concept of election. The individual soul was predestined either to heaven or hell. Regardless of good works or intentions, God's grace was bestowed on the Elect. In radical Puritanism, this Calvinistic doctrine could sometimes mutate into the heresy of antinomianism. This is the idea that for the 'pure all things are pure'. Because the Elect cannot fall from grace, then, the moral law is deemed to have no relevance. Whereas traditional Puritans attempted to withstand the beleaguerments of carnality, heterodox groups succumbed entirely to them. Indeed, paradoxically, the more you flaunted your sinful behaviour the more it was thought of as a sign that you were one of the Elect.

Much academic interest has centred on the Ranters and their literature. Their works give expression to heretical beliefs and sentiments and include accounts of orgiastic sex, the consumption of prodigious amounts of tobacco and alcohol, compulsive swearing and the frenzied, ranting speaking in tongues which gave the sect their name. The sect's belief that divine grace resided within all individuals in the form of an 'inner light', 'spirit' or 'Christ within' could be anarchocommunistic in its implications. If all things came from God, then, all things belonged to God, thus challenging the whole basis of private property. In such a view, those who accrued vast reserves of capital or acquired property were thieves, stealing God's property.

However, the concept of the 'inner light' could also make for the kind of messianic posturing that John of Leyden went in for. If you manage to persuade yourself that God is working through you, then it is not such a big step to conceive of yourself as an actual incarnation of Him. Many succumbed to self-deification amidst the tumult of the 1640s and 1650s. During these extraordinary decades, historical events were viewed through the lens of apocalyptic literature like never before. A steep rise in literacy and a communications revolution helped fan the flames of apocalyptic fantasizing. A flood of privately printed religious tracts was eagerly consumed by the masses. On street corners, self-styled prophets, messiahs and millenarians whipped up a frenzy of lay religiosity. It was also the age of radical social visionaries. Radical democratic beliefs and heterodox religious ones often went hand-in-hand with each other.

At the centre of the storm was the Bible itself. Once the preserve of a Latin-reading priestly clerical class, the Word of God was now no longer a closed book. This was a process that had been set in motion since the Reformation and the translation of the Bible into the vernacular languages of Europe. In the early 1640s, the Bible had been available in English translation for a century. Mid-seventeenth-century England was one of the most literate societies there had ever been. Because it was considered to be the fount of all wisdom, ordinary folk were encouraged to read the Bible, thus exposing them to some pretty radical and potentially dangerous doctrines. Old Testament prophets routinely denounced the rich; in the New Testament the Gospels suggest human equality in the notion that we are all God's children.

And then of course there were the explosive apocalyptic texts, *Daniel* and *Revelation*. Passages from them could be read in tracts sold by sectarians, passages about how God would finally lay low the rich and the powerful and reward and recompense the lowly and the faithful. Thus inspired, a Leveller might demand a wider extension of the suffrage; a Digger demanding the building of heaven for the poor on earth might point to *Revelation* 20. And the Ranters, rejecting all orthodox forms of moral restraint, could point to passages in the New Testament about the drama and the ecstasy of the operation of the spirit within the individual. Different forms of radicalism – personal, political and religious – shaded into each other when imbued with the all-pervasive apocalypticism of the time.

Ecstasies, signs, portents, prodigies, outpourings of the Spirit: all these were everyday events in these wild and tempestuous times, particularly during that period of political instability and uncertainty which followed the execution of the king and lasted until the establishment of the Protectorate. Cromwell himself was infused with some of these millennial beliefs, particularly before he assumed high office; certainly large numbers of his New Model Army were convinced that the violence of the Civil War was the preordained convulsions which were to precede the Kingdom of the Saints. In their apocalyptic scenario, God's elected Englishmen were going to establish a New Jerusalem on English soil under an English sky. Such a patriotic conception of the apocalypse even infused that soberest of geniuses, John Milton. In his great prose work *Areopagitica* (1644), he wrote: 'God is decreeing to begin some new and great period . . . What does he then but reveal himself . . . as his manner is, first to his Englishmen?'[4]

Born and raised in Warwick, Abiezer Coppe (1619–72) was the most celebrated – and the most notorious – of the Ranters.

A former Anabaptist minister, he had gone forth into the West Country with apostolic zeal, baptizing vast numbers of people. In 1646, he ended up in prison for his pains. His growing eccentricity estranged him from his wife and family. Then in 1649 came his conversion to Ranterism. This heterodoxy believed that God inhered in all matter – whether in heaven, hell or on earth. Such beliefs could issue in all kinds of bizarre behaviour and practices. Clothes were ritually shed because they were thought to betoken a return to primal innocence. The Adamic contagion of sexual shame was thought to be exorcized through orgiastic sexual practices.

An archpriest of Ranterism, Coppe himself had a reputation for prodigious bouts of drinking, smoking, whoring and swearing. But because Coppe regarded himself as one of the Elect on whom God bestowed his grace, when he swore he was merely hearkening to the deepest promptings of the Spirit within. Coppe's coprolalia – obsessive use of bad language – might nowadays be put down to a bad case of Tourette's syndrome. For Coppe and his swearing disciples, the bad language coming from their mouths had been cleansed by God and could not be judged to be bad. For the Elect, for the pure for whom all things are pure, swearing and cursing was more glorious than pious prayers and preaching. Similarly, the pub and not the pulpit was the proper arena for religious worship. The Ranters were great frequenters of the common alehouse, having the power to transfigure such places into theatres of apocalyptic struggle and striving.

The gloriously long-winded title of Coppe's most significant work, *A Fiery Flying Roll*, announces the author's apocalyptic intention:

A Fiery Flying Roll: A Word from the Lord to all the Great Ones of the Earth, whom this may concern: Being the last

Warning Piece at the dreadfull day of JUDGEMENT. For now the Lord is come to 1) Informe 2) Advise and warne 3) Charge 4) Judge and sentence the Great Ones. As also most compassionately informing, and most lovingly and pathetically advising and warning *London*. With a terrible Word, and fatal Blow from the Lord, upon the Gathered CHURCHES. And all by his Most Excellent MAJESTY, dwelling in, and shining through AUXILIUM PATRIS, alias *Coppe*.[5]

The end-time furies are to be specifically unleashed on the 'Great Ones'. This reflects Coppe's beliefs that all private property belonged only to God alone. Those who had appropriated more than their fair share of the world's resources were guilty of the 'worst and foulest of villanies' – stealing from God. In comparison, traditional vices and sins – fornication, swearing, blaspheming, drunkenness – were deemed to be of no consequence in the new moral order. In the Last Days, 'Sin and Transgression is finished and ended', supplanted by the 'everlasting Gospell'. The language suggests the Joachite Third Age, the Age of the Spirit, recast and reconfigured in antinomian terms. In their version of Joachim's triadic division of history, the Ranters would be the inheritors of the Third Age on earth. Having reached perfection here there would be no need for the Last Judgement and the destruction of the world.

In the preface, Coppe gives a vivid account of his conversion to Ranterism:

First, all my strength, my forces were utterly routed, my house I dwelt in fired; my father and mother forsook me, the wife of my bosome loathed me, mine old name was rotted, perished; and I was utterly plagued, consumed, damned, rammed, and sunke into nothing, into the bowels of the still Eternity (my mothers wombe) out of which I came naked, and whetherto I returned again naked. And lying a while there, rapt up in silence, at length (the body or outward forme being awake all this while) I heard with my outward eare (to my apprehension) a most terrible thunder-clap, and after that a second. And upon the second thunder-clap, which was exceeding terrible, I saw a great body of light, like the light of the Sun, and red as fire, in the forme of a drum . . . whereupon with exceeding trembling and amazement on the flesh, and with joy unspeakable in the spirit, I clapt my hands, and cryed out, *Amen, Halelujah, Halelujah, Amen.*[6]

God then grants Coppe a vision of hell where he makes the discovery that, amidst all the darkness, there is a small spark of transcendent glory, a testament to the unity and universality of all things in heaven, hell and on earth. God then tells him about how the 'spirits of just men [are] made perfect'. Perfection proclaimed, Coppe is now one of the Elect; he is the receptacle for the visions and revelations of God. Inner voices assail him, uttering violently apocalyptic messages:

Blood, blood, Where, where? upon the hypocriticall holy heart, &c . . . Vengeance, vengeance, vengeance, Plagues, plagues, upon the inhabitants of the earth; Fire, fire, fire, Sword, sword, &c. upon all that bow now down to eternall Majesty, universall love; I'le recover, recover, my wooll, my flax, my money. Declare, declare, feare thou not the faces of any; I am (in thee) a munition of Rocks, &c.[7]

Ranting is raised here to the level of artistic utterance. Non sequiturs, the fractured syntax, repetition and eccentric punctuation enact out the experience of revelatory ecstasy.

The voices then tell Coppe to go to London and to write. A roll of a book is handed to him, only to be snatched back and

thrust violently into his mouth. Coppe eats the paper, whereupon he suffers violent indigestion – 'it lay broiling, and
burning in my stomack' – until he vomits it up on to the page
and thus completes the process of composition. Such excesses
recall the extreme behaviour of the divinely inspired Ezekiel.
The point is that the divine word is rooted in sordid bodily
reality, thus testifying to the universality and unity of all things
– the key Ranter tenet.

For Coppe, the pen was definitely mightier than the sword
or Münzter's scythe. Like his German counterpart, Coppe
conceived of himself as a purveyor of revelation and revolution
but he used words rather than weapons to help usher in the
millennium. In Chapter 1, Coppe figures the rich and the
powerful as 'High Mountaines' and 'lofty Cedars'; and like
the loftiest cedar of them all, Charles I, they are about to face
the chop.[8] The jealous and wrathful God of the Old Testament
is now a violent insurrectionary, hell-bent on levelling and
felling forests of vain cedars. Here the apocalyptist is the
metaphorical lumberjack, a variation on the grape-stamper
from *Revelation*. In the wholly extraordinary Chapter 2 of *A
Fiery Flying Roll*, rich people are enjoined to embrace, literally,
beggars and prisoners; they are the flesh of their flesh and so
should be acknowledged as their brothers and sisters.[9] That
Coppe meant quite literally embracing the poor there can be
little doubt. Sleeping with female beggars and convict women
is not just a case of sexual slumming or the thrill of rough
trade. Sexual transgression is seen as an agent of social and
moral regeneration. In the physical contact of flesh-on-flesh,
malefic social divisions and barriers would dissolve. In preparation for this sexualized version of the millennium, prisons
needed to be emptied and the destitute and the starving fed and
housed.

Radical sectarian groups like the Ranters helped turn the

world upside in the 1640s and 1650s. It was the end of the world (at least in England) for absolute monarchy and the old ruling elites. The repercussions of this social and political revolution were to play out across the centuries. Literary critics have noted how the Ranters' rhetoric of apocalyptic has resurfaced in later writers like D.H. Lawrence.[10] An earlier Romantic writer, William Blake, has also been associated with the Ranters. Liberation from the orthodoxies of religion and social and moral restraints were common concerns for both writers. Like the Ranters, both Blake and Lawrence were products of English Puritanism. Like Coppe, both created their own religious alternative to mainstream orthodoxy.

The convulsions of the English Civil War era had huge cultural, social and political repercussions. In the post-Restoration years, a biological catastrophe added to the apocalyptic mix. At its peak, the Great Plague of London, which hit the capital from 1665 to 1666, killed two thousand Londoners a week. Mercifully, it lasted only a few weeks, but it was followed by a uniquely catastrophic event – the Great Fire of London. Accounts of the Great Fire by Samuel Pepys and John Evelyn strike an apocalyptic note. The fire is described as a conflagration devouring the city like some ravenous apocalyptic monster. Pepys's entry for 2 September 1666, describes how 'a most horrid malicious bloody flame' engulfs the City.[11] Along with water, fire is an apocalyptic element which can also destroy, cleanse and regenerate in equal measure. In *Genesis*, first the world is destroyed and purified through water; in *Revelation* fire serves a similar function. From a public health point of view, the historical Great Fire of London was a godsend; warrens of medieval streets, incubators of the plague, were destroyed in one fell swoop.

For doomsday date-setters and numerologists, the fire was also providential. They had already been disappointed by the year 1656, which was believed to be a possible date for the end of the world, being the number of years calculated between the Creation and the Flood. A decade later they had a new focus for their millennial expectations. Add together the talismanic figure of 1,000 and 666, the mark of the Beast, and you came up with the figure 1666. Recent historical events had provided many provocations to support the view that the end was nigh. The Lord's Anointed, Charles I, had lost his head a decade and a half or so earlier, followed by a period of civil war and political and social strife. Then the plague paid a brief but deadly visit to the capital in 1665–6, only to be followed by the Great Fire. For many, such a sequence of events could only mean one thing.

The Jewish mystic Sabbatai Zevi of Smyrna (Turkey, 1626–76) also believed that 1666 was to be the Great Year. Earlier, in 1648, he had proclaimed himself the Messiah and gathered together a host of Jews from Europe and the Turkish Empire to form the Sabbatean sect in the expectation of a great national revival. Landing in Constantinople, he was captured and given a stark choice by the Sultan; either convert to Islam or face death. Ever the pragmatist, he chose conversion. Despite such an apostasy, the influence of the Sabbatean movement survived for many years, well into the eighteenth century.

Other seventeenth-century doomsday dates reveal how science, maths and apocalyptic beliefs often combined together. John Napier (1550–1617), the mathematician who discovered logarithms, also went in for more metaphysical calculations. The year 1668 was the date he set for the end of the world, basing his prediction on the *Book of Revelation*. When this was disconfirmed, he fell back on that other mainstay of apocalyptic speculation, the *Book of Daniel*, and came up with the figure of 1700. Isaac Newton was the man who discovered calculus, founded modern physics and wrote the *Principia* and the

Opticks – two of the most revolutionary books in the history of science. Less well known is that Newton was also a keen student of the Apocalypse (2060 was his *annus mirabilis*). His biographer, the Cambridge economist John Maynard Keynes, found reams of Newton's writings about esoteric theology. The man who discovered the force of gravity was also a believer in a less scientific explanation of the world; he believed that hidden in the Bible was a code which would unlock the secret of the divinely fore-ordained future.

In our world, science and religion seem to be in permanent conflict with each other. Very often the former becomes a cudgel with which to beat the latter. In Newton's age, however, the demarcations between science, religion and the occult were far less clear cut. Modern science had grown out of the work of the alchemists, a debt Newton repaid by writing about the occult. Surveying nature or the sky for end-time signs could also be seen as good preparation for the empirical inductive method. For centuries, prophets of the Apocalypse had been observing, classifying and recording signs in nature.

The Age of Reason may have been about to dawn but this did not stop a flurry of date-setting activity as the seventeenth century drew to a close. In the New World, there was the Woman in the Wilderness cult. Drawing from theology and astrology, the German prophet Johann Jacob Zimmerman determined that the world would end in the autumn of 1694. The location for Christ's return, he prophesied, would be America. He and the other sect members planned to cross the Atlantic and put on a welcome party. When the day of departure came, however, in February 1694, he fell down dead. Undeterred, the pilgrims got themselves a new leader, Johannes Kelpius; he successfully completed the journey with the other sect members. Unfortunately Christ failed to keep the appointment.

Such failed prophecies often called into question the whole

legitimacy of date-setting. Newton believed that when prophecy failed the sacred prophecies themselves were discredited.
On this point at least Newton was orthodox; he could point to
the New Testament's condemnation of date-setting in *Acts* 1:
6–7. It is not in man's remit to know when the end of the world
is to take place. Viewed kindly, date-setters were simply
irresponsible and rash. Others took a dimmer view. For them,
date-setting prophets were attempting to steal God's thunder.
All would be revealed in the fullness of time when God wills it.

The kind of panic which prophecy could engender has been
well documented. One such incident occurred on 13 October
1736. A certain William Whitson earned his place in the Hall
of Fame of failed prophets when he predicted that a deluge
would engulf London. Mass panic seized many Londoners,
leading to an armada of boats being launched into the Thames.
These were their very own arks. The dangerously delusional
William Bell whipped up a similar case of millennial mass
hysteria. The end would come courtesy of an earthquake, he
proclaimed, predicted to occur on 5 April 1761. There had
been an earthquake on 8 February and another on 8 March.
That must mean there would be another one in 28 days' time.
Despite the rudimentary nature of Bell's date-setting many
Londoners believed him and braced themselves for Last Days'
convulsions. Many sought protection in boats on the Thames
or headed for the hills. When the Day of Doom passed without
anything noteworthy happening, the atmosphere turned re-
criminatory. This was one failed prophet who couldn't explain
away his failure to the London citizenry. Bell ended up being
incarcerated in Bedlam, London's notorious lunatic asylum.[12]

*

The life and work of Emanuel Swedenborg (1688–1772) was
an attempt to synthesize mystical and millenarian beliefs with

the Age of Reason. Starting life as a groundbreaking natural scientist, he also had a second career as a mystic and theosophist. Visited by a mystical illumination in 1745, Swedenborg claimed a direct vision of a spiritual world underlying the natural sphere. Unlike many mystics, Swedenborg believed that modern science and religion could be synthesized; he proposed an approach to spiritual reality and God through material nature rather than in rejection of it. In response to a new vision of the Last Judgement and the Second Coming, Swedenborg predicted the end of the world would happen in the year 1757. He proclaimed the advent of the New Church, an idea that found social expression in the Swedenborgian societies and in the Church of the New Jerusalem. Swedenborg was to exert a formative influence on one of the great figures of English Romanticism – the poet, painter and visionary William Blake.

Blake was born in Swedenborg's Great Year, 1757 – a fact not lost on him. But the year was also significant for social and cultural reasons. Born mid-century, Blake is one of those seminal figures who bridges two ages – the Age of Reason and the Age of Romanticism. Like Rousseau in philosophy, Thomas Gray in poetry and Goya in painting, Blake's work helps to define the age that he left behind and the age he so signally helped to bring into being. The Age of Romanticism was the age of revolution and Blake was both romantic and revolutionary. He hailed both the American and French revolutions of 1776 and 1789 as apocalyptic events. Like the Puritan revolution in mid-seventeenth-century England, these great historical events were readily converted into end-time myths. Apocalyptic scriptures were useful to the American and French revolutionaries – like they had been to the peasant revolutionaries in the fourteenth century or to Münzter in the sixteenth and the radical sectarians of the English Civil War era – because they could be used to both inspire and legitimate the political aspirations of disaffected and dissident groups.

How the American Revolution contributed to the collective apocalyptic imaginings of the American people will be dealt with in a later chapter. For its part, the French Revolution was more radical and far-reaching in its political, social and cultural consequences. Commentators often reached for apocalyptic images and types in order to figure the momentousness of the events. Long recognized as one of the defining moments in the shaping of the modern world, the French Revolution represents a before and an after: human values, beliefs and attitudes would never be the same again.

When the Paris mob stormed the Bastille on 14 July 1789 the shock waves sent through Europe were seismic. The end of the *ancien régime* was commonly construed in violently apocalyptic terms. Blake caught the zeitgeist in his work during this period. In the first book of *The French Revolution* (1791), he traces the history of the revolution shortly before and just after the fall of the Bastille. David Erdman has noted how Blake converts recent political events in France into apocalyptic myth:

> All the revolutionary events of June and July are treated as a single Day of Judgment or Morning of Resurrection during which the dark night of oppression lingers and fades in the marble hall of the Old Order while the Sun of democracy rises above the city streets and the people's Assembly.[13]

The revolutionist and statesman Abbé Sieyès is used by Blake as a speaker through which he predicts the end of all forms of oppression, including the slave trade, and the coming of a millennial kingdom in which 'men walk with their fathers in bliss'. In the coming millennium, soldiers are envisioned throwing down their weapons and embracing the peasantry; monarchs strip themselves of all the panoplies and appurtenances of power ('the red robe of terror, and the crown of oppression'); priests will bless rather than curse the 'wild raging millions', their joys and desires.

For Blake, the Apocalypse is essentially a state of mind or an imaginative construct rather than a literal fact to be enacted at the end of time. In his Notebook draft exposition of his painting 'A Vision of the Last Judgement', Blake expounds upon his vision of the Apocalypse:

> I assert for My Self that I do not behold the outward Creation & that to me it is a hindrance & not Action; it is as the Dirt upon my feet, No part of Me. 'What', it will be Questiond, 'When the Sun rises, do you not see a round disk of fire somewhat like a Guinea?' O no, no, I see an Innumerable company of the Heavenly host crying 'Holy, Holy, Holy is the Lord God Almighty.' I question not my Corporeal or Vegetative Eye any more than I would Question a Window concerning a Sight: I look thro it & not with it.[14]

The poetic imagination is seen here as essentially eschatological in nature. Like the apocalyptic visionary, poets destroy and re-create the world anew in their texts. Blake's exposure to the radical and heterodox fringes of English Puritanism has been well attested to. The cultural historian, A.L. Morton, saw Blake as a late manifestation of an underground, dissident tradition, stretching back to the Ranters of the English Civil War and beyond to the medieval Brethren of the Free Spirit.[15] The key text here is the late poem, 'The Everlasting Gospel' (c.1818). The title is an allusion to the apocalyptic beliefs of Joachim of Fiore, that great seedbed of heterodoxy. For Blake, Jesus is not so much a great ethical teacher or philosopher but the very incarnation of an amoral poetic spirit, the sort of tablet-breaking revolutionary Nietzsche would later extol. Jesus the ranting antinomian banishes the rational moral figure so beloved of the Enlightenment. Like the Ranters before him, Blake posits a vital and non-dualistic relationship between divinity and humanity. Perfection can be found in the flesh. Divinity and gratified desire go hand-in-hand.

Others followed where Blake had led. The future Poet Laureate, Robert Southey (1774–1843), was also so enthused by the French Revolution that he came to see it in millennial terms. In conservative middle age, he looked back nostalgically at his younger rebellious and romantic self, declaring that

> few persons but those who have lived in it can conceive or comprehend what the memory of the French Revolution was, nor what a visionary world seemed to open upon those who were just entering it. Old things seemed passing away, and nothing was dreamt of but the regeneration of the human race.[16]

Wordsworth too saw the Revolution as a new chapter in human history. In his great autobiographical poem, *The Prelude* (1805), he remembered the early years of the Revolution as a time when all Europe 'was rejoiced, /France standing on the top of golden hours, /And human nature seeming born again'.[17] Like Southey, however, Wordsworth's radicalism and millennial yearning was something he left behind in his conservative old age. Another commentator on the French Revolution, Thomas Carlyle, used apocalyptic types to figure the momentousness of the events even though he had abandoned an early Evangelicalism. Long after he had lost his faith, the Bible continued to pervade his thinking to such an extent that the whole of reality was viewed through a biblical lens. In

On Heroes, Hero-Worship, he uses the *topos* of the shipwreck to figure the death throes of the *ancien regime*:

> We will hail the French Revolution, as shipwrecked mariners might the sternest rock, in a world otherwise all of baseless sea and waves. A true Apocalypse, though a terrible one, to this false withered artificial time; testifying once more that Nature is preternatural; if not divine, then diabolic; that Semblance is not Reality; that it has to become Reality, or the world will take fire under it – burn it into what it is, namely Nothing! Plausibility has ended; empty Routine has ended; much has ended. This, as with a Trump of Doom, has been proclaimed to all men.[18]

In *The French Revolution*, the apocalyptic colouration of Carlyle's imagination inflects the rhythms and peculiar structures of his writing. The Terrors are described as a 'black precipitous Abyss' to which all have been tending towards 'till Sansculotttism have consummated itself; and in this wondrous French Revolution, as in a Doomsday, a World have been rapidly, if not born again, yet destroyed and engulfed'.[19]

In the immediate post-revolutionary years, romantics and radicals really did believe that human nature and society could be remade. Such utopian dreaming is particularly evident in the thoughts and writings of Samuel Taylor Coleridge. The son of a minister, the whole cast of Coleridge's mind was profoundly metaphysical. In the summer of 1794, Coleridge became friends with Robert Southey, the future Poet Laureate. Together they planned to establish their very own utopian community that would fulfil the idealistic goals of the revolutionaries. 'Pantisocracy' was to be located in the New World, by the Susquehanna River in Pennsylvania, on land bought by the radical Joseph Priestley after his exile from England.

Priestley was not only a great chemist but also a founder of the Unitarian Society. He too had interpreted the events in France apocalyptically.

As has been noted, Coleridge's major early poem 'Religious Musings' (1794–6) is nothing less than the whole of human history, viewed apocalyptically. It begins with the Creation of the world and finishes with the consummation of history in the form of the French Revolution, an event that is explicitly seen as the fulfilment of the prophecies in *Revelation*. In one memorable passage, Coleridge launches into a jeremiad against the universal corruption of the late eighteenth-century world that is worthy of an Old Testament prophet. 'Fiends' cast spells that 'film the eye of faith', causing us to lose God and degenerate into 'an anarchy of spirits'. Before the French Revolution, the poor were cast out of life's feast, young women prostituted, old women pauperized, and young men condemned to die in a mangled heap on the battlefield. But deliverance for the 'Children of Wretchedness' is at hand: 'Yet is the day of Retribution nigh'.[20]

The kind of end-times scenario Coleridge had in mind is indicated in the prose argument of the plot of 'Religious Musings' in which he refers to the subject matter of the close of the poem under the following headings: 'The French Revolution. Millennium. Universal Redemption. Conclusion'. Coleridge's notes accompanying the text quote and cite *Revelation* in support of his conviction that the establishment of an earthly millennium is imminent. As so often, the decadence of the age is seen as a sure-fire sign that divine deliverance is on its way.

Utopian visionaries are usually much better at imagining the perfect society than in taking practical steps in order to realize it. In this respect, Southey and Coleridge were no exception. Pantisocracy was put on hold (permanently) due to pressing family obligations. Southey gave up utopia for the law. For his part, Coleridge did not end up on the Susquehanna River; instead, in 1795, he met William Wordsworth with whom he was to collaborate on the *Lyrical Ballads*. Social revolution and building paradise could wait. He was too busy revolutionizing English poetry.

Whereas the gentle but chaotic figure of Coleridge could only dream of paradise in his work, there were those across the Channel all too determined to build it, whatever the human cost. The political idealism of the early years therefore mutated into the Reign of Terror. Increasingly, the diktats of the new regime took on an apocalyptic colouration. Time itself was to be reformulated in a bid to lend a cosmic significance to the regime's seizure of power. In 1793, the National Convention instituted a revolutionary calendar, proclaiming that September 1792 was to be regarded, retrospectively, as the beginning of Year One, with all future years to be numbered and named accordingly. Thus the impression was conveyed that time began with the abolition of the monarchy and the birth of the new republic. To reorder time in this way is also to rewrite history for propaganda purposes. If time begins again from year zero, then, the break with the pre-revolutionary past and the post-revolutionary future is absolute. Inscribed in the date and the calendars we compile is a powerful ideological message. Just as in the Gregorian calendar time begins with the advent of Christ, so secular societies construct calendars which exalt the current regime's achievements. What happened prior to the new regime coming to power is analogous to the state of Chaos which existed before God's creation.

When one century ends and another opens, apocalyptic speculation and millennial yearning are often rife. The cataclysmic events of the 1790s cast a long and dark shadow over the opening decades of the nineteenth century. The French Re-volution had so shaken the powers-that-be across the English Channel that they introduced the Combination Laws of 1799 and 1800, forbidding any gathering of employers or employ-ees. Conservatives spoke about the example of the French Revolution and whether or not it could happen here. In the event, political revolution did not take place in Britain as it did in France and America; but the so-called Third Revolution, begun in the eighteenth century, proved unstoppable – the Industrial Revolution.

The new capitalist economic order called forth a new theory of the end of the world. Marx and Engels were now the new apocalyptic visionaries, albeit of the secularized variety. Their conception of history essentially displaces a Judaeo-Christian apocalyptic view of history on to a material and secularized vision of the world. Like the four-part division of history in *Daniel*, Marx's theory of history posits four great periods. Each of these is associated with a particular form of economic activity and class domination.

In the Marxist model of history, the collapse of one age and the coming into being of another was often figured in quasi-apocalyptic terms. The Marxist equivalent of the Last Days is the end of the fourth age which sees the collapse of capitalism, and the return of the great golden age of communism. In such a secularized apocalyptic scenario, the middle-class capitalists are the equivalent of the demonic hosts: 'Like the sorcerer, who is no longer able to control the powers of the nether world whom he has called up by his spells', the bourgeoisie, through the very success of the material advance it had accomplished, had 'forged the weapons that bring death to itself'.[21] As in the Jewish and Christian apocalyptic tradition, Marx views his-tory as unfurling along a linear axis. However, it is the social scientist and not the apocalyptic prophet who is now capable of forecasting the future through his scientific methods. For Marx, the destined end is not a divinely appointed Big Bang but the internal contradictions of capitalism which will bring down the current world order. The Marxist equivalent to the third and final Age is the new communist world order, the millennial kingdom made manifest in the real material world.

Born a Jew, Marx came to hate religion because he felt it anaesthetized people to their pain. It was opium that made the pain of being exploited by others bearable. For Marx, waiting for a posthumous reward from a God that did not exist was the height of delusional behaviour. What he would have made of the mass religious movements in nineteenth-century England is easy to surmise. For him, this would have been just another case of man handing over the task of radical social reform to God when it should be placed fairly and squarely in the hands of men.

Nevertheless there were many in the nineteenth century that persisted in looking to God, not man, as the agent of apocalyptic transformation. A wholly extraordinary figure from this period is Joanna Southcott. At the ripe old age of sixty-four she announced she was pregnant with an immaculately conceived Messiah, to be called Shiloh. He was to be born on Christmas Day 1814. Witnesses claimed she looked as though she were pregnant. In the event, there was no nativity; in fact she was to die very shortly after the day the Messiah was supposed to be born. Followers insisted that her body be kept warm for four days and four nights before a dissection could take place in order to ascertain the truth of the pregnancy claim and establish the cause of death. The autopsy revealed that it was not an embryonic Messiah that caused the bump but trapped wind. No discernible cause of death was established.

In the 1920s Mabel Barltrop, an ex-inmate of a lunatic

asylum, founded the Panacea Society in Bedford in order to carry out the prophetess's final works. A wholly unremarkable town, Bedford was proclaimed by Barltrop to be the ancient site of the Garden of Eden. She bought up houses in Bedford so as to create compounds in which sect members could carry out their divinely appointed roles at the end of the world. To this day, members of this extremely secretive sect claim to have the 'Ark' containing Southcott's prophetic writings from 1792, when the Lord first visited her to 1814, the year of her death. For sect members these writings were divinely authored and constitute a new covenant which will save England and the world from all ills – hence the name Panacea.

The use of the term 'ark' to denote a box recalls the original ark the Children of Israel used to contain the original covenant with God.[22] The new covenant contained in the ark in Bedford can be read only when twenty-four bishops from the Church of England are brought together; in preparation for such an event they have built a house in Bedford with twenty-four bedrooms and a special ark opening room. Then the Lord will manifest His glory to all present, making the British people the 'Covenant People'. However, just like their founder, modern South-cottians are not immune to misprophecy; some set the date for the end of the world in 2004. Some sect members also seemed to be convinced that only Diana, Princess of Wales was pure enough to be the 'Second Eve' and bear the Godhead i.e. be worthy enough to be the mother of Shiloh. How they reacted to her untimely and tragic death, in the company of a Muslim man, is not on record. The elderly members of the society are still waiting for the bishops to oblige so we can all be delivered collectively from evil.

In the first and second halves of the nineteenth century, apocalyptic faith galvanized two great mass religious movements. If religion was the opium of the people, then it was still

proving to be highly addictive to a great many people. In the
first half of the century Wesleyanism swept the country. Under
the influence of German Pietism, John Wesley believed that
Christ's millennial kingdom would begin in 1836. In com-
menting on *Revelation* 12:12, he wrote: 'We live in the *little
time* wherein Satan hath great wrath; and this *little time* is now
upon the decline. We are in the "time, times, and half a
time".'[23] In the second half of the nineteenth century, the
Salvation Army took up the apocalyptic mantle. Salvationist
eschatology saw the world as an arena in which the devil and
the Holy Ghost were locked in perpetual conflict: William
Booth's *In Darkest England and the Way Out* (1890) pictures
London as a vast black ocean of iniquity, from which the
fortunate slum-dweller is plucked and resettled ('the Way
Out') in rural England.[24] It is not piecemeal socialist policies
that save the slum-dweller but the miraculous intervention of a
supernatural power.

The theories of Herbert Spencer provide a striking contrast
to such metaphysical explanations of the world. Today Spencer is a name that does not mean much to too many people. In
his day, however, he was one of the great prophets of his age –
albeit of the secular variety. His vision was informed by the
post-Darwinian stress on the essential continuity between man
and the rest of the universe. In works such as *System of
Synthetic Philosophy* (1860–90) Spencer took the Darwinian
lineal model of history and recast it in order to put forward his
theories about progress and society. History is seen as march-
ing triumphantly forward, in perfect uniformity and harmony.
Science, not God, will deliver us from the forces of evil –
disease, poor sanitation and poverty. By improving people's
living conditions, you are not simply improving man's material
lot. Just as modern sanitation methods delivered the Victorian
pedestrian from filth, so would progress deliver us from our

own evil nature. In Spencer's view, the moral and spiritual dirt would be washed away. This notion of incremental improvement in human history flatly contradicts the Christian doctrines of Original Sin and its corollary, the absolute need for universal redemption.

Myths about social and moral progress could issue in a peculiarly homespun utopianism. Often in the second half of the nineteenth century utopia was not to be found in some far-flung destination but closer to home. Take, for example, the model English industrial village Port Sunlight, Liverpool, founded in 1888 by the soap tycoon W.H. Lever for the factory workers of his firm of Lever Brothers. They would be housed in neat little Tudor-style houses. It was a world of Mechanic's Institutes, Morris dancing, floral basket displays, village cricket greens; periodically conservative politicians in Britain invoke such images of the English New Jerusalem as a way to rally support behind the Tory flag. Lever's social utopia greatly influenced subsequent industrial villages such as Bournville in Birmingham, and Ebenezer Howard's garden-city movement. These were very English utopias which attempted to reconcile the fact of industrialization with a rural conception of 'organic' communities living in their very own little castles.

The idea of progress being divinely underwrit is particularly evident in the extraordinary expansion of the British Empire during the second half of the nineteenth century. Through spreading British culture, religion and scientific/technological knowhow abroad – by 1900 four hundred million of the world's inhabitants were lit by the British imperial sun – Britain began to conceive of itself as a special nation, earmarked for God's work on earth. Like the American doctrine of manifest destiny, British notions about empire and divine destiny gave a huge impetus to painting the global map red. Military conquest based on naval power, the extension of territory in every continent except Antarctica, the subjugation of less 'advanced' peoples, the establishment of a British equivalent of a *Pax Romana*: empire builders imbued all these with a metaphysical significance. The ideology of Anglo-Saxonism legitimated the occupation, spoliation and dispossession of supposedly inferior nations and cultures because it was seen as all part of God's divine plan.

But it was not only the Christian right who exalted in the white man's superiority over other races. Secular prophets too constructed myths about progress and racial superiority. A disciple of Darwin after he lost his Christian faith, H.G. Wells was thought to be in the vanguard of progressive social and political thought. But this thinker held some pretty detestable views about race. In *Anticipations* (1902) he envisages a 'New Republic' in which eugenics and genocide play the same kind of role as they do in the Nazis' New Order:

> the ethical system of these men of the New Republic, the ethical system which will dominate the world-state, will be shaped primarily to favour the procreation of what is fine and efficient and beautiful in humanity – beautiful and strong bodies, clear and powerful minds . . . And the method that nature has followed hitherto in the shaping of the world, whereby weakness was prevented from propagating weakness . . . is death . . . The men of the New Republic . . . will have an ideal that will make killing worth the while.[25]

Race war becomes the equivalent to Armageddon, a battle not so much between good and evil but an unequal battle between the weak and the strong. Salvation here comes in a biological form. The brisk cheeriness with which Wells views such a prospect is utterly repellent. Nevertheless, Wells died a broken man, his hopes about racial superiority and the efficacy of science evaporated. In the end, he was left to contemplate not the salvation of mankind but its extinction.

After reading Wells, it is salutary to remind yourself that apocalyptic beliefs from the Jewish and Christian tradition challenge myths of secular progress. Postmillennialism emphasizes the darkness, decadence and danger in human history and the absolute need for divine intervention to counter it. At the end of the nineteenth century, age-old apocalyptic beliefs about the increasing decadence of the world were reformulated for a world that was becoming more secularized. Suddenly, epochal gloom, studied cynicism and decadent attitudinizing became all the rage. *Fin de siècle* attitudes and values informed a broad artistic and cultural movement. Here was an end of a century for connoisseurs, dilettantes and artists and writers who delighted in inverting the narrow social and moral codes of the Victorians. Presiding over the revels was that master of immorality, Oscar Wilde. His celebrated plays and essays glorified the figure of the metropolitan dandy and the *saloniste*, a kind of highly articulate Antichrist-figure who gleefully inverted traditional morality. Wilde's glittering social comedies of the 1890s shocked, entertained and challenged in equal measure.

For those young men born in the 1890s a terrible fate lay in store. Many of them were destined to be members of that Lost Generation who reached adulthood just as the Great War of 1914–18 started. Wells had envisioned an apocalyptic showdown between different races. In the event, it was the so-called master races who were to tear each other to pieces. The great God of Science and Technology which the Victorians believed would deliver them from evil, instead made killing possible on an unimaginable scale. Modern arms would make possible a man-made Armageddon.

5

WAR AND APOCALYPSE IN THE TWENTIETH CENTURY

'War is the locomotive of history', Trotsky once claimed. It's an agent of social change, fast-tracking revolutions, derailing old social orders, shunting women into men's jobs, and consigning centuries-old empires to the scrap yard. If Trotsky's metaphor is an apt one, then, we could say that the Great War was the bullet train of social and historical change. In earlier chapters we looked at how wars and revolutions rewrote the political and territorial maps of their age. In contrast, however, the events of 1914 to 1918 dwarfed any previous conflict. The demographic, political, cultural, social and diplomatic consequences of it changed the continent forever.

But it was not just the old geopolitical maps of the nineteenth century that needed to be torn up when the soldiers left the trenches and returned home. Paul Fussell's *The Great War and Modern Memory* charts the remapping of human consciousness that took place during and after the conflict. Fussell's grand narrative takes in Great War poetry, drama, fiction, memoirs and even letters and general culture as he advances his theory that consciousness itself was radically altered by the war.[1] The birth of a modern sensibility came out of the deaths of millions of combatants and civilians. Myths about the March of History, progress and the White Man's Burden would be hard to sustain in the face of such terrible and unparalleled suffering.

Earlier, we saw how that other locomotive of history – revolution – inspired apocalyptic visions and imaginings in previous centuries. The English peasants in the fourteenth century, Münzter and the Anabaptists in sixteenth-century Germany, the radical sectaries in the English Civil War, the *sans culottes* in eighteenth-century France: all these revolutionaries turned their various societies and times upside down. But the 1914–18 conflict was on a vastly different scale from any upheaval, revolutionary or military, the past. Here was the first war in which the technological advances of modern western industrialized countries could be tried and tested. Barbed wire, trenches, tanks, zeppelins, chemical weapons, aeroplanes, machine guns, heavy artillery: all these were products of the huge technological advances made in the nineteenth century when, according to Social Darwinists, industry and technology were supposed to liberate mankind from barbarity. The first total, mechanized war in history quickly put paid to such optimistic fantasies.

It was not merely the nature of the conflict, but also its magnitude, which distinguished it from all previous wars. The frenzied empire building of the last century meant that the Great War had a global reach. It is often remembered in terms of the principal theatre, the western front in Belgium and France, but many societies and cultures worldwide were sucked into a conflict which spanned continents. Because of European colonial possessions, the war was fought in Africa, the Middle East and Asia. These are the forgotten fronts. Many of the fallen in the Great War were not just German, French or British; the French deployed African troops on the western front; more than 800,000 Indian soldiers fought for the British in the war.[2]

The casualty rate among the combatants was staggeringly high: some nine million or so troops died in the war. Of those, 750,000 were British. Estimates for civilian deaths range from seven to ten million. Not to be outdone by the human predilection for killing one another, Mother Nature got in on the act and killed off twenty or so million people in the influenza epidemic of 1918. Wartime food shortages and malnutrition had weakened people's resistance. Imagine then: after having suffered the most calamitous man-made disaster in history, a pandemic struck which was as deadly as the Black Death in the fourteenth century. It was a double whammy of apocalyptic proportions. No wonder belief in a providential God evaporated for many in the post-bellum years.

But it was the long-term political fall out of the Great War that was most terrible. 'Ours is essentially a tragic age', D.H. Lawrence wrote in the opening to his last great novel, *Lady Chatterley's Lover*.[3] The third and final version of this novel was begun in December 1927; Lawrence died in 1930 and so did not live to see how things were about to get a whole lot more tragic before the decade was out. Out of the collapse of the Russian Empire stepped Bolshevism in 1917. Out of the defeat of the Central Powers (Germany, Austro-Hungary and the Ottoman Empire) stepped Nazism in Germany in the early 1920s. So the fuse to the gunpowder keg had been lit in the interwar period. When it eventually exploded in 1939, it was the start of the greatest and most destructive war in history.

The epithet 'great' was used to describe the war of 1914–18 because of the unique magnitude of the destruction and suffering. In the Second World War a whole new dimension, however, was added to the concept of global conflict. Gigantic struggles engulfed not only Europe but Asia, Africa and the far-flung islands of the Pacific. This time more than seventeen million members of the armed forces of the various countries involved perished. Then there were the countless millions of civilians – ordinary men, women and children who were systematically bombed from the skies, gassed in extermination camps, shot in mass graves, raped and pillaged, deported and dispossessed. In total, another fifty to sixty million could be added to the list of the dead in the Great War. Some historians argue that the First World War and the Second World War were part of a continuum and should be subsumed under the title of the New Thirty Years War.

In such a view, peace in the interwar years was really a long armistice, a respite, before round two got under way. Hitler indicated as such way back in 1922–4 when he was composing *Mein Kampf*. In it he predicted that Germany would one day have a 'final active reckoning with France'. In his mind, and countless millions like him, the Great War had not been lost; the front line had been 'stabbed in the back' by the folks back home. Later, in his 'Political Testimony', written in the bunker under the Reich Chancellery, with the Red Army only streets away, Hitler spoke of how he had served his country for over thirty years, tracing his career back as the saviour of his people to 1914. For him, that was the crucial year, the year zero when his reign began, ushering a new era of history which was to violently alter the subsequent course of European and world history.

The final descent into world war was swift. On 1 August 1914 Germany declared war on Russia and on the 3rd on

France. On the 4th, Great Britain declared war on Germany. The following day, Austro-Hungary joined the fray. When the war broke out in 1914 the mood was mixed. Some jingoists danced in the street, having swallowed the official line that the conflict would be over by Christmas. Others took a gloomier, more philosophical view. They saw the war as a necessary evil, a cleansing of the decadence and moral corruption besetting western civilization. Later, Wilfred Owen would become justly famous for his haunting poems about the horrors of the trenches and for striking a fiercely anti-war attitude. At the outset of the war, however, he expressed the sentiments of many when he wrote to his mother just after the outbreak of hostilities:

> While it is true that the guns will effect a little useful weeding, I am furious with chagrin to think that the Minds which were to have excelled the civilization of ten thousand years are being annihilated – and bodies, the product of aeons of Natural Selection, melted down to pay for political statues.[4]

Encoded into the metaphor is the notion of the English garden which has become overgrown and full of weeds. Killing is euphemized as 'weeding', a necessary purifying of the garden/body-politic of the impurities and baser elements. In contradistinction to the weeds are the finest English blooms, the pick of the crop among the current generation. Here the model is a late Victorian one, a popularized version of Darwinian evolution applied to human society. What seems to particularly irk Owen is the sheer arbitrariness of modernized, mechanized warfare. Shells raining down from the skies do not distinguish between the blooms and the weeds as they pulverize the earth.

Paul Fussell brilliantly demonstrates how in the literature of the Great War Owen was part of a movement towards myth and 'a revival of the cultic, the mystical, the sacrificial, the prophetic, the sacramental, and the universally significant'.[5] In such a view, the enemy became the demonic other, the dead were euphemized as the 'fallen' and the killing fields of the western front transposed metaphorically into 'theatres' in which good and evil do battle. Describing the landscape of the front, Siegfried Sassoon reached readily for familiar apocalyptic language in order to render the unparalleled situation in which he found himself: 'On wet days, the trees a mile away were like ash-grey smoke rising from the naked ridges and it felt very much as if we were at the end of the world. And so we were: for that enemy world . . . had no relation to the landscape of life.'[6]

In fact, the western front was more like some demonic stockyard, a human abattoir in which the killing was carried out on an industrial scale. There were 60,000 British casualties on the first day of the Somme, 20,000 of who were 'fallen'. Faced with such a disaster the opposite of apocalyptic rhetoric could also come into play. Official communiqués are full of duplicitous euphemisms and pallid circumlocutions intended to disguise and mitigate the full horror of the western front. The *Daily Mirror* managed to turn the first day of the Somme, the bloodiest single day in British military history, into a 'general situation [which] is favourable'. The *Daily Chronicle* for 3 July 1916 speaks of how the British 'have already occupied the German front line . . . as far as can be ascertained our casualties have not been heavy'. In his book, *The Battle of the Somme*, John Buchan resorted to Noachian flood metaphor to disguise the true nature of the disaster:

> The British moved forward in line after line, dressed as if on parade; not a man wavered or broke ranks; but minute by minute the ordered lines melted away under the deluge of high-

explosive, shrapnel, rifle, and machine-gun fire. There was no question about the German weight of artillery. From dawn till long after noon they maintained this steady drenching fire . . . . The splendid troops . . . now shed their blood like water for the liberty of the world.[7]

What about those genuine writers and artists who fought and died or returned home from the western front and bore witness to the horror? In their writing and paintings, they depicted a nightmarish world of mangled corpses, debris and flattened landscapes. The carnage described takes on an hallucinatory and apocalyptic quality worthy of the most violent and lurid passages in *Revelation*. The Reverend John M.S. Walker witnessed the first day of the Somme offensive at a casualty clearing station. He writes of how the 'heavens and earth were rolling up' as every gun was fired at the German front line for an hour.[8]

A French writer described the terrible aftermath of battle:

It was a dreadful squalid mass, a monstrous disinterring of waxy Bavarians on top of others already black, whose wrenched and twisted mouths exhaled a breath of corruption, a whole accumulation of slashed and mangled flesh, with corpses that you might have fancied unscrewed, knocked awry, the feet and knees twisted completely round; and to watch over them all, one single dead body remaining on his feet, propped up with his back against the face of the trench, and buttressed by a monster with no head.[9]

In the past, the apocalyptic imagination created monsters whose 'otherness' to the human form was absolute: beasts with multiple horns, fire-breathing dragons etc. Now the mangled forms of dead soldiers became the new monsters of apocalyptic imaginings. In the 1920s, the German expressionist painter George Grosz depicted hideously disfigured war veterans as demonic figures. The human form divine, which had inspired centuries of great western art, was now reduced to a grotesque composite of mechanical body parts. Shattered by technology and then reassembled through it, the body came to symbolize the age's profoundly ambivalent attitude to scientific and technological progress.

D.H. Lawrence's work during the Great War depicts this disillusionment in explicitly apocalyptic terms. Along with William Blake, Lawrence is the greatest apocalyptic visionary in English literature. The last book that he ever wrote, *Apocalypse* (1930), was an idiosyncratic commentary on the *Book of Revelation*. It was an exploration as to why the supposedly 'least attractive' of all the books of the Bible should have exerted a lifelong influence over him even though he had lost his Christian faith as a young man. For Lawrence, as for so many of his generation, the answer lay in his Nonconformist background. As a child, he had the Bible 'poured everyday into [his] helpless consciousness, till there came almost a saturation point'.[10] As Lawrence admits ruefully, he may have lost his faith but apocalyptic images and symbols remained and continued to permeate his writing. His two wartime novels, *The Rainbow* and *Women in Love*, confront the horror of the Great War and recast it in apocalyptic terms. In many ways, Lawrence's use of the apocalyptic types is paradigmatic of twentieth-century writers and artists generally. Having lost their childhood faith, they still nevertheless avail themselves of the apocalyptic types in order to express their sense of the uniquely destructive nature of the age in which they lived.

The title of *The Rainbow* is an allusion to the rainbow God sets in the sky as a sign of his new covenant with Noah that he will not send another deluge to wipe out most of the human and natural order. In the end, Lawrence settled on the more commercial but slushy sounding title *Women in Love* for his next novel. The title suggested by his wife would have been far more apt – 'Dies Irae'.[11]

Like a medieval *magna propheta*, Lawrence made no secret of his messianic message. Time and again, he casts himself as a saviour-figure who would change the world for the next thousand years or longer. A charismatic personality who compelled attention, many people fell under Lawrence's spell and became followers. The critic John Middleton Murray was for a time a disciple of the cult of Lawrence. In his last book he suggests that Lawrence's suffering during the winter of 1914–15 was absolutely different from his own, labouring as he did 'under a prophetic vision of the war as a portent of the imminent doom of modern civilization and modern man'.[12] On another occasion, Murray records how he felt he was in the 'presence of a man of destiny, a prophet, a Messiah; one in whom life itself was making an experiment towards a new kind of man, and that the experiment was crucial'.[13]

Lawrence's first attempt to rewrite Christian apocalyptic beliefs was in the early *Study of Thomas Hardy*. Begun in 1914 out of 'sheer rage' at the war, the work is a systematic attempt to put forward an alternative belief system to the Christian one. In order to do this Lawrence draws on an apocalyptic view of history that goes right back to the medieval period. At the heart of the *Study* is a form of trinitarian thinking which has its origin in the apocalyptic beliefs of Joachim of Fiore in the twelfth century. Like the medieval mystic, Lawrence divides history up into three separate ages – the Ages of Law, Love and the Holy Ghost. The ages of Law and Love, associated with the Father and the Son respectively, are related to the Old and New Testaments.

For Lawrence, the Age of Law is a time of physicality

associated with the Jews and with women. The second age, the Age of the Son, is associated with spirituality and separateness which Lawrence takes to be the 'male principle' and which he associates with the Christian era. Usually in a phase of cultural history, either Law or Love predominates over the other; there is rarely a creative balance between the two. In Lawrence's world-view, the Renaissance represents a moment of great cultural richness because it is associated with just such a creative and life-affirming reconciliation of opposites. More often than not, however, Law and Love are pitched against each other. Since the Renaissance, Europe has followed the Male Christ alone, proclaiming the one way of Spirit and thereby denying the Flesh of the Law.

For Lawrence, it is this dissociation of the body and the spirit which is the real cause of the Great War. Thwarted in the flesh, modern man throws down his life in a lemming-like rush towards death. The early war years, therefore, are endowed with apocalyptic significance. These are the death throes of the Age of Love which will finally usher in a new age in which all the old polarities – the body and the spirit, man and woman – will be reconciled. In the *Study*, then, the great catastrophe of the Great War is not deemed to be purely destructive – in Lawrence's prophetic scheme of things it is 'destructive-consummating' because it will finally bring into being a new moral and spiritual order. The death-worshipping spirituality of the Christian era will finally come to an end.

Lawrence's reformulated version of the Joachite Third Age pervades his thinking to an extraordinary extent. This self-styled 'priest of love' repeatedly proclaims that the millennial kingdom will only come into being once man and woman have perfected their relationship in a consummate marriage. Re-conciling Law and Love, the flesh and the spirit, the Holy

Ghost will preside over this golden age, the 'crown' of human existence.

Lawrence's letters at this time continually proclaim his own sense of apocalyptic purpose. In a letter to Lady Ottoline Morrell, dated 27 January 1915, he writes: 'It is an Absolute we are all after, a statement of the whole scheme – the issue, the progress through Time – and the return – making unchangeable eternity.'[14] Caught up in the horror of history, Lawrence seeks solace by imagining the contemporary situation as part of a larger cyclical pattern – there will be a return to some sort of eternal realm. To usher in this new age requires a wholesale abandonment of the Christian faith and a thoroughly new conception of 'God', the old one having been knocked for six by the catastrophe of the Great War. Viewed apocalyptically, the Great War is a symptom of the spiritual and religious malaise of modern man.

Lawrence considered his early masterpiece, *The Rainbow*, 'supreme art' because, he believed, it brought a new religious dispensation into being by reconciling Law and Love. When revising the typescript of *The Rainbow* in March 1915, he proudly proclaimed its prophetic purpose to one correspondent: 'It really puts a new thing in the world, almost a new vision of life.' Later he uses a horticultural metaphor to figure his messianic purpose. We need to 'cast off the old symbols', he writes, 'the old traditions . . . like a plant in growing surpasses its crowning leaves with higher leaves and buds'.[15]

This sense that the Great War is an apocalyptic moment, ripe with possibilities, is triumphantly expressed at the end of *The Rainbow*. When the heroine Ursula Brangwen crosses 'the void, the darkness which washed the New World and the Old', she is ready to receive the rainbow as a sign that the living God will institute the 'earth's new architecture'. Her home town, a drab Midlands mining community, is transformed into a New

Jerusalem. The dirty, dust-coated bodies of the miners become 'new, clean, naked bodies' swaying in the wind and rain.[16] Ursula's individual regeneration therefore has a paradigmatic significance. Her ritual dying and regeneration takes on a general apocalyptic significance for the fate of society as a whole. In such a view, the Midlands mining town becomes a microcosm of industrial civilization. The old corrupted town is destroyed only to rise again – like the miners who die chrysalis-like only to be born again with new clean bodies. As a projection of Lawrence's own apocalyptic hopes, the end of *The Rainbow* is one of the most beautiful and moving pieces in the whole of his work. As in all genuinely apocalyptic visions, a literal belief in the imminent destruction of the world is also the correlative of a literal belief in the resurrection of the world, or at least a chosen remnant of it. After having completed the latest version of the novel, he stated in a letter: 'I have finished my Rainbow, bended it and set it firm. Now off and away to find the pots of gold at its feet.'[17]

Such optimism, however, was to be short lived. Rather than ending in glorious renewal, the war rumbled on remorselessly. The darkness of the middle war years pervades Lawrence's next novel and perhaps his supreme masterpiece, *Women in Love*. It is a work full of apocalyptic destruction but little sense of millennial renewal. The interplay between history and apocalyptic imaginings is reflected in the events of July 1916. That month saw the carnage of the Somme offensive and Lawrence revising and typing the penultimate draft of *Women in Love*. The horror of those months is figured in the dark demonic flood which threatens to engulf the characters in the novel completely. In November 1916 he writes apropos of *Women in Love*: 'The book frightens me: it is so end-of-the-world.'[18] When writing the sixth version of *Women in Love* in July 1917, he proclaimed that there was 'no rainbow' in

Europe: 'I believe the deluge of iron rain will destroy the world here, utterly: no Ararat will rise above the subsiding iron waters.'[19]

During these terrible middle war years, Lawrence imbued the most seemingly random and commonplace events with an apocalyptic significance. The sight of autumn leaves being burned on Hampstead Heath stirs thoughts of dead soldiers undergoing ritual immolation. A zeppelin raid is recast into the war in heaven envisioned by John on Patmos.[20] He is constantly on the lookout for 'any signs' of the 'new world to come'. Often his apocalyptic imaginings strike a Blakean note:

> The sun is just sinking in a flood of gold. One would not be astonished to see the Cherubim flashing their wings and coming towards us, from the west. All the time, one seems to be expecting an arrival from the beyond, from the heavenly world. The sense of something, someone magnificent approaching, is so strong, it is a wonder one does not see visions in the heavens.[21]

While Lawrence was writing about the end of the old world, official artists were actually witnessing it at first hand on the western front. When Paul Nash went to France in 1914, he was so appalled at the carnage that when he returned to England, his style had changed completely. His haunting work, *We are Making a Better World*, mixes elements of Vorticism and Surrealism to evoke a strange, post-apocalyptic landscape. The remains of shattered and carbonized trees testify to the previous presence of a wood. The pulverized earth is peppered and pockmarked with shell-holes which undulate and swirl in a weird and disturbing manner. The sun breaks through the sky, rust-red, like a seeping wound, radiating a cold and bleak light. What Nash liked to call the 'genius loci', the spirit of place, is powerfully present. Nash takes the remade world myth and harshly inverts it. The theme of the destruction and the rebirth of the world has existed for centuries; phoenix-like a new world is supposed to emerge from the ashes of the old. In Nash's painting we journey through a wasteland created by a cataclysm. But there is no mythical pattern of birth, death and rebirth. The title of the painting is harshly ironic; we are marooned amidst the ruins of a post-catastrophic world.

The realities of modern warfare clashed violently with the widespread perceptions and anticipations of the pre-war era. At the beginning of the war, cavalry units rode bravely into battle as though it were still the era of flashing sabres, plumes and gold-braid epaulettes. Machine guns and heavy artillery soon put pay to such romantic notions. Out of the pits and pools of no man's land was to emerge an ironclad monster, firing death and destruction from its sides – the tank. Patrick Wright describes the peculiarly apocalyptic fervour which surrounded the war machine when it made its belated entrance in 1916.[22] In bygone eras, the soldier could expect to die a heroic individual death in man-to-man combat; now killing had been mechanized you might be mowed down by one of these Behemoths; or be cut down by machine gun fire from an enemy you did not even see; or be blown to pieces by shells falling out of the skies. Or, most ignominious of all, drown in the ocean of mud, either side of the duckboards, your passing unnoticed as you slipped into the filthy ooze.

The experience of collective, anonymous, mechanized death left a deep imprint on the modern mind. In the 1930s, the bomber dropping death and destruction from the skies became the focus of apocalyptic fears. Stanley Baldwin, the architect of 1930s appeasement, believed that the bomber would 'always get through'. But in the Great War it was artillery that was responsible for the majority of battlefield deaths. The German 150-mm field howitzers could fire five rounds per minute and were particularly lethal. Air-burst shrapnel shells rained down hot flying metal which could penetrate helmets. Shells pulverized earth and human flesh. Body parts were strewn across no man's land, a quagmire of shell-holes and feculent pools. Killing was carried out on an industrial scale on the western front. In 'Anthem for Doomed Youth', Wilfred Owen compares death on the western front to the slaughter of cattle: anonymous, collective and debasing.

Such mechanized killing took on a terrible resonance in the work of C.R.W. Nevinson. Having been influenced by the Futurists before the war, Nevinson was well versed in the new visual language of the time. He had gone out to France to drive an ambulance with the Red Cross in 1914 and was thus one of the first to experience the horrors of the western front. What he does so brilliantly in his wartime paintings is to take the Futurist glorification of the machine and turn it into an apocalyptic nightmare. The belief that science and technology would be the salvation of man is inverted to shocking effect. Instead, man and machine meld together in the act of killing, twentieth-century style. In his famous painting, 'La Mitrailleuse', an automaton-like machine gunner embodies Nevinson's vision of the war as the apotheosis of the demonic machine. It was exhibited above the following statement: 'Man made the machine in his own image. The machine has retaliated by remaking man in its own image.'[23] Nevinson was particularly fascinated by the special effects produced by the new firepower. Explosions are rendered into resonating geometric shapes – sharp and glittering, cold, angular and eerily beautiful.

The guns finally fell silent on the eleventh hour, on the eleventh day of the eleventh month. For the soldiers who fought in the trenches a home fit for heroes had been promised

them. In the event, for many the post-war years were characterized by dole queues and soup kitchens. For a privileged
few, it was the Roaring Twenties in which the 'bright young
things', fresh from elite institutions like Princeton or Oxford,
rejected the old Victorian values of their parents and flicked
their modern ways and morals in the face of convention.

But in Germany it was a different story. The newly established Weimar Republic soon suffered spiralling inflation and
mass unemployment. The great German expressionist painters
of that era, George Grosz and Otto Dix, had their work cut out
recording Germany's collective descent into the depths. Beneath their smart metropolitan cynicism lies a real sense of
acute apocalyptic foreboding. Amputees and hideously de-
formed ex-servicemen are their equivalent of the apocalyptic
monstrosities of previous eras. The tortured flesh of multiple
paraplegics, glass-eyed and cicatrized, conveys the fractured
and broken nature of the larger society. Inflation, mass unemployment, and an embittered generation of ex-servicemen:
these were the raw ingredients a demagogue and rabble-rouser
like Hitler could go to work on. From the outset, there was
always the enemy within to blame – the Jews. International
Jewry was responsible for the post-war social and economic
malaise in Germany. Even the Treaty of Versailles was ultimately their responsibility. Didn't they, along with the Bolsheviks, foment a revolution at home in 1918 which led to
Germany's defeat?

For those still grieving the loss of loved ones, there was
always spiritualism. In the 1920s séances became an alternative to traditional forms of religious consolation. My grand-
mother, who lost two brothers in the Great War, attended
séances in the hope of contacting them. After the carnage,
many people lost faith in a providential God and sought
alternatives to mainstream Christianity. In T.S. Eliot's 'The

Waste Land' (1921–2) the search for alternative belief systems is seen as symptomatic of the emotional and spiritual sterility of the wasteland which is the modern world. Such a climate calls forth fake fortune-tellers like Madame Sosostris. The image of the city clerks, the walking dead, trooping over London Bridge from the railway station to their offices is unforgettable. It's a Dantesque scene, the modern metropolis as medieval inferno.[24]

This all-pervading sense of cultural decline is most brilliantly and systematically worked out in Oswald Spengler's *The Decline of the West*, first published in two volumes between 1918 and 1923. Its central conceit of organic growth and decadence and decline presents a deterministic view of history. In the great cosmic march of things cultures are analogous to seasons: the unrolling cycle of spring, summer, autumn and winter is unstoppable. Our culture finished its summer phase at about the beginning of the nineteenth century. We are now in the autumn, a world characterized by mega-cities, corrupt religion and politics, frenzied artistic experimentation, imperial rivalry and despotic rule (a prophesy perhaps of the Nazi regime). We are running headlong to decay, carried along by the impetus of a civilization doomed by destiny to decline.

That cultures are born, flourish and perish in a predictable way is a view informing W.B. Yeats' great apocalyptic poem of 1922, 'The Second Coming'. Using the Christian myth of the Second Advent, Yeats imagines a demonic version of the nativity. A 'rough beast' will be born in Bethlehem bringing an end to the Christian epoch, characterized as 'twenty centuries of stony sleep'. A new era with a new religious dispensation, one of power and might, will replace the Christian democratic world. The poem dramatizes Yeats' highly conflicted view; a nightmarish 'blood-dimmed tide' engulfs the world. The 'worst' are extremists full of fervour and self-belief.[25] Yet the terrifying sphinx-like beast that is going to be born is also apocalyptic in nature. This new life force will destroy the old dispensation but also help to bring into being a new one to re-invigorate the culture. The mixture of hope and fear, exhilaration and panic, is typical of the apocalyptic visionary. The consummation of all history is also the end of history; out of destruction comes regeneration.

Such myths of cultural decadence appealed to the apocalyptic imagination of Hitler. Having served in the Great War as a corporal, Hitler came to see the conflict as the product of racial struggle. International Jewry was responsible, not old-style Prussian militarism, for the catastrophe. In Hitler's apocalyptic imagination the Jews were the enemy within, a latter-day incarnation of Antichrist, secretly sowing the seeds of conflict among the western powers so as to win racial mastery. The myth of cultural decay was thus given a new and deeply sinister racialist element. In the first volume of *Mein Kampf*, Hitler articulates one of his cherished and deeply rooted beliefs – in the absolute evil of the Jewish race. From the time of writing his Nazi 'bible' in prison to the last days of the Third Reich in the bunker in Berlin in July 1945, this was the one and only abiding theme. All the problems of the world could be laid at the Jews' feet – communism, international capitalism, Germany's defeat in the war, racial degeneration, modernist art etc. etc. They were the German nation's true enemy, he wrote. They had no culture of their own, he raved, but perverted existing cultures such as Germany's with their parasitism. As such, they were not a race, but an anti-race intent on bastardizing and polluting the pure stock of the Aryan line.

Implacably opposed to this inferior race, Hitler believed, were the German people, descendants of the Aryans, people of the highest racial purity. The Aryan was a figure invested with apocalyptic significance. If the Jews were the equivalent of the Antichrist, then, the Aryan was the saviour-figure of humanity:

> He is the Prometheus of mankind from whose bright forehead the divine spark of genius has sprung at all times, forever kindling anew that fire of knowledge which illumined the night of silent mysteries and thus caused man to climb the path to mastery over the beings of this earth. Exclude him – and perhaps after a few thousand years darkness will again descend on the earth, human culture will pass, and the world turn to a desert.[26]

To maintain that pure Aryan bloodline, it was necessary to avoid intermarriage with subhuman races such as Jews and Slavs. In *Mein Kampf*, Hitler often uses the old apocalyptic imagery to figure the racial order supposedly rooted in nature: 'All who are not of good race in this world are chaff.'[27] Germany's millennial role was to exorcize the Jewish demonic host from the body politic (in this sense, the Nazis were similar to the crusaders who massacred Jews along the Rhineland in the belief they were ushering in the Last Days). Only by doing so could the master race fulfil its destiny of finding *Lebensraum*, living space, in the east. This was a life or death struggle; without this land, the superior German culture would atrophy and die. This living space would come from conquering Russia (controlled by Jewish Marxists) and the other racially inferior Slavic countries. Once democracy had been eliminated (another invention of the accursed Jews) and a saviour-type Führer established, then, the German people could start building their empire in the east.

The Third Reich is itself a term heavily inscribed with apocalyptic meaning. In 1933, when Hitler came to power, he immediately issued the 'Proclamation of the Third Reich'. On one level, the term was used to indicate the latest phase in a numerical sequence – the first Reich or empire was the Holy Roman Empire, beginning with Charlemagne; the Second Reich was the German Empire of 1871–1918, founded on Bismarck's 'blood and iron'. In using the term the Third Reich, then, the Nazis were consciously associating themselves with the imperial glories of the past. But it was also a way of signalling an absolute break with the past and, in particular, with the despised Weimar Republic. The Third Reich has a distinctly millennial ring to it, recalling as it does the Joachite concept of the Third Age. Unlike Joachim's millennial kingdom, however, Hitler's thousand-year Reich represented the apotheosis of violent, apocalyptic action. He believed he could save the world only by destroying a significant proportion of it.

It was the Jews that Hitler particularly wanted to destroy. To legitimate his war on them, he drew on a cosmic conspiracy theory that had been doing the rounds since the beginning of the twentieth century. Since its appearance in 1905, *The Protocols of the Elders of Zion* has served to stir up apocalyptic fears about the Jews. Norman Cohn called it the Nazis' Warrant for Genocide.[28] A forged report on the first Zionist Congress in 1897, the *Protocols* describes a 3,000-year-old conspiracy of the Jews to enslave mankind. Hitler drew on such toxic conspiracy theories to promote himself as the saviour of the Aryan race. As he ranted and raved about Jewish plots to take over the world, the age-old spectre of a Jewish Antichrist was once again being invoked. It helped to move his millennial movement from the fringes to the centre. Only extreme ruthlessness, Hitler proclaimed, could save the day against their merciless enemy. In casting the Jews as a demonic host, hell-bent on world domination, Hitler was using the same kind of apocalyptic motifs that had proved so murderous during the Middle Ages. Killing or converting the Jews for the crusaders was a sure-fire way to hasten the end of the world and book a place for yourself at the top table in heaven. Hitler's end-times scenario also gave the Jews an important role to play. Only the Final Solution would bring to an end racial and cultural degeneration. Quite simply, the destruction of the Jews meant salvation for the Aryans.

Like other militant millenarians, Hitler attempted to re-order time itself. Deluded despots fondly turn back the clocks to year zero in the hope of lending apocalyptic significance to their seizure of power. Hitler's accession to power in 1933 – a shabby backdoor affair – was supposed to be the dawn of a new thousand–year Reich (in fact it lasted only 12 years). When Hitler was appointed Chancellor on 30 January 1933, he proclaimed that this was the beginning of the Third Reich, a term which differentiated the new regime from the much despised Weimar Republic and associated it with the glories of Bismarck's Second Reich. Time had effectively begun again with the thousand-year reign of the master race.

Presiding over this new age was the Führer, a redeemer-figure who would lead the biologically chosen people, the German *volk*, to the Promised Land in the east. The *drang nach Osten* ('drive to the east') was a divinely appointed task. There an organic community, based on the blood-ties of a racial elite, would create the perfect society on earth. Before the Germanic people could settle in these Slavic lands they had to be cleansed of the Jews and the 'sub-human' Slavs. What distinguished Hitler from other racist utopianists was that he was actually in a position to turn theories, visions and pro-phecies into brutal reality. The outbreak of war in 1939 represented a key turning point in the Nazi policy towards the Jews. For Hitler, it was they who had caused the war and for that they would pay a heavy price. In a speech to the Reichstag on January 1939, Hitler unveiled his sense of his prophetic purpose and his plans for the Jews in Europe – nothing less than annihilation:

> In the course of my life I have very often been a prophet, and have usually been ridiculed for it. During the time of my struggle for power it was in the first instance only the Jewish race that received my prophecies with laughter when I said that I would one day take over the leadership of the State, and with it that of the whole nation, and that I would then among other things settle the Jewish problem. Their laughter was uproarious, but I think that for some time now they have been laughing on the other side of their face. Today I will once more be a prophet: if the international Jewish financiers in and outside Europe should succeed in plunging the nations once more into a world war, then the result will not be the Bolshevizing of the earth, and thus the victory of Jewry, but the annihilation of the Jewish race in Europe![29]

In the first stages of Hitler's racial war, the murdering was carried out by *Einstzgruppen*, special murder squads who would go in after the *Wehrmacht* and the SS battalions to mass murder the Jews and other non-desirables. Shooting men, women and children at the side of vast burial pits took such a terrible psychological toll on the killers that a more humane method of extermination was required – humane for the perpetrators of mass murder, that is, not the victims of it!

Between the German invasion of Russia in June 1941 and the beginning of the mass gassing of Europe's Jews in March 1942, the decision was taken that the killings should be carried out by more scientific and efficient methods. In order to eliminate what Hitler termed the Jewish 'bacillus', specially built extermination camps equipped with gas chambers would be erected in Central-East Europe. In hindsight, the term the 'Final Solution' for the Holocaust has a sinister apocalyptic ring to it. At the time, it was simply a euphemism to mask evil. In Germany, 'euthanasia' programmes – the gassing of mentally ill patients and other defectives – had been in operation since the beginning of the war. Later the Nazis were to experiment and perfect their methods of mass murder with carbon monoxide being pumped into mobile vans. The next step was the employment of the fumigant Zyklon B. In camps such as Auschwitz industrial- scale gas chambers were built in which millions of men, women and children from all round Europe met their end.

The cold-blooded rationality with which the murderers went about their business is chilling in the extreme. In order to be implemented, the killing programme required a vast bureaucracy – governmental and other administrative agencies. Viewed as an apocalyptic event, the Holocaust is atypical. Normally the end of the world is figured as an orgy of irrationality and violence. In the Nazis' apocalypse, the bureaucrat filling out the forms was to play a decisive role. Everything was to be done as orderly and rationally as possible. The notorious Wannsee Conference, held on 20 January 1942, provides a shocking insight into how one of the most technologically sophisticated and bureaucratic of countries went about the irrational business of eradicating another race off the face of the earth. Presiding over the co-ordination and implementation of the greatest planned mass genocide in history was Reinhard Heydrich. In his brilliant account of 'the Meeting', Mark Roseman reveals how lists were drawn up of the Jewish populations in every country in Europe, including those not yet conquered by the Nazis.[30] These were to be cleansed of the Jewish presence at some point in the future. In the fullness of time, the whole of

Europe would become 'Jew-free'. After the total racial re-ordering of Europe, humanity would then enter a biologically golden age, in which only the fittest members of the master race would be allowed to flourish.

Although Hitler never bothered himself with the specifics of mass murder, in all this could be detected the presence of the Führer. Race was to Hitler what class was to Marx. The concept of racial struggle as the central fact of world-history is as central to Nazism as class struggle is to communism. Both ideologies emphasize the need for violent revolution in order to usher in their millennial kingdoms – a new racial order for the Nazis and a new social and political order for the communists. Although characterized as mortal enemies, both ideologies have a teleological, end-oriented view of history. Time speeds towards a cataclysmic event which will herald the complete re-ordering of society.

The Nazis' idea of *Rassenkampf*, or 'race war', is heavily infused with such an apocalyptic notion. It is the Nazis' equivalent of Armageddon. In the Nazis' apocalyptic scenario, the forces of goodness are all blond and Germanic-looking; the forces of evil are racist caricatures – all hooked noses and the like. It is a battle on which hangs the fate of the world. In June 1941, the idea of race war caused Hitler to commit the greatest military blunder in his career. The invasion of the Soviet Union lost the war; because the Nazis had not secured victory in the west, it meant fighting on two fronts. For Hitler, however, apocalyptic concerns were uppermost, not military tactics. Code-named Operation Barbarossa, the Russia campaign was to be Hitler's crowning glory; it was to be a crusade not only against Bolshevism but also the Jews who supported such a despicably egalitarian system. Victory would usher in a racial paradise on earth.

In this ideologically driven war, then, killing was seen as an act of salvation. When Aryan killed Jew or Slav, they were destroying an inferior race that endangered their own. A deliberate programme of racial extermination was carried out from the western frontier of the Ukraine to Stalingrad – all in the name of good over evil. The murderous violence of such apocalyptic fantasizing, however, was not just confined to the Nazis. Antony Beevor relates how devout Ukrainians, who suffered one of the most catastrophic man-made famines under Stalin, greeted the 'arrival of military vehicles with black crosses as symbolic of a new crusade against the anti-Christ'.[31] Such was the loathing many had for the Stalinist regime that they welcomed the German invaders as saviours. Many of them were all too happy to join the Nazis' murder squads.

The circumstances of Hitler's last days continue to fascinate. Holed up in his bunker, surrounded by the ruins of his millennial kingdom, Hitler played out Wagnerian apocalyptic scenarios in his mind as the Red Army moved in. He felt the German people had not been resolute enough in their life-and-death struggle with lesser races and so therefore deserved to be defeated. He even countenanced the possibility that the imminent Russian victory meant that the hated Slavs were actually stronger racially than the Aryans and so deserved to prevail. One thing was sure, though. In his last political testimony, the belief that animated him from the very beginning still burned brightly – hatred for the Jews.

Two years after the end of the war, the despised Jewish people finally got their own state while Hitler's country, meanwhile, was divided between the Soviets and the Allies. That the creation of Israel in 1948 was as a direct result of the Holocaust is one of the great ironies of history. In attempting to eradicate European Jewry, Hitler had helped to create a Jewish homeland. Thus the dual nature of apocalyptic once again manifests itself. A uniquely destructive event, the Holocaust, is followed by consummation – the founding of the state of Israel.

The impact of technology on warfare was important in all spheres in the Second World War, but was most marked in the air. In this phase of the twentieth century the end of the world was frequently envisaged as a bomb dropping out of the skies. The apocalyptic fear of the potency of the bomber in the 1930s certainly contributed to the British policy of appeasement. Bombers were viewed as invincible super weapons capable of laying whole cities to waste. H.G. Wells' *The Shape of Things to Come* stoked the fires of apocalyptic fear as did its movie adaptation, *Things to Come*.

Picasso's monochromatic masterpiece *Guernica* (1936) depicted allegorically the horror of an air raid in the Spanish Civil War when the Luftwaffe practised their dive-bombing on defenceless civilians. In successive campaigns during the Second World War, the bomber lived up to its destructive reputation: the Blitz of 1940, the massed concentrations of RAF four-engine bombers raining incendiary bombs down on Berlin, Hamburg and Dresden, B-29 Super Fortresses reducing one Japanese city after another to rubble, the German bombardment of Britain with V2s, the so-called flying bombs, in 1944–5. If the tank was the Behemoth, the earth-bound monster, of the Great War, then the bomber of the Second World War was like one of the four horsemen of the Apocalypse, dealing death and destruction from the skies.

One new strategy proved particularly lethal. 'Area bombing' and 'fire-storms' were part of a new terror campaign waged as much against the civilian population as against the military. In one single raid on Hamburg in 1943 the RAF killed over 30,000; in 1944-5 American bombers destroyed over 30 per cent of the buildings in Japan. In February 1945, RAF incendiary bombs generated a fire-storm which engulfed the magnificent city of Dresden, turning it into a vast crematorium in which many thousands of men, women and children perished. And yet these conventional weapons, terrible as they were, did not prove all conquering. The onslaught seemed to steel the will of the civilian population rather than buckle it. It would take an entirely new bomb to defeat Japan.

The events that took place in a remote area of New Mexico, in America's south west, during the predawn hours of 16 July 1945, forever changed the world and how we conceive its ending. Code named 'Trinity', the testing of the first atomic bomb vividly demonstrated that mankind had finally usurped God as the agent of universal destruction. On the day of the test, Robert Oppenheimer, known as the father of the atomic bomb, fully realized the enormity of what he had just accomplished. As he stood watching the mushroom cloud ascend into the heavens, he recalled how a phrase from the *Bhagavad Gita*, the Hindu scripture, popped unbidden into his mind: 'I am become death, the destroyer of worlds.' The atomic age had just been born.

The American atomic attack on Nagasaki and Hiroshima resulted in the deaths of over 280,000 people, some of whom died straightaway while others succumbed later to the radiation poisoning. Allied forces would certainly have won the war against Japan with conventional weapons. By 1945, Super Fortresses roamed freely in Japanese airspace unimpeded. Victory in Asia was a foregone conclusion. Like the RAF's fire-bombing of Dresden, the atomic attack on the two Japanese cities had more of a symbolic significance than a military one. America used the bomb in order to terrorize the enemy into surrendering sooner rather than later. The invasion of the Japanese island of Okinawa had given the military leaders a terrible insight into what would be the human cost of an invasion of the mainland. The Japanese, quite literally, were capable of fighting to the last man. So Japanese civilians were sacrificed en masse in order to save American military lives. This was indeed a dirty 'total' war in which such calculations had to be made.

Unlike the furnaces of Dresden, however, the symbolism of the mushroom cloud ballooning over civilian targets was extremely effective. It was so dreadful, so awe-inspiring, that Japanese surrender was swift in coming. Jonathan Schell's classic account of the bombing in *The Fate of the Earth* brilliantly evokes the aftermath of a nuclear strike:

> In that instant, tens of thousands of people were burned, blasted, and crushed to death . . . The centre of the city was flattened, and every part of the city was damaged . . . Half an hour after the blast, fires set by the thermal pulse and by the collapse of the buildings began to coalesce into a firestorm, which lasted for six hours . . . a 'black rain' generated by the bomb . . . fell on the western portions of the city, carrying radioactive fallout from the blast to the ground. For four hours at midday, a violent whirlwind, born of the strange meteorological conditions produced by the explosion, further devastated the city.[32]

With this final and terrible instalment, the so-called 'Age of Catastrophe' had come to an end.[33] The destructive potential of American air power plus atomic bomb had now been fully revealed. Bombs now became *the* Bomb, the definite article being a testimony to the singular power of this new weapon. The advent of the atomic age would forever change the way in which the End of the World would be conceived. And because the race to develop the nuclear bomb had been won by the Americans it was now their turn to play God. As Oppenheimer had so quickly grasped, God may have created the world but it was the Americans who had been the first to develop the capacity to destroy it.

Given the appalling nature and scale of the suffering in the twentieth century, it is hardly surprising that the word Apocalypse has become synonymous with destruction, pure and simple. The trench warfare in France, Stalin's Reign of Terror in the 1930s, the Second World War and the dropping of the atomic bomb: for many, these terrible historical events are popularly described as apocalyptic as a way of conveying their uniquely destructive nature. The Holocaust is viewed as an apocalyptic event because of the unprecedented scale of the killing and destruction. In this respect, the word Holocaust to describe Hitler's war on European Jewry is an entirely appropriate one. Originally derived from the Greek for 'burned whole', the word Holocaust then became a biblical word for 'burnt offerings' – sacrifices made in the Temple to assuage a jealous Jehovah. Later, in the nineteenth century, it was given the secondary meaning of a massacre, the destruction of a large number of people.

It was only in the 1950s that the term Holocaust started to be used specifically about Hitler's war on the Jews. Prior to that, it had been referred to as *Shoah*, 'catastrophe'. Inscribed into these two terms – Holocaust and *Shoah* – is the sense of the complete destructiveness of the events. When viewed biblically, however, a new perspective emerges. In the Bible, apocalypse is not just about destruction but also renewal. The world is destroyed and then saved. The Jews who perished in the concentration camps were often tormented by the belief that no one would believe them about the enormity of their suffering. Cremating their bodies and then disposing of their remains in the way that they did, the Nazis were intent on erasing a people as though they had never existed. However, out of the ashes of Auschwitz arose the phoenix of Israel. The Holocaust helped to drive the Jews back to the Promised Land. In attempting to wipe the Jews off the face of the earth, Hitler had simply accelerated the return of Israel to Palestine. A nation state now exists dedicated to commemorating the memory of the nameless millions that perished.

For Jews, this was nothing short of a miracle. It was a miracle that a nation that had once been destroyed in ancient days should be re-established nearly two thousand years later; a miracle that its people who had been dispersed to the ends of the earth and then systematically burned, gassed and murdered in massacres and pogroms down through the centuries should be gathered from among all the nations and returned; a miracle that the nascent state fought off seven hostile nations in the 1948 War of Independence; a miracle that a barren, empty, desolate country should bloom. For many Jews, settling in Israel, such miracles were simply the fulfilment of biblical prophecies: passages in *Deuteronomy*, *Jeremiah*, *Isaiah* and *Ezekiel* could, and were adduced, in order to prove the existence of a God who acts in history to save the Chosen People.

In the following two chapters, we shall see how guilt over the Holocaust and the birth of Israel triggered an extraordinary messianic reaction among many Christians in America. This shift in Christian millennial theology represents the opposite of the apocalyptic demonizing of the Jews popular at the time of the Crusades and revived in our own era by Hitler.

6

APOCALYPSE IN AMERICA: PART ONE

Religion gave birth to America, Tocqueville observed long ago.[1] America's sense of itself as a unique nation with a unique role to play in divine history was there from the very outset. When the Mayflower Puritans crossed the Atlantic in 1620, they were inspired by the belief that aboriginal America was a place to be conquered and colonized for God. In New England, the first Puritan settlers wielded the sword of the spirit as much as they did the axe to clear the forests for settlement. It was here, on 'pure' 'virgin' land, they would build a model society, a type of new heaven and earth. In 1630 John Winthrop (1588–1649) wrote a sermon entitled 'A Model of Christian Charity' while voyaging towards the New World on board the *Arbella*. Destined to become the first governor of Massachusetts, Winthrop outlined his vision of the new polity based on divine law and principles. He was convinced of God's divine purposes for the colony. Like the Israelites, the settlers were God's covenanted people; as the 'chosen people' they had spiritual and earthly duties. The Puritan mission in New England was therefore seen in typological terms; Winthrop famously proclaimed that the new colony must be 'as a City on a Hill', a beacon of light that other generations would follow as they pushed forward the frontiers of Christian civilization. If, however, they apostatized then New England would become Babylon, a byword for moral and spiritual degradation.

Winthrop's utopian vision has resonated down through the ages. It has contributed greatly to enduring myths about America's special status as a chosen nation and its role as an example to the rest of the world. More than any other immigrant group the Puritans have historically been considered the starting point for the United States' national culture. It's where the genesis of the American Dream took place. So when John F. Kennedy and Ronald Reagan invoked Winthrop's 'City on a Hill' image in the late twentieth century, they were tapping into one of the most enduring myths Americans have about their country – their divinely ordained duty of dominion. As the covenanted people, the Puritans were infused with a sense of the uniqueness of their national destiny. They had to build a society from scratch in a place they regarded as the frontier of 'white' civilization. Initially, the Native Americans they encountered were not seen as their natural enemies, but rather as potential friends and converts. But their Christianizing efforts met with little success and evangelical fervour soon gave way to bitter disillusionment and fear. Known for their cruelty and ruthlessness, the Pequot tribe were soon recast as the deadliest of foes. In 1639, after the murder of several colonists, hostilities between the Pequots and colonists finally erupted into open warfare.

In these crisis-ridden years, many turned to the *Book of Revelation* for comfort and solace. Out of John's frenzied

vision of destruction comes order and renovation. The steadfast are blessed and finally rewarded. The forces of darkness
are defeated. In their premillennial eschatology, the more
terrible the tribulation the nearer the glorious consummation.
In such an apocalyptic scenario, the Native Americans themselves now figured as the devil's legions.

As in Europe, 1666 was deemed to be the Glorious Year. When
the first thousand years of the Christian era were added to 666,
the number of the Antichrist, the number 1666 came up. In this
apocalyptic time-line the New World had not long to run. For
those who had arrived in 1630, it was all of thirty-six years.
When the miraculous year came and passed without incident,
new apocalyptic scenarios came to the fore. Having survived the
terrible early years, the colonists began to see themselves in a
new light. They were God's elect, commissioned to bring about
the end of the world through building a millennial kingdom
worthy of Christ on American soil. The names of original
Puritan settlements in the New World – New Canaan and
New Haven – bear the imprint of such apocalyptic expectation.
Christ's millennial kingdom would not drop from the heavens in
a blink of an eye. Rather it would be gradually and systematically introduced through their human efforts in harmony
with God's plan. The end of the world was projected into an
indefinite future. Paradise would have to be placed on hold.

Central to Puritan theology was the concept of election, the
idea that some individuals were predestined by God to be
saved and taken to heaven while other individuals were
doomed to hell-fire. God had extended his covenant of grace
to his chosen people who would attain thereby everlasting
salvation. God's final judgement therefore had relevance not
just to their individual selves but also to their community as a
whole. All around them comets, eclipses, forest fires and other

'wonders' and prodigies were read as signs portending an imminent Final Judgement. Puritan ministers performed exegetical contortions in order to make historical facts conform to scriptural predictions in order to pinpoint exactly when the Great Day would be, the time at which Christ would return and usher in a millennium. This would be the end of history when the earth would be destroyed and the Elect would be ushered into heaven while all the others would be cast into hell.

Published in 1662, Michael Wigglesworth's poem 'The Day of Doom' was a bestseller among seventeenth-century Puritans. Consisting of over two hundred eight-line stanzas, Wigglesworth's verse jingles along merrily despite its doom-laden theme. Its primary purpose was to act as a catechism, drumming rhythmically into people's minds the key doctrines of righteousness and eternal punishment. Eighteen hundred copies of Wigglesworth's poem were circulated in New England in its first year. It has been estimated that at one time every other New England family must have owned a copy of 'The Day of Doom'. It was still being re-issued and bought well into the eighteenth century. Such popularity reveals a great deal about the religious climate of the age. In the poem theological abstractions are given concrete form. On Judgement Day, a vengeful Christ divides humanity up into two groups. On the right are the blessed sheep who will ascend to heaven; on the left, the wicked goats who are bound in iron bands and cast down to a burning lake in hell where they are to be tormented for eternity. Such a vision was meant to strike fear into the stoutest of Puritan hearts. Although the doctrines of election and the covenant of grace fortified the communities collectively, on a personal level many individuals were unsure as to what would be their final destiny. Only in death would the truth be fully revealed. The end of your life therefore was conceived of as an apocalyptic event, in the sense that it revealed, 'uncovered', once-and-for-all and incontrovertibly the fate of your soul. Would you be numbered among the sheep and be saved or would you spend an eternity in the company of the other goats? A heaven of boundless beneficence or a hell of perpetual torment: the metaphysical polarity was stark and was at the heart of the Puritan Manichean scheme of things. In the Puritan hell, there was no fire escape. Ever mindful of death and the fleeting nature of time, the world was viewed as a journey back to God. For the Elect, the road was straight and narrow and led directly to Jerusalem the Golden, the heavenly equivalent of the Christian communities they had attempted to build on earth. For the reprobate, it was a one-way journey to a terminus of perpetual torment.

Bernard McGinn is alert to the dangers of the nature of the apocalyptic imagination: 'Its moral absolutism forms the most disturbing (and historically the most destructive) aspects of apocalypticism.'[2] The sense that the devil and his legions are here in our midst, stalking the streets and about to recruit new members, can create paranoia and hysteria. The notorious witch-hunts of 1692 in Salem Village, New England, typify such a world-view. These notorious events occurred during a period of great crisis in the life of a small rural community. The colony was waiting for a new governor and had no charter to enforce laws; New England towns were under attack by Native Americans and French Canadians; smallpox epidemics, floods and droughts were a constant threat.

Such threats, real or imaginary, racked the villagers with fear. Many began to seek a metaphysical explanation as to why they should be so afflicted with misfortune. Soon events yielded them the evidence that absolute evil was in their midst. Several local adolescent girls began to behave in a bizarre and alarming fashion: they suffered convulsions, contortions and spoke gibberish. Nowadays these would be considered psychosomatic symptoms; in the New England colony in the seventeenth century, however, there could be only one explanation: evil spirits possessed them. Under cross-examination, the girls claimed they had been bewitched. They pointed the finger, first at their neighbours and then at the wider community at large in the Massachusetts Bay area.

Act two of the drama began with the entrance of Cotton Mather. A Boston minister, Mather had recently written *Memorable Providences*, a book about witches in his home town. Aside from being a demonologist, Mather was also a prolific writer of apocalyptic prophecies and jeremiad-like sermons. The recent events in Salem Village, therefore, offered Mather a wonderful stage on which to display his witch-hunting prowess. He was also in a position to influence the trial, being a friend and minister to three of the five judges. He made suggestions to them as to how they might approach evidentiary issues at the upcoming trials.

As the weeks passed, Mather became firmly convinced that 'an Army of Devils is horribly broke in upon the place which is our center'. On 4 August 1692, Mather whipped up a storm of apocalyptic fear and expectancy when he delivered a sermon warning that the Last Judgement was imminent. Ever mindful of his public image, he portrayed himself as a part of a holy triumvirate – the other two members were Chief Justice Stroughton and Governor Phips – spearheading the battle against the Devil's legions. The kind of influence Mather could exert was a matter of life and death. This is illustrated in the case of George Burroughs, a former pastor of Salem Village. He had been accused of the ultimate apostasy, turning turtle and working for the Devil. Just before he was hanged, Burroughs faced the crowd and perfectly recited the Lord's Prayer – a feat that was deemed to be impossible for either a witch or a wizard. The crowd gathered round the gibbet began to waver and weep. Richard Calef describes Cotton Mather's reaction in his account, *More Wonders of the Invisible World* (c.1700): 'Mr Cotton Mather, being mounted upon a Horse, addressed himself to the People . . . That the Devil has often been transformed into an Angel of Light; and this did somewhat appease the People, and the Executions went on.'[3]

When the witch trials finally came to an end in October 1692, twenty people had been executed: nineteen had been hanged while one was pressed to death after having refused to plead guilty. As for Cotton Mather, he was more successful at sending innocent people to their deaths than at apocalyptic prophecy. Mather's prophecies failed in 1697, 1716 and 1736.

*

The early Puritans lived in the daily expectation that Christ would return at any moment. In the eighteenth century, this hardline premillennialism gave way to something softer. The revivalists of the Great Awakening of the 1730s and 1740s promoted a sense that the millennial kingdom was not something about to happen in future but that God was now working on earth to establish it. In such a post-millennial view, human effort as well as heavenly intervention would be instrumental in bringing about the millennium. Christ would return when the faithful had built a truly righteous kingdom here on earth. In the sermons of revivalist preachers from Georgia to New England, the thirteen colonies were recast as the biblical Israel. The waves of mass immigration from Europe to the New World were viewed as the apocalyptic ingathering. A sense of superiority infused the colonists. The old world was viewed as corrupt; the new one was regenerate. Such a polarity was religiously inspired but it also helped later to inspire the political revolution of 1776.

The Great Awakening of the 1730s and 1740s was a great

catalyst then for religious as well as political change. It was the American equivalent of the great religious revival that swept through England, for the most part due to the evangelizing efforts of John and Charles Wesley, the founders of Methodism, and George Whitefield. For the ambitious evangelist, the new world offered unprecedented opportunities: it was a realm filled with potential converts and a vast arena for heroic spiritual striving. Whitefield himself visited the colonies in 1738 and made six more preaching tours of the country before his death in 1770. A charismatic preacher, Whitefield went out into the field and delivered sermons to vast audiences about how they too could become a 'new man' and be 'born again' under the influence of the Holy Ghost. If Whitefield was the messenger, delivering the good news to the people, then Jonathan Edwards was the writer of that message. He provided the theological core to evangelical Christianity. A Massachusetts Congregational minister, Edwards was so encouraged by the early successes of the Great Awakening that he believed God was working on earth to establish the millennial kingdom in America.

As colonists awoke to the possibilities of the spiritual life, so they started to formulate new ideas about their duty to pursue political liberty. From the outset, this correlation between religious striving and political struggle had been present. In the Founding era the individual's pursuit of salvation became indistinguishable from the collective pursuit of political liberty. God had endowed individuals with rational faculties which they were at liberty to use in order to distinguish good from evil. If an oppressive colonial power was identified as evil, then surely it was incumbent on the individual to pursue political liberty in accordance with the divine principle? This melding of political beliefs and religious doctrine is reflected in the reaction to the Stamp Act of 1765. Someone calculated that the words 'Royal Supremacy in Great Britain' was a secret code which, when decoded, meant

'666' in Greek and Hebrew – the mark of the Beast in *Revelation*.

In the minds of some, King George III was now the very living embodiment of evil. The melding of politics and apocalyptic, revolution and *Revelation*, proved to be explosive. In the modern era, the Iranian revolution has similarly demonstrated that religion, far from being the opium of the people, can also radicalize them and make them take to the streets. This is because apocalyptic faith paints the world in stark and uncompromising chiaroscuro: the forces of darkness and light, Babylon and the New Jerusalem, the blessed and the damned. Such polarities can form the basis of great political propaganda. In the end, the American Revolution was fought with bayonets and bullets but it was also a war of words, fought with speeches and sermons. In such a climate, radical politics and religion become indistinguishable from each other. In the speeches of the revolutionaries, apocalyptic rhetoric fuelled the political and vice versa. In our era, George W. Bush has revived such religious language in the political realm. He has spoken about God's 'gift of freedom to every human being in the world'.

In insurance terms, flash floods, earthquakes and forest fires are known as 'acts of God'. For the early Americans, God was acting up in all manner of ways. For example, on 19 May 1780, large forest fires are the most likely explanation for convincing a whole New England community that the End of the World had arrived. A late spring day had started ordinarily enough. By midday, however, a mysterious cloak of darkness descended over a large part of New England. So dense and dark was it that many were convinced that this was the End. In Hartford, the Connecticut Governor's Council was meeting. Andrew Gardner takes up the story: 'When the darkness became overwhelming, it was suggested the men adjourn their deliberations. Colonel Abraham Davenport objected. "Either the Day of Judgment is at hand or it is not", he said. "If it is not, there is no cause for adjournment. If it is, I wish to be found in the line of my duty. Bring me candles." [4]

Not all could muster such equanimity. Many locals were aflame with a mixture of quaking fear and ecstatic expectation. By mid-afternoon, the darkness began to roll back, allowing the early evening sun to break through. Then banks of clouds accumulated, enshrouding that part of New England into a darkness so deep that it blanked out a full moon. It was now night, but the memory of the Day of Darkness lived on for generations in the folktales and legends of those who had lived through it.

In apocalyptic myth the corollary of darkness is the realm of radiant light bestowed upon the blessed. Whereas doom-mongers emphasize the destructive aspect of apocalyptic myth, utopianists are alive to the possibilities of paradise on earth. America has always been a country that has attracted such utopian visionaries. Coleridge's utopian colony was to be established in the heartland of American Puritanism – Pennsylvania. Later, D.H. Lawrence thought of setting up his utopian colony, Rananim, under the big sky of the American southwest. The epic landscapes of America appeal greatly to those of an apocalyptic cast of mind. Vertiginous valleys and cloud-capped mountains, endless plains and sweeping panoramas: all provide a suitably heroic stage for the apocalyptic drama. The freedom to move into vast open spaces enabled cult leaders, utopian visionaries and messianic oddballs to uphold the First Amendment – freedom of religious worship.

One of America's most famous utopian experiments illustrates this interplay between millennial yearning and the American landscape. John Humphrey Noyes founded the infamous 'free love' Oneida Community in 1848. Noyes believed that perfection could be achieved here on earth if man was in a perfect environment. For Noyes such a location was not to be found out west but in the more homely climes of Oneida Creek in upstate New York. For some thirty years this was to be the location for one of the most successful utopian communes in history. Rejecting all forms of personal wealth and private property, members were also encouraged by Noyes to share-and-share alike sexually with each other. The two hundred or so adult members considered themselves 'married' to the entire community rather than to one single monogamous partner. Noyes' thinking behind group marriage, or 'complex marriage', was to foster harmonious group relations. Monogamous sex was deemed selfish and harmful because it excluded others. Like the Ranters in seventeenth-century England, polygamy and 'free love' (Noyes coined this term) was seen to be a sign of perfection – a state of spiritual and physical perfection in which all that Adamic contagion of shame surrounding sexuality would be expiated.

In this new sexual order, *coitus reservatus* was to be practised; male members were allowed to ejaculate only while having sex with women who were post-menopausal. This was not just an effective method of avoiding unwanted pregnancies à la Roman Catholics. 'Male continence', as it was rather primly termed, was a physical as well as spiritual discipline, the counter to unbridled sexuality. But it also had a more sinister purpose; it was part of Noyes' eugenics programme which decreed that only the most spiritually ascended members could have sex for procreative purposes with each other.[5] Out of their couplings, a new spiritual master race would issue. So whereas antinomian groups like the Ranters indulged in indiscriminate sex, Noyes' communitarians were allowed to have procreative sex only with carefully selected members. Overseeing the bedroom arrangements was Noyes himself.

Noyes' utopian experiment was a heterodox offshoot of a wider religious fervour seizing the east coast of America.

Known as the Second Great Awakening, this was a period of intense religious revival, similar to the first one in the early eighteenth century. Such was New York's reputation for being a hotbed of revivalist preaching that it came to be known as the 'burned over district'. Out of this religious tinderbox emerged the Millerite movement – one of the most famous millenarian movements to come out of the revivalist spirit of the Second Great Awakening. A farmer from upstate New York, William Miller was an avid Bible student. Based on his extremely complicated system derived from his reading of the *Book of Daniel* and *Revelation* Miller proclaimed that Christ would return sometime between 21 March 1843 and 21 March 1844.

In Millerite apocalyptic prophecy the Second Coming was renamed the Advent and that was what the movement came to be known as – the Adventists' movement.[6] For Miller, it was not so much the Advent as a whole series of advents: all the events of the *Book of Revelation* have not yet taken place but are still to come in the future. In such a prophetic view, the weight of expectation is immense. The events described between Chapters 12 to 21 in *Revelation* – the arrival of the Antichrist, the battle of Armageddon and the descent of the New Jerusalem from the heavens – most compelled his attention. All of these events will occur only after Christ returns (other prophetic systems had claimed that at least some of these end-time events had already happened in human history). Miller's brand of premillennialism was one of the most important new developments in American religious history. His legacy still lives on to this day among apocalyptic groups in the United States.

Miller's literal biblical prophecy was based on an interpretive system that was extremely elaborate. A key passage was 'Unto 2,300 days; then shall the sanctuary be cleansed' in *Daniel* 8. For Miller, the cleansing of the sanctuary was a metaphor for a conflagration that would annihilate the earth and thus purge it. A similarly symbolic interpretation was given to the 2,300 'days'. Interpreted as years, not days, Miller's date for the end of the world was about to roll round: 'I was thus brought, in 1818, at the close of my two years' study of the Scriptures, to the solemn conclusion, that in about twenty-five years from that time all the affairs of our present state would be wound up.'[7] As the Great Year of 1843 drew near, Miller's followers were infused with millennial fervour. The very imminence of the End created a great sense of urgency. Many left their jobs and gave away their property in order to dedicate themselves to the 'midnight cry' – the final call to repentance before the End arrived.

With Miller, the millennial fringe had gone mainstream. Thousands attended a series of camp meetings. Adventists could not be dismissed as religious fanatics. Many were ordinary men and women, often involved in the movement for women's rights and the abolition of slavery. What appealed to these people about Miller was his very ordinariness. A former soldier and farmer, Miller was no rapt charismatic spouting bible-babble. Square-jawed and broad-shouldered, he was reassuringly stolid in his appearance. True, he had grown up in millennial country – on the frontier of New York and Vermont – but he had been an upstanding farmer who had served as a sheriff and justice of the peace.

What transformed this local dignitary into one of the most important religious leaders of the nineteenth century were his organizational skills. Rather than relying on charismatic preaching or in-the-field evangelizing methods, like the great revivalist preachers, Miller was quick to see the importance of the latest communications technology to get across his apocalyptic message. High-speed printing presses churned out pamphlets, tracts, newsletters and newspapers. Based on reasoned discourse and arithmetic calculation, Miller's brand of

literal biblical prophecy lent itself very well to the new communications technology. And then there was Miller's sober
public demeanour. Here was a case of the apocalyptist as
number-cruncher. With the aid of coloured charts, he would
take his audience through the calculations lecture-style

Through such techniques a local flare up of millennial fervour
was transformed into a mass movement. In today's world,
Miller's heirs are the TV evangelists working the cable channels
in America or the apocalyptic prophets who proselytize through
the worldwide web. Instead of the Internet, Miller had the latest
print technology at his disposal, enabling him to disseminate his
message far and wide. Being able to mobilize a mass millennial
movement, however, is not the same as successfully predicting
the End of the World. As a millennial cult leader Miller was
spectacularly successful. As an apocalyptic prophet, he was a
spectacular failure. In fact, few prophets in our story have failed
so publicly and so spectacularly.

Although Miller did not specify an actual date when the
Second Coming would take place but only an interval of time,
his followers had other ideas. Some pinned their hopes on 23
April 1843, others at the end of that year. Both passed without
incident. Finally 21 March 1844, the end of the year of the
Second Coming according to the official position, rolled round
without incident. Now the world was ready to mock. Some
believers fell by the wayside; others hunkered down and
swallowed their disappointment. Soon they were re-invigo-
rated with a new sense of hope and purpose. By the summer,
evangelizing had reached fever pitch. Missions to England
were planned. Most importantly, a new date for the Second
Coming was set – 22 October 1844.

In northern New Hampshire farmers abandoned their farms
and let the fields go fallow because of their certainty about the

Lord's arrival. The October date now became the be-all and the end-all. A Millerite editor commented: 'It swept over the land with the velocity of a tornado, and it reached hearts in different and distant places almost simultaneously, and in manner which can be accounted for only on the supposition that God was [in] it.'[8] Some fifty thousand Adventists gathered together in prayer on the expected day, singing into the night fully expecting God to roll back the darkness and usher in a new millennial dawn. It did not happen and the followers were left having to face 23 October in the knowledge that the great prophecy had failed. Known as The Great Disappointment, the failure of Millerite prophecy was a collective trauma for thousands of people. For many, disappointment soon turned to anger. The air was thick with scoffing and recrimination. A breakaway group went on to form the Second Adventists who later mutated into today's Seventh Day Adventists. As for Miller, his career as head of a millennial cult was at an end. Like many biblical prophets before and since, he had fallen foul of date-setting.

While New York and Massachusetts burned in the revivalists' fire, many sought heaven on earth in the west. Homesteaders were filled with a sense of manifest destiny as they began their heroic trek to the Promised Land. No matter that they were appropriating other people's land and spoiling their culture. Whites were God's 'chosen people' and their destiny was to win back the vast expanses of western wilderness for Him. During the 1840s hundreds of thousands of whites made the Oregon Trail. For the Native Americans, the land was not empty but filled with the spirits of their ancestors. In their creation myth the earth was created by the assistance of the sun; it was made without boundaries or lines of demarcation. Now the vast herds of buffalo on the western plains were disappearing fast, along with the antelope. Now the tepees were being burned. Soon whole communities would be rounded up into Native American reservations. Later, such a collective trauma for the Native Americans would be interpreted in apocalyptic terms.

One of the greatest migrations west during the 1840s was made by a group of religious outcasts with extremely unorthodox beliefs and doctrines. The great Mormon trek from Illinois to the Great Salt Lake in Utah was undertaken in 1846–7. In Mormon mythology it is the equivalent to Moses leading the Israelites out of captivity into the Promised Land. The church's unorthodox beliefs had led to persecution in the east. The west held out the promise of vast open spaces and religious freedom. Precisely why the Mormons needed to beat a hasty retreat from Illinois becomes clear when you consider their beliefs. The founder of the faith, Joseph Smith (1805–41), claimed to have been instructed by the angel Moroni to translate a secret history of North America, written on a series of golden plates. These were to be the basis for the *Book of Mormon*. This Holy Scripture makes amends for what many Americans regard as a glaring omission in the Bible – namely the lack of Americans in it. In the *Book of Mormon*, we learn that it was not Columbus who discovered America but various Hebrew tribes who migrated from Jerusalem to the New World in about 600 BC, led by the prophet Lehi.

Originally there were two such groups in America. The Nephites were virtuous, industrious-types who prospered for a time and even built great cities. The second group were the Laminites. They were sinful, destined to become heathens and the ancestors of the Native Americans. Eventually the Laminites prevailed over the Nephites and ended up exterminating them. Before this happened, though, Jesus appeared in America and taught the Nephites. The prophet Mormon abridged the history and the teachings and wrote them down on gold plates.

Mormon's son, Moroni, made additions to the Holy Scripture and then buried the plates in the ground, where they remained for about 1,400 years. Now a resurrected being or angel, Moroni directed Joseph Smith on the night of 21 September 1823 to a cave on a hillside. It was here that Smith claimed he found the gold plates on which were inscribed strange characters, deemed to be 'reformed Egyptian'. Through the aid of a pair of magic 'peep stones' named Urim and Thummim, thoughtfully provided for him by the angel, Smith was able to decipher the text (any one else attempting to read the plates would have been struck down basilisk-style). When Smith finished his translation, he returned the plates to Moroni.

In such home-grown American beliefs, the concept of manifest destiny takes on a whole new colouration. Biblical history is recast in order to give American people a starring role in it. The Holy Land is transplanted across the Atlantic and the Mormons, styling themselves as 'Saints', become the 'chosen people'. Salt Lake City becomes their Jerusalem. The *Book of Mormon* replaces the Torah and the Gospels. Joseph Smith becomes a latter-day Moses receiving not common-or-garden tablets of stone but actual gold plates! And Jesus even gets the opportunity to cross the Atlantic and walk on American soil.

But it was not just the heretical nature of Mormon scripture that brought them into conflict with the authorities. The practice of taking 'plural wives' was an important part of nineteenth-century Mormonism and was widespread. Joseph Smith claimed that God gave him a revelation that polygamy was to be practised by the Mormons. When the practice was outlawed in 1890, it occasioned a quick change in mainstream Mormon doctrine. However, the practice is now making a comeback among fundamentalist Mormon splinter groups who are determined to keep true to the tenets of their first prophet. In 2001, the fundamentalist Mormon Tom Green was prosecuted for polygamy (five wives and twenty-five children). The polygamous groups believe that they are providing bodies for waiting heavenly spirits, thus swelling the numbers of Mormons both in this world and the world to come. Multiple wives ('plurality of marriage') means more children which, in turn, means that many more future Saints will be saved. Those who practise a righteous 'plurality of marriage' can look forward to a place at the top table in the Celestial Kingdom.

When it comes to the End of the World Mormon doctrines and practices are truly fascinating. In the Mormon faith, the sealing principle plays an important part. For example in Mormon marriage a sacred ordinance binds husband and wife in time and in eternity, symbolized by white under-garments worn by the wife. Further ordinances tie children to parents, parents to grandparents and so on across the generations. But the Mormons have taken the notion of family togetherness one step further. There are ordinances which bind and seal the living with the dead. Through baptism, the souls of the dead are invited to join the Mormon Church. This is how posthumous conversion works. A living Mormon takes the name of a dead person and undergoes a sealing ceremony on their behalf. During their lives, zealous Saints may have had numerous identities, as they introduce one dead person after another into the Mormon Church. Mormons argue that the dead are free to reject the offer of church membership; they are simply being given the opportunity to convert before the Day of Judgement.

This doctrine of posthumous baptism is not based on some vague notion that we are all descendants of Adam and Eve. Instead, as Steve Jones has noted, 'painstaking genealogical research'[9] is conducted in order to tie a dead person genealogically with a living Saint. In fact, a vast scientific and technological enterprise is underway to ensure that, come the Day of

Judgement, the Mormon faithful will be well represented. The highly secretive Granite Mountain Record Vault lies buried 22 miles southeast of Salt Lake City in the ragged rock of Utah's Wasatch Range. It contains a vast data bank consisting of hundreds of millions of dead people's names, recorded on millions of rolls of microfiche, costing millions of dollars to assemble. Entombed beneath 700 feet of granite and six humungous Mosler doors, this vast necropolis could probably survive a nuclear strike. In fact, the bunker has not been built to protect the records of the dead from human destructiveness. It is the flood God will send in the Last Days that Mormons fear.

The Jehovah's Witnesses are often confused with the Mormons, due perhaps to their adoption of similar door-stepping techniques. Known originally as the International Bible Students Association, the sect was founded in 1872 by Charles Taze Russell. A former Adventist, Russell learned from Miller the importance of using the latest printing technology to get across his message. The name of Russell's publication, *The Watchtower Announcing Jehovah's Kingdom*, states forthrightly its apocalyptic orientation. The sect was then renamed the Jehovah's Witnesses in 1931 under the leadership of Russell's successor, Joseph Franklin Rutherford.

Sect members are considered to be God's specially selected witnesses to the true faith, hence the 'Witness' part of their name. The faiths of the other Christian denominations are deemed to be false, manifestations of Babylon the Great, *Revelation*'s world-empire of false religion. Needless to say such a hostile and sectarian mentality does not endear them to the religious mainstream. But it is not just other churches or faiths the Witnesses have dissociated themselves from. Secular powers are also regarded as having thrown their lot in with Satan. Consequently, Jehovah's Witnesses refuse to vote, salute the flag, sing the 'Star Spangled Banner' and won't join the armed forces. Believing that this is the 'Time of the Gentiles', when dark forces are at work, believers rigidly divide the world between the wicked 'them' and the blessed 'us'.

Such a Manichean view of the world imbues every aspect of their faith and is central to their sense of history. Convinced that these are the Last Days, Jehovah's Witnesses are forever on the lookout for signs that the glorious consummation is at hand in which they will take their rightful place in God's Kingdom on earth while the rest of us are annihilated en masse. But there is at least one consolation for non-believers: they won't have to suffer the torment of hell for all eternity. The damned will simply be annihilated, thrown into the lake of fire where they will become extinct forever.

For those who are saved, two types of salvation are on offer – an earthly one and a heavenly one. The first of these is reserved for those believers that faithfully spread the *Watchtower* message and put up with years of having doors slammed in their face. Paradise Earth awaits them where they will have 'everlasting life', their resurrected bodies existing in a corporeal state. In this regenerate world, a new social and economic order of communal caring and sharing will replace corrupt and soul-destroying business. Because Jehovah is such a whiz at man-management and maximizing productivity, the Elect will have to labour for only three hours a day.

Paradise Earth, however, is only second best. For those Jehovah's Witnesses who are among the 144,000 – variously known as the 'remnant', 'little flock' or 'anointed class' – another fate awaits. Members of this exclusive group form the heavenly, spiritual nation of God who rule with Christ in the new heavens. These are the ones who are born again and who alone are allowed to take communion in their annual communion service. They will have immortal life bestowed upon them, not having resurrected bodies like those on earth, but spirit bodies.

With such rewards on offer for the faithful, it is little wonder that Jehovah Witnesses are so obsessed with the End of the World. Few apocalyptic groups have come up with so many dates and therefore been so consistently wrong. Russell's *The Time is at Hand* predicted that the end of the 'Time of the Gentiles' and the establishment of God's kingdom on earth would be firmly established by 1914.[10] When the world did not end in 1914 (it was engulfed instead in a global conflict), many Jehovah's Witnesses experienced a severe case of cognitive dissonance. The turn of events did not match prophetic projection. Faced with such a situation, the editorial team got to work. In the next edition of *The Time is at Hand*, Russell had to effect some nifty back-pedalling to account for the failure. In the 'Foreword', written in 1916, he even resorted to landlord metaphor:

> We could not, of course, know in 1889, whether the date 1914, so clearly marked in the Bible as the end of the Gentile lease of power or permission to rule the world, would mean that they would be fully out of power at that time, or whether, their lease expiring, their eviction would begin. The latter we perceive to be the Lord's program; and promptly in August, 1914, the Gentile kingdoms referred to in the prophecy began the present struggle, which, according to the Bible, will culminate in the complete overthrow of all human government, opening the way for the establishment of the Kingdom of God's dear Son.[11]

Reading the 1914 winter issues of *The Watchtower* is a squirm-inducing experience.[12] As Festinger demonstrated, when an apocalyptic group comes up with a prophecy and it fails, then they simply come up with another one. For the Jehovah's Witnesses, 1918 now became the focus of their predictions. When 1918 proved disappointing – it was the

year of the Armistice not Armageddon – prophecies proliferated apace: 1920, 1925, 1941, 1975 and 1994 have all been
years freighted with apocalyptic significance.

The 1925 prophecy is particularly noteworthy because of
the Beth Sarim saga. The second president of the group, Joseph
('Judge') Rutherford explained the significance of the year in
the booklet, *Millions Now Living Will Never Die* (1920):

> . . . there will be a resurrection of Abraham, Isaac, Jacob and
> other faithful ones of old . . . we may expect 1925 to witness
> the return of these faithful men of Israel from the condition of
> death, being resurrected and fully restored to perfect humanity
> and made visible, legal representatives of the new order of
> things on earth.[13]

The prediction that in the autumn of 1925 all the Patriarchs, as
well as the individuals named in *Hebrews* 11, would be raised
to life was certainly an audacious one. But it also turned out to
be a foolish one. When 1925 came round and no one from
Hebrews 11 showed up, some felt compelled to leave the
movement. For others, it was just a question of waiting . . .
and then waiting some more.

By 1929, there was still no show. Nevertheless the leadership was becoming increasingly preoccupied with the question
of accommodation. Where were Abraham and the others in
Hebrews 11 going to stay? Rutherford's solution was to build
them their very own hacienda-style villa in San Diego, California, known as Beth Sarim, Hebrew for 'House of the
Princes'. This well-appointed residence, in an up-and-coming
neighbourhood, was thought to be suitable for such illustrious
guests. Rather than leave the property empty, Rutherford
would act as a sitting tenant. Presumably he did not want
Abraham and co. to be faced with squatters when they turned

up. In the event, the Patriarchs and prophets never did show up and Rutherford got to occupy the house until his death in 1942. Eventually, the villa was sold in 1948.

Nowadays the Watch Tower Society is more circumspect when it comes to setting a date for the End of the World. The experience of disconfirmation seems to have clipped its prophetic wings. A general position, one which does not commit it to any particular date but which also cranks up expectancy, is that we are now living in the Last Days, 1914 marking that apocalyptic milestone. Believers are enjoined to keep waiting and watching – and also proselytizing. Unlike other apocalyptic groups the Jehovah's Witnesses do not believe in the End of the World as such. When Armageddon finally breaks out it will be a mini-end of the world – corrupt political and religious institutions, businessmen and financiers, landlords and estate agents will all go up in smoke. What's left, purified and cleansed, will be a fit abode for Christ and his true believers.

The Jehovah's Witnesses and the Mormons have a worldwide following. The global appeal of these two home-grown American groups is that they seem to offer an alternative to a consumer society and its values. From San Francisco to Shanghai, the pursuit of happiness is being increasingly associated with the latest mobile phone, or a Starbuck's café latte. Some people are so out of kilter with this McDonaldized world that the message of the Witnesses and the Mormons falls on receptive ears. In contrast to those who demonize the whole of the modern world are groups and individuals whose apocalyptic faith arises out of a struggle with a particular set of political, social and economic circumstances. In the past the apocalyptic faith of the exilic Jews arose out of a particular situation. Likewise the black slaves in America were particularly receptive to an apocalyptic message which promised an instantaneous and miraculous deliverance from their misery.

Whites too saw the struggle to free the slaves in apocalyptic terms. In the closing words of his Second Inaugural Address of 4 March 1865, Lincoln linked America's suffering during the Civil War to divine chastisement for slavery:

> Fondly do we hope – fervently do we pray – that this mighty scourge of war may speedily pass away. Yet, if God wills that it continue until all the wealth piled by the bondsman's two hundred and fifty years of unrequited toil shall be sunk, and until every drop of blood drawn with the lash be paid by another drawn by the sword, as was said three thousand years ago, so still it must be said: 'The judgments of the Lord are true and righteous altogether.'   (Psalm 19:9)[14]

The story of the Native Americans demonstrates how combustible apocalyptic and politics can be. For them, the great western migrations of the 1840s were an unmitigated disaster. They led to the disappearance of the buffalo on the western plains, to dispossession and cultural spoliation. For many historians, this was just the latest chapter in a deliberate policy of extermination that the English and their American successors had been following for many centuries.[15] For some 'genocide' is the only appropriate term to describe how white settlers treated the Native Americans over the centuries. That America's suffered horribly is indisputable; it is a firmly established fact that a mere 250,000 Native Americans were still alive in the territory of the United States at the end of the nineteenth century. Such a catastrophic decline was not just due, however, to the white man and his weaponry. The most lethal killers were the pathogens the Europeans brought with them in their breath and in their blood. Highly contagious diseases such as smallpox laid low whole tribes because of their lack of immunity.

The violent collision between the whites and America's native population was not just simply a struggle over land. Gaping social and cultural differences fuelled the conflict. Many of the millions who arrived in the New World from Europe were instantly infused with the idea that it was *their* manifest destiny to fill the vast spaces of the west and stake out land for themselves and God.[16] In contrast, the Native Americans did not regard the great western plains as empty and waiting to be filled. Instead they believed that the spirits of their ancestors roamed the great tracts of land, untrammelled by property rights and fences. In the nineteenth century, the battle between the settlers and the native inhabitants expressed itself in simple spatial terms: expansion and enclosure. White expansion westward resulted in the Native Americans being rounded up and enclosed in reservations.

Faced with such a catastrophe, Native Americans turned to apocalyptic faith for a miraculous deliverance. It led to one of the most haunting and tragic episodes in modern American history – the last major massacre of Native Americans by white soldiers in the 1890 Battle of Wounded Knee. Outbreaks of millenarianism had flared up before among converted Native Americans. In this respect, the plight of the Native Americans was similar to the medieval peasants in Europe. In both cases the experience of dispossession and social oppression had inspired millennial fantasies of turning the tables once-and-for-all on their oppressors. During the late 1860s and early 1870s, the Ghost Dance ritual had spread among tribes in California and Oregon. But these had been localized flare ups which soon burned themselves out.

The emergence of Wozoka, the so-called 'Indian Messiah', in 1889, however, changed all that. During a solar eclipse, he claimed he had received a prophetic visitation from God. God had instructed him to teach the Ghost Dance and proclaim its millenial message to his people. This combination of Christian apocalyptic belief and Ghost Dance lore galvanized the Native Americans. All the long-standing grievances, all the suffering and killing could now be turned to good account. If the Native Americans separated themselves from the world and performed the Ghost Dance, then, the ghosts of their ancestors would return, the land would be released from its curse and restored to its former glory. Plains of grazing buffalo would reappear; the white man would disappear. Such a miraculous vision could not fail to appeal. The movement spread like wildfire from Texas to the Canadian border, as Native Americans dropped tools and engaged in frenzied dancing which induced ecstatic trances and rapt visions. The whites were becoming increasingly nervous and interpreted the movement as a general call to war. When the movement reached the Sioux, a new belief took hold: special 'medicine shirts' would protect the faithful from the white man's bullets. For the whites, however, this visual accompaniment to the movement simply worsened their fears about the Native Americans' intentions.

When Sitting Bull, the legendary leader of the Sioux, lent his support to the 'Indian millennium', local white government representatives became particularly alarmed. After all, here was the supposed killer of General Custer at Little Bighorn supporting a movement perceived by whites as a call to racial war. The authorities therefore thought it was time to take pre-emptive action. They would arrest Sitting Bull. The operation, however, was seriously botched. It left six policemen and eight of Sitting Bull's supporters dead, including the old chief himself.

So much then for scotching the movement. Worse, however, was to come. The government took the decision to round up Chief Big Foot's independent band of Lakota Sioux and confine them in a reservation. Such a task would require great sensitivity and diplomacy. Instead it was left to an inexperienced band of trigger-twitching army recruits. The result was another horrendous botch up ending in butchery. On the morning of 29 December 1890, mayhem and murder broke out just as with the arrest of Sitting Bull but this time on a much larger scale. After the Hotchkiss machine-guns had done their worst, firing almost a shell a second, spraying the Native American camp, ripping through tepees and flesh, 150 or so Sioux lay dead. Sixty of them were women and children. Some historians claim many more were killed.[17] Whatever the final figure one thing was sure: the ghost shirts had been unable to stand up to modern weaponry.

*

The one thing history should have taught us is not to predict. The prophet proudly proclaims his prophecy, goes to great trouble to persuade a sceptical public that this time it is for real, only to see the date pass and nothing happen. Certainly the failure of the Millerite prophecy in 1844 led to a discrediting of date-setting generally. But the general premillennial position that the world is irrevocably deteriorating as we speed towards the end of days was not discredited. In fact, its pessimistic outlook tallied with what was happening to American society in the middle to late nineteenth century. The trauma of the American Civil War, the horrors thrown up by rapid industrialization and urbanization and the dislocations and ruptures caused by mass immigration: all these could, and were, read as signs that we were about to enter the final countdown to the time of tribulation. In other words, the kind of post-millennial optimism that had animated previous generations simply did not accord with the Signs of the Times.

What was needed was a new type of pre-millennialism – one

which avoided the pitfalls of tying yourself to a particular hour and day while also whipping up a fervour of millennial expectation. The work of the British theologian and evangelist John Nelson Darby performed just such a feat. Seldom read except by specialists, Darby's works put forward tenets which have proved remarkably influential on American Evangelicals down to the present day. Known as pre-millennial dispensationalism, Darby's scheme offers a vision of the future which is thrilling and dramatic while also remaining conveniently open ended.

Darby was a leading force behind the Plymouth Brethren in Britain. However, his prophetic beliefs never met with the same success in his homeland as they did in the United States. In all, Darby made six trips to the United States and Canada during the mid-nineteenth century, visiting all the major cities where he made many converts through his preaching and theological works. But what really got his core doctrines and ideas on to the religious map was the publication of the *Scofield Reference Bible* in 1909. A bestseller in its day, this landmark publication helped to popularize and spread many of Darby's ideas and doctrines which might otherwise have remained locked away in vast and weighty theological tomes.

Like Joachim of Fiore, Darby saw human history as unfolding in a series of stages or dispensations. But whereas Joachim believed in only three dispensations, Darby's prophetic scheme was more complex; in his brand of dispensationalism there were to be no less than seven dispensations.

The world had experienced six dispensations already, ranging from the fall to the flood and to the crucifixion of Christ. According to Darby, the end of the 'Church Age' is the one we currently occupy. The passing of this dispensation will be marked by a series of events, the culmination of which will be Christ's first return when he will 'rapture the saints', snatching them up into heaven and thus sparing them the terrible upheavals and suffering of the seven-year tribulation. Precisely when the Rapture will take place still sharply divides dispensationalists to this day. Some incline to the belief that the Rapture happens prior to the tribulation (pre-tribulationists). Others believe that it will happen mid-way through the seven-year period (mid-tribulationists). Then there are those dispensationalists who believe that they are going to have to do the whole seven-year stretch before being beamed up into the heavens by Christ (post-tribulationists). Darby's pre-tribulationist doctrines have proved particularly influential in today's America. It is the majority position of the Evangelicals who exert such political sway in Bush's America.

For Darby and his followers, there would be signs portending the end. These were not the usual stock-in-trade disasters and calamities of your bog-standard apocalyptic prophet. In Darbyist prophecy, modernity itself became a sign that the glorious consummation was at hand. Secularism and technological advances such as steam locomotives and the telegraph were freighted with apocalyptic significance. Similarly, some Christian fundamentalists today regard the Internet, the great communications tool of our day, as the Devil's work. Imbuing technological advances with apocalyptic significance makes for a thrilling end-times scenario. As the march of technology advances forever forward, so does the Great Day of reckoning draw ever closer. In Darbyist eschatology time is hurtling towards its consummation. Then one earth-shattering event after another will occur: the Rapture, the descent of Satan to earth, the Great Tribulation, Christ's return to earth, Armageddon and the defeat of Satan, followed by the Seventh Dispensation and peace and harmony for a thousand years.

The Great Tribulation is particularly dramatic and has proved to be especially influential on today's Evangelicals.

During this time, a figure will emerge who appears to be a man of peace; however, he soon reveals himself to be an arch-impostor, a demonic simulacrum of Christ. The belief that Antichrist will be a Jew has a long history in apocalyptic thought. The point about Antichrist is that he is a demonic counterfeit of Christ who was, after all, born a Jew. Modern Darbyists such as Jerry Falwell have repeated this belief and provoked many accusations of anti-Semitism. Darbyist beliefs about the unique apocalyptic role of the nation of Israel in the end of history have also proved to be remarkably influential in today's America. The Israelites' return to the Promised Land, he said, was a requirement of the Second Coming. For many Evangelicals today, the creation of the modern state of Israel in 1948 is the ingathering which is a sign that the end is near.

But it is Darbyist beliefs about the Rapture that have proved so influential. The prospect of being whisked up to heaven in the blink of an eye is irresistible to many Americans. It is a belief that has helped to knit together a wide variety of dispensational beliefs and styles in today's America. In the Bible Belt, bumper stickers on cars carry the alarming message that 'In case of rapture, this car will be unmanned'. Falwell has conjured up visions of a Carmageddon: all round the world cars career into each other on highways as the faithful are called away from the driver's wheel. In popular television ministries watched by millions, in films and videos, on the Internet and in the bestselling novels of writers like Timothy LaHaye, visions are conjured up of what will come to pass when John Nelson Darby's prophecies about the end come true. That an obscure British theologian and evangelist should exert such an influence on modern America is truly astonishing. In the next chapter we shall how Darbyist beliefs have infiltrated politics to such an extent they their presence can even be detected in the Oval Office itself.

7

APOCALYPSE IN AMERICA:
PART TWO

In the early decades of the twentieth century prophets and visionaries in America came in many different shapes and sizes. Historical events stimulated a sombre version of premillennialism: the Depression and two world wars all stimulated prophetic speculation which was deeply sceptical about reform and challenged fundamentally the entire contemporary social and intellectual order. Darby's dispensational premillennialism, in particular, sounded an apocalyptic warning about the ravages of modernity which appealed to the disparate elements in American Evangelicalism. It was a valuable if sobering way of interpreting the swirl of history and divining the mind of God. The belief that soon the righteous and the chosen would enjoy sweet revenge over their enemies lent a triumphalist tone to their sermons.

Discussing 1 *Thessalonians* 4:16, the great travelling evangelist Dwight L. Moody glosses the rapture passage in such a way as to bring out the radical dualism of the belief. For the righteous the trump of God is not to be feared but for the 'poor wretch waiting his trial' the trumpets are a 'knell of despair' because he will have to stand at the bar of justice and hear witness after witness testify against him. When the verdict is reached, 'there will remain nothing for him but punishment and disgrace'.[1] This brand of premillennialism stands in judgement on American culture and awaits in eager anticipation for its overthrow through apocalyptic judgement. Rather than being the city on the hill American civilization is a Babylon riddled with corruption and decadence. Nothing less than divine intervention will vanquish and destroy the enemies within. In the early decades of the twentieth century these were identified as being the liberals and secularists who questioned the fundamentals of the evangelical faith. The Scopes trial in 1925 served to draw up the battle lines in the ideological war that was raging within American society. On one side stood the serried ranks of those who upheld the inerrancy of the Bible and believed that the world was only six thousand or so years old; on the other, were those who were defending the right of science teachers to teach Darwin in high school. In 1925, Darwin and scientific rationalism was victorious. However, this was only a battle won in a long and bitter campaign. To this day true believers from the evangelical heartlands are still waging an ideological war against the godless intelligentsia of the east coast. At stake, is the spiritual and moral heart of America.

In the new century, new prophetic configurations emerged. The Seventh-Day Adventist Church, which survived the stigma of its Millerite origins, became an important premillennialist denomination. During this period the Jehovah's Witnesses flourished as never before. The rise of modern American Pentecostalism in the first decade of the new century also evidenced the all pervasiveness of premillennialism. The distinctive practice of speaking in tongues – the Holy Ghost speaking through those that have received the baptism from him – was interpreted as a sign that we were about to enter the Last Days.

The outbreak of war in 1914 seemed to confirm Russell's prediction that the world was going to end that year. The year war broke out also saw the founding of a leading Pentecostal denomination, the Assemblies of God Church. A bastion of premillennial belief, the Church is still going strong in the heartlands of evenagelical America. While liberal religious leaders spoke optimistically of Christianizing the whole of the social order, premillennialists offered a bleak vision of American society generally. The ship of state was not sailing gloriously and resplendently into the new and unchartered waters of human progress. Instead it was sailing, full steam ahead, towards an iceberg that would send it plunging into the darkest depths.

Bound for New York from England, the *Titanic* did actually sink off the coast of Newfoundland in 1912. At the time, some Evangelicals and prophecy believers interpreted the disaster as a sign of divine displeasure. The ship was not a triumph of technology and human ingenuity but a monument to vanity. Its fate was interpreted as a sign of man's utter helplessness without God. Mankind's only hope lay not in technology and human ingenuity – there would always be an iceberg waiting to scupper such vainglorious enterprises – but in the Second Coming and the miraculous transformations effected by Christ.

As Paul Boyer has noted, in the pre-First World War era premillennialism flourished in American society at the grassroots level, 'fed by a shadowy but powerful network of itinerant evangelists, prophecy conferences, Bible schools, books, and magazines – and Scofield Bibles'.[2] It was not just the poor and the dispossessed who held such beliefs. The late twentieth century and the early years of the new millennium are also years in which premillennialism is flourishing like never before. Large segments of American society today are similarly convinced about the certainty of a Second Coming in which, respectively, the good and the wicked will be rewarded and punished everlastingly.

America's century has also been dubbed the 'Age of Catastrophe', a century scarred by the bloodiest and most destructive conflicts in the history of the world. The thirty-odd years between the beginning of the Great War and the end of the Second World War were times of great crises both at home and abroad. The traumatic events of these three decades gave an enormous impetus to premillennialism. Apocalyptic prophets and Bible students produced a vast outpouring of material – books, articles and pamphlets – speculating about the war's meaning and its eventual outcome. In such times, apocalyptic faith enables people to believe that there is a moral order centre to the world, despite all evidence to the contrary – that the forces of good will eventually prevail over the forces of evil. Identifying your country's enemy as evil is a useful myth with which to galvanize support and create national solidarity. Certainly this was what happened in America during the Great War. The Kaiser was recast as the Antichrist, hell-bent on the overthrow of Christian civilization.

Paul Boyer has noted how the geopolitical configurations thrown up by the conflict seemed to confirm prophecy believers. Events affecting the Middle East were particularly significant. At the end of 1917, as the Ottoman Empire collapsed, the British were able to recapture Jerusalem without firing a shot. Earlier, the British Foreign Secretary Arthur Balfour had declared that the British government viewed with favour the establishment of a homeland in Palestine for the Jewish people. For premillennialists, the long-anticipated Jewish restoration to Palestine seemed suddenly a distinct possibility. The Balfour Declaration of 1917 did not come to fruition until 1948 with the creation of Israel. But it was during the last years of the Great War that the germ of the idea was sown. Later we shall see how in today's America the return of the Jews to the Holy Lands is a key element in the end-time scenario.

Like a future Jewish state, Russia also became a vital part of current apocalyptic scenarios in the later years of the war. Down through the ages Russia had been identified as the northern power that, according to Ezekiel, would invade Israel in the Last Days. The 1917 Russian Revolution crystallized this identification. Viewed through an apocalyptic lens, the godless communism of the Bolsheviks was regarded as another piece of the prophetic puzzle that slotted right into place. Later the spectre of the Soviet Empire would inspire generations of American prophecy believers during the Cold War era.

After the war, premillennialists looked at the new world order that had emerged from the Versailles peace conference as simply another one of humanity's misplaced hopes. The League of Nations, created in order to prevent another world war from erupting, was deemed to be nothing more than a palliative. Along with its successor, the United Nations, it was deemed by some to be satanic. Later the European Union would occupy the same position in apocalyptic thought. Such international organizations were deemed to be Antichrist's New World Order, a demonic simulacrum of Christ's millennial kingdom.

The world was diagnosed as being terminally ill and could not be cured through social reform or international organizations. Only its imminent demise could bring about the kingdom of Christ. Much of the discourse surrounding the collapse of the New York stock market in October 1929 had an apocalyptic colouration to it. When a spectacular bust followed the speculation boom of the 1920s it was the economic equivalent of the Big Bang. Black Tuesday was the day of reckoning after several years of boom based in large part on credit. The scale of the catastrophe was not cosmic but it ruined people – big and small, old and young – across continents.

As the Great Depression followed swiftly in its wake, many Americans came to regard their economic destitution as divine chastisement for all the hedonism and consumerism of the Jazz Age. According to Paul Boyer, the apocalyptic novel has been a feature of American popular culture since the 1930s.[3] The theology of crisis found in such novels offers those suffering deprivation and hardship a sense there is a meaning to their suffering. Soon Christ will intervene violently and suddenly in order to right the wrongs suffered by the reader. The worse things get the closer the day of deliverance. Then the old corrupt world that begot capitalism and cycles of boom and bust will be swept away; it will be replaced by a new social and economic order founded on justice and mercy.

For those who sought another kind of solution to America's ills there was always political extremism. For the American left, the Bolsheviks in 1917 had held out the promise of a secularized millennium, an uncorrupted world of brotherly equality and love as envisaged by Karl Marx in *Das Kapital*. In the 1930s, however, American communists and radical socialists did not get paradise but the horrors of Stalin's Reign of Terror – purges, massacres, famines and deportations. For their part, the American extreme right could always look to that other great dictator of the age, Adolf Hitler.

Hitler's hatred of America was deep and abiding. Like the white supremacist groups in America, everything that made America great – democracy, racial and cultural diversity, its embracing of the modern world – was anathema to him. New York and its spectacular skyline were a particular focus of his apocalyptic fantasies. Run by Jewish financiers, the Big Apple was regarded as a latter-day Babylon, a melting pot of races. In a telling passage from his Spandau prison diary, Albert Speer recalled the following about the Führer's apocalyptic fantasizing and pyromania:

> I would unhesitatingly say that fire was Hitler's proper element . . . what he loved about fire was not its Promethean aspect, but its destructive force . . . fire itself, literally and directly, always stirred a profound excitement in him. I recall his ordering showings in the Chancellery of the films of burning London, of the sea of flames over Warsaw . . . I never saw him so worked up as toward the end of the war, when in a kind of delirium he pictured for himself and for us the destruction of New York in a hurricane of fire. He described the skyscrapers being turned into gigantic burning torches, collapsing upon one another, the glow of the exploding city illuminating the dark sky.[4]

Hitler never got to bomb New York but he did succeed in provoking a war with two future superpowers – the United States and the Soviet Union.

For many Americans, the war against Nazism was another instance of America's divinely appointed role in world affairs. As in 1917 when America had come to the rescues of the Allies, it was being forced out of isolation to sort out the problems of the old continent. The old apocalyptic dualism came in handy for the government – the forces of democratic light were pitted against the forces of totalitarian darkness. After the war, the new geopolitical realities of the Cold War era also lent themselves very well to this configuration. In western propaganda, realms of light and darkness could be found either side of the Iron Curtain.

The threat of a global thermonuclear war gave fresh impetus to prophetic speculation. The early 1950s saw the Soviet Union successfully test its own nuclear weapons and thereby up the pace of the arms race. As the decade progressed, so too did the proliferation of atomic weapons. American movies from this era very much reflect the fear engendered by this situation. The 1954 film *Them!* featured gigantic mutant ants mauling the good people of a small desert town, 'atmospheric fallout' from the Bomb being responsible for mutating the ants to such a size. Roger Corman's *The Day the World Ended* (1956) depicts a post-nuclear world populated by hideously disfigured people and an atomic monster killed at the end of the movie by a spell of 'pure rain'.[5]

The years 1960 and 1961 saw an acceleration of the arms race as the Soviets matched the Americans warhead for warhead. The superpowers were spending money on armaments as though there was no tomorrow. The Cuban Missile Crisis of 1962 was the nearest two superpowers came to using their nuclear arsenals against each other. Those fourteen days in October, when Khrushchev and Kennedy squared up to each other and played atomic brinkmanship, had an enormous social and cultural fallout. Bob Dylan provided the soundtrack to the crisis, albeit retrospectively. Released 27 May 1963, his classic album *The Freewheelin' Bob Dylan* is heavily freighted with apocalyptic foreboding. In such songs as 'Blowin' in the Wind', 'Masters of War', 'Talkin' World War III Blues' and 'A Hard Rain's A-Gonna Fall', Dylan the doomsayer captures the fears and anxieties of the atomic generation. In his autobiography, Dylan writes about the fallout shelter craze that swept America but somehow never caught on in northern Minnesota. He wrote a song about that too – 'Let Me Die in My Footsteps'.[6]

For his part, Stanley Kubrick dealt with impending nuclear annihilation as an absurdist farce. In his classic film, *Dr Strangelove Or: How I Learned to Stop Worrying and Love the Bomb* (1964), he created iconic images for the atomic generation: phallic-shaped missiles, B52 nuclear bombers, cigar-chomping paranoid military men, the Pentagon War

Room, the Soviet 'doomsday machine' which guarantees 'MAD' (Mutually Assured Destruction). Designed to be fail-safe, this vast scientific and technological enterprise is actually the instrument of apocalyptic destruction. Science without conscience is the moral and spiritual condition which allows for such an eventuality. Not surprisingly, *Dr Strangelove*'s whoops-apocalypse scenario did not meet with approval of the authorities. The première had to be delayed because of the Kennedy assassination. When it was released eventually, Columbia Pictures felt obliged to put out a disclaimer at the beginning to the effect that the United States Air Force would not allow any of the events depicted to actually happen. They also reassured audiences that none of the characters portrayed in the film were based on any real-life person, alive or dead.

The alien-invasion film also provided America with an imaginative space in which they could express their fears about science and technology and rival ideological systems. The mother of all alien-invasion scenarios is H.G. Wells' novel, *The War of the Worlds*. Orson Welles' infamous 1938 adaptation of it for radio switched the location from England to America. The Martians land in small-town America – Grover's Mill, New Jersey. Later, a reporter on the spot in Grover's Mill, describes what the Martians look like as they emerge from their spaceships. Such was the authenticity of the performance many listeners who had just tuned in believed it was a genuine news bulletin.

Panic ensued when, horror-stricken, the news reporter dropped down dead at his mike. Before the programme was even halfway through, the CBS switchboard was lit up with callers demanding verification that the end of the world was nigh. Pockets of millennial frenzy burst out across the nation: Simon Callow relates how 'in Indianapolis a woman ran screaming into a church where evening service was being held and shouted "New York has been destroyed. It's the end of the world. Go home and prepare to die." '[7]

The latent fears of the American audience gave plausibility to such an improbable scenario. At the time, the threat of invasion was uppermost in many American minds – not from Mars but from a Europe increasingly dominated by the Nazis. What Americans feared were not the death-rays of Martians but very real bombs falling out of the skies. According to Callow, these fears were justified. The government had failed to implement a system of civil defence against aerial bombardment. By imitating actual newscasts, Welles was able to play on the audience's fears about the worsening international crisis.

This displacement of very real fears on to imaginary monsters reached its apogee in the 1950s. In Cold War America, the red planet and the red scare could easily be conflated. An alien monster is so utterly the 'Other' that it can be remarkably malleable like the traditional bestiary in apocalyptic literature. It can be shaped and twisted into whatever form you so wish and be inscribed with all kinds of political, cultural and social meanings. In American alien-invasion movies from the 1950s, the extraterrestrial is a menacing and predatory figure: it is analogous in fact to exponents of the 'alien' political system that was threatening to take over the world – communism. A Cold War psychosis was fed by such classic sci-fi schlock as the 1951 *The Thing From Another World* (last lines: 'Watch the skies, everywhere! Keep looking. Keep watching the skies!') and the 1956 *Invasion of the Body Snatchers* ('They're here already! You're next! You're next, You're next . . .').

By the late 1960s, American fears about an imminent nuclear attack had somewhat abated. There were new and more immediate concerns to contend with. The Vietnam War was one fought in the media spotlight like no other war before. Americans now had a new focus for their collective fears and anxieties. The opening sequence of Francis Ford Coppola's 1979 film, *Apocalypse Now* depicts helicopters napalming Vietnamese jungle to the tune of Jim Morrison's doom-laden masterpiece, 'The End'. For an entire generation, Vietnam was a source of national soul searching and hand-wringing. In the fullness of time, Americans got to learn some pretty horrifying facts about their nation's mission to roll back communist expansion in southeast Asia. The indiscriminate use of napalm and anti-plant agents was responsible for the destruction of some 30 per cent per year of food production in Vietnam. For many, it was the end of America's sense of itself as a nation with a divine mission abroad. This was one conflict America did not win.

On the domestic front, the Nixon administration was engulfed in a political scandal which also seriously challenged America's sense of itself as a nation with a divine destiny. From the original 1972 break-in to Nixon's resignation in 1974, Watergate was a political scandal that just grew and grew. The social and political fallout of Vietnam and Watergate was profound. Having polluted the wellsprings of American political life, Nixon left the country bereft and demoralized, anxious for a new sense of its unique role in the world as the Redeemer Nation. By resigning Nixon spoke of how it would begin that 'process of healing which is so desperately needed in America'.

After Watergate and Vietnam, America was in desperate need of a new set of myths with which to re-invigorate itself both culturally and spiritually. In terms of popular American culture, a new type of film was very much the order of the day – the sci-fi fantasy. Some of the great blockbusters of the late 1970s were films which displaced apocalyptic fears and millennial yearning into the distant past or an imaginary future. George Lucas' *Star Wars* (1977) had the famous tagline 'A long time ago in a galaxy far, far away . . .'. The first in an enormously successful trilogy, the film has a depth and resonance because of the way in which Lucas recasts apocalyptic scenarios and elements. Led by the messiah-like figure, Luke Skywalker, the Rebel Alliance is pitted against the empire of the evil Emperor Palpatine and Nazi-helmeted Darth Vader. In the final instance, simple faith ('the Force') triumphs over superior technology in the final Armageddon-style climactic battle.

Such simple oppositions appealed to Ronald Reagan, reportedly a fan of the *Star Wars* movies. His election win in 1980 demonstrated just how damaging Vietnam and Watergate had been to the collective American psyche. After such a trauma, America desperately needed to reaffirm a sense of its divinely appointed role in the world. It was the former Governor of California, a B-list movie star and a 1950s anti-communist crusader, who managed to do just that. In his first inaugural address on 20 January 1981, the 40th President of the United States, Ronald Reagan, linked national destiny with religious beliefs: 'We are a nation under God, and I believe God intended for us to be free. It would be fitting and good, I think, if on each Inaugural Day in future years it should be declared a day of prayer.'[8]

The apocalyptic cast of Reagan's mind had been formed a decade earlier. While Governor of California in the 1970s, Reagan was fascinated by Hal Lindsey's *The Late Great Planet Earth*, which imagines Armageddon in terms of a nuclear exchange between the superpowers occasioned by a Soviet invasion of the Middle East. The number one non-fiction bestseller of the 1970s, the book was even made into a film narrated by a lugubrious-sounding Orson Welles. Lindsey's jeremiad caught the doom-laden zeitgeist of the early 1970s when the oil crisis and the arms race created a strong sense of apocalyptic foreboding. A dispensationalist, Lindsey believed that an elect would be spared the horrors of nuclear annihilation (circa 1988) through Rapture. In the twinkling of an eye the saints are going to be caught up to meet the Lord in the sky while the rest of us are left behind to fry. In his follow-up book, *There's a New World Coming*, Lindsey grants those lucky few a vision of what awaits them in heaven. 'I wouldn't be at all surprised or disappointed', he writes, 'if the *new* song which the hosts of heaven sing to extol the incomparable Son of God has a "country music" style'.[9]

Country and western fans might feel a little closer to God; the rest of us were put out of continence that an author like this could exert such an influence on Reagan. The man with the finger on the world's largest nuclear arsenal repeatedly cited and quoted Lindsey's work with approval as though its vision of a nuclear showdown between the Soviets and the Americans was not only inevitable but also somehow desirable because it had been ordained by God. Who needed a nuclear shelter if you had divine protection in the form of the Rapture? Who needed to worry about global radioactive contamination when you were going to be sitting pretty in heaven listening to country and western music? Armageddon – bring it on, Armagettin-out-of-here!

Reagan's opponents were particularly concerned about Jerry Falwell's influence on the President. A born-again fundamentalist leader of the Moral Majority, Falwell met with Reagan more than with any other religious leader. Falwell's anti-communism was apocalyptic in nature; his pamphlet, *Armageddon*, shows a nuclear explosion mushrooming into a reddened sky. Because of their need for oil and their hatred for Israel, Falwell predicted that the Soviets were going to move into the Middle East, precipitating a nuclear holocaust. Another Cold War crusader, closely affiliated to the Reagan administration, was James Robison. Reagan chose the funda-

mentalist born-again minister to deliver the opening invoca-
tion at the 1984 Republican convention in Dallas. What
Lindsey, Falwell and Robison et al. had in common was a
belief that the world was about to end very shortly in a nuclear
showdown with the Soviet Union.

Those who believed in Armageddon theology would not
only cite *Revelation* 16:16, the only mention of the great battle
in the Bible, but would also refer particularly to *Ezekiel* 38 and
39. There Magog appears, a great country far to the north and
which was assumed to be the land of the Russian bear. In one
passage God speaks of many people 'all of them riding on
horses, a great host, a mighty army . . . [who] will come up
against my people Israel'. A few verses later, God says, 'I will
rain upon him and his hordes and the many people that are
with him, torrential rains and hailstones, fire and brimstone.'
According to fundamentalists, this was a description of a
nuclear war. The weapons in *Ezekiel* 39 are the weapons of
the time – shields, spears, pikes etc. For literal prophecy
believers, however, these weapons of a bygone age are in fact
the hi-tech weaponry of the modern age: bombs, missiles and
tanks. God is therefore given a nuclear makeover. He nukes his
enemies off the face of the earth.

This link between Armageddon, the Christian Right and the
Presidency was illustrated in Reagan's notorious 'evil empire'
speech of 1983. Reagan used the phrase for the first time when
he addressed the National Association of Evangelicals in
Orlando, Florida. For the faithful in the audience, it was
redolent of the *Book of Daniel*. Such a characterization of
the Soviet Union allowed Reagan to introduce a metaphysical
dimension into the Cold War. Like the succession empires in
Daniel, godless Soviet totalitarianism was destined to fall
because it went against God's will. In such a view, America's
nuclear weapons were instruments of God's will, saving the

world from the forces of darkness. By claiming the moral high ground for America, Reagan was restoring America's sense of itself as a special nation with a special mission.

On the international front, Reagan's great political ally was the British Prime Minister Margaret Thatcher who had come into power in 1979. Under their leadership, an era of high budget military spending was inaugurated on both sides of the Atlantic. Cruise missiles were deployed to Western Europe and Reagan got to dream about his own pet project, the so-called 'Star Wars' initiative when incoming nuclear missiles would be miraculously zapped from satellites in space. A famous photomontage of the time depicted Reagan as Clark Gable in *Gone with the Wind*, holding a supine Margaret Thatcher/Scarlett O'Hara. Instead of Atlanta burning in the background, there is a vast nuclear mushroom cloud. The caption reads, 'I will love you until the end of time.'

The revival of Cold War tensions in the early Thatcher and Reagan years was reflected in other forms of popular culture. In film and television, 'hard' apocalypse was back on the menu. The 1983 television film *The Day After* was a disturbing portrayal of nuclear war and its aftermath in a small town in central Missouri. Its transmission was one of the biggest media events of the 1980s. Half the adult population watched it, the largest audience for a made-for-TV film to that time. The apocalyptic nuclear war scenario makes for compelling viewing. Signs of impending doom include shoppers panic-buying and jammed interstates as people attempt to flee the major cities. When nuclear war does eventually break out between the superpowers, Minuteman missiles are fired off from local silos in Missouri, swiftly followed by 300 inbound intercontinental ballistic missiles from the Soviets. After the bombs have dropped, the dust in the air blocks out the sun and creates a perpetual twilight. In this post-apocalyptic world, those who survived the attack have only the grim prospect of succumbing to a silent killer – radiation sickness: 'You can't see it . . . you can't feel it . . . and you can't taste it. But it's here, right now, all around us. It's going through you like an X-ray. Right into your cells. What do you think killed all these animals?'

In the event, such grim prognostications never came true. Instead, at the end of the decade, something quite miraculous happened. The collapse of the Berlin Wall was the outward manifestation of the internal collapse of the Soviet Union. The evil empire seemed to vanish overnight, after having menaced the free world for generations. Pat Robertson summed up the prevailing triumphalist mood at the Republican National Convention in 1992. 'Seventy-five years ago a plague descended upon the world and covered the nations of Eastern Europe like a dark cloud', he thundered in his best Old Testament tones. 'Slowly but surely, this dreaded menace grew and spread until it threatened the freedom of the entire world.'[10] Thankfully, the Redeemer Nation was on hand to slay this particular apocalyptic dragon.

Now the sole superpower, America was to spend the rest of the decade casting round for new enemies to demonize. Granted there was no great ideological eastern bloc which could menace the West through ICBMs. Yet the weapons still existed and, by the end of the 1990s, there were eight members of the nuclear club: the United States, Russia, Great Britain, France, India, Pakistan, China and North Korea. Increasingly, the fear was that nuclear annihilation would not come from an old-style nuclear exchange between the superpowers but from terrorist attacks in big cities using small devices. The age of *the* Bomb had given way to the age of portable nuclear bombs and 'dirty bombs' – conventional bombs coated in plutonium.

With the Soviet threat removed, some Americans cast around for new manifestations of the Evil One. They did not have to look very far. Before, godless communism had threatened their divinely appointed American way of life. Now a new enemy, in many ways far more insidious, was threatening their values and way of life. What if Antichrist and his ministers were closer to home than initially believed? What if the Destroyer had disguised himself as the American government and its federal agents? Those who hold extreme beliefs about the satanic origin of all secularism often feel compelled to form militias, paramilitary organizations in which killing for God is deemed to be a divine mission. Guns and food are stockpiled and bunkers built in the expectation that, sooner or later, a holy war will break out between the faithful few and apostate majority – an entity they characterize as 'Babylon'.

For Christian militias, there is enormous significance in the first and second amendment – the right to freedom of worship and the right to bear arms. They are prepared to defend with arms their right to practise whatever form of worship they so choose. For such organizations, these rights, enshrined in the American constitution, have the kind of unassailable authority normally reserved for divine writ. In defending their rights to worship freely and carry firearms they see themselves as divinely appointed guardians of the constitution. These latter-day Last Days warriors do not wield scythes or axes like their sixteenth-century counterpart, Thomas Münzter. Instead they have available to them some fearsome modern weaponry: AK47s and rocket propelled grenades and the like. But like Münzter, these militants wish to emulate the Christ who re-appears to do battle with the forces of evil. This time Christ is not the victim who is crushed in the winepress at the Crucifixion but a vengeful Messiah who triumphantly slays the armies of Antichrist with the sword of his mouth. The earth is then reaped. Into 'the great winepress of the wrath of God' are tossed those ripe grapes – people who have reached maturity but who have rejected the grace of God. They are to be trodden under foot, crushed and bruised until blood flows out of 'the winepress, even unto the horse bridles'.[11]

Such astonishing brutality and mercilessness appeals particularly to those on the margins of American life. For them, biological and disease metaphors more aptly describe the uniquely decadent nature of the times rather than ones involving grapes and winepresses. They might speak of the 'cancer' of the US government and its law enforcement officers, killing the divinely appointed nation from within. Then there's the IRS fleecing God-fearing folks of their hard-earned cash. Other sources of disease include secular humanists, liberals, particular minorities like the Jews, or racially mixed couples, or those of a sexual orientation other than heterosexual. In schools, educationalists infect the minds of young people by teaching Darwin's theory of evolution. Health-care experts prescribe the pill to underage girls or arrange for them to have abortions. The list goes on for potential candidates for the role of Antichrist and his ministers of darkness.

For some militia groups, racism is absolutely central to their belief system. Often biblical history is revised in order to give theological justification to it. For example, some racist ideologues have constructed an alternative genealogy for whites. Such beliefs originated in Britain in the 1840s. Rev. John Wilson's *Our Israelitish Origin* (1840) was the founding text of British Israelism. Wilson, along with other religious thinkers at the time, advanced the idea that Anglo-Saxons were God's 'chosen people' who were direct lineal descendants of the Lost Tribes scattered by invasion and exile in biblical times. These 'true' Israelites had made the long trek to the chilly climes of northern Europe where their descendants became the Anglo-Saxon peoples of northern Europe and the British Isles.

Being descended from the British, many Americans also

readily subscribed to a belief which cast them as descendants of the true Israelites. However, as the doctrines and ideas of British Israelism spread in America, a new sinister strain emerged. When British Israelism mutated into Christian Identity a virulent anti-Semitism emerged. The key figure in this process was Wesley Swift (1913–70), a former Methodist minister from southern California. In the 1940s, Swift started his own church, known tautologically as the Church of Jesus Christ Christian. He was associated with a number of extreme right-wing groups, including the Ku Klux Klan. It was his ideas which were to provide the 'theology' to Christian Identity and neo-Nazi groups in the post-war period. Bizarre beliefs about the demonic origins of the Jews lie at the heart of such a world-view. The 'two-seed' theory is perhaps the most notorious one of all. Developed in the 1960s by Swift and his disciples, this theory holds that the seduction of Eve by the Serpent in Eden was not just metaphorical. From their coupling came Cain who, in turn, became the progenitor of the Jewish people. Consequently, all Jews are seen to be direct lineal descendants of the Devil, 'Satan's Spawn'. In contrast, the other seed line in the two-seed theory derives from Abel, Adam and Eve's good son. He is the father of the Lost Tribes and thence the white Europeans/Americans.

Such a racist world-view has a particularly pronounced dualism. On the one hand, there are the Devil-derived Jews and the 'mud people' (non-whites created before Adam and Eve); on the other, there are the descendants of a pure bloodline who are now members of neo-Nazi groups like Aryan Nation, the Ku Klux Klan and some of the anti-government militia. Members of such groups perceive themselves as God's warriors, intent on saving the world from racial mixing, anti-gun law, gay rights, abortion, the US government, a punitive tax system . . .

Like many Evangelicals in America today, Identity adherents believe that Jesus will return to the earth following a period of tribulation. Unlike Evangelicals, however, they reject the notion of pre-tribulation rapture. They believe that the tribulation must be lived through. This is because their violent form of apocalyptic faith glorifies the role they will play in the Last Days. In the final showdown, they will be fighting the demonic forces of racial interbreeding. With the help of semi-automatic weapons, these congeries of white separatist groups will finally prevail and defeat Satan's non-Aryan children and the United States government which they often refer to as 'ZOG' (Zionist Organized Government). Only a complete withdrawal to a wood cabin on a mountaintop in deepest Idaho, say, or a similarly remote location can save them from racial and religious contamination. To prepare for this supreme struggle, insiders are put through an intensive Rambo-style military training cut off from the outside world.

Elohim City in eastern Oklahoma is a Christian Identity community that has severed all links with the outside world. It gained national attention for its ties to members of the neo-Nazi Silent Brotherhood in the 1980s and with convicted Oklahoma City bomber Timothy McVeigh in the 1990s. Similarly, Dan Gayman's Church of Israel, another offshoot of Christian Identity, has separated itself from the cultural and social mainstream of American life. Located five miles outside the small town of Schell City, Missouri, Gayman's group gives a racist spin to traditional Christian apocalyptic beliefs. For Gayman, a leading racist ideologue, Armageddon is a Nazi-style race war involving Aryan Christians and the demonically inspired other races. In his rabid rhetoric, the spirit of Adolf Hitler lives on:

> The fall of the American government is imminent. We are living already in the preparatory throes of a national and world wide revolution . . . as the agents of Satan who head their world wide

conspiracy of anti-Christ, plot and plan the total demise of
Christian civilization and of the white race . . . A blood-bath
will take place upon the soil of this great nation, that will end only
in victory for Christ or Satan. We of the Nordic race who believe
in Jesus Christ are determined that this nation will remain ours.[12]

While white supremacist groups relish the day they can exact
revenge on the rest of us, other cults and groups are more likely to
turn the violence on themselves. One of the most famous
examples of mass suicide in American religious history was
one that took place in Jonestown, Guyana in 1978. Over nine
hundred men, women and children perished, when they gulped
down a purple fizzy drink which had been laced with cyanide and
sedatives.

Originally from Indianapolis, Jim Jones grew up a Pentecostalist who had visions of a nuclear holocaust which was to
occur in 1967. Undeterred by his failed prophecy, Jones went
on to found the People's Temple in San Francisco. The Gospel
According to Jones, was a heady and intoxicating brew of
apocalyptic beliefs, counter-culture politics and attitudes with
a strong dash of Jesus' social gospel. 'Apostolic socialism' was
its official name. Seeing himself as the messiah, Jones warned
his San Francisco congregation of the coming cataclysm – a
period of race war, genocide and nuclear holocaust. For Jones,
the great enemy was American capitalism which was recast as
the Babylon of *Revelation*, an irremediably corrupt nation.
The only thing for the Elect, the saving remnant, was to
withdraw to a place of safety to survive the coming catastrophe. Out of the ruins of the old world, a communist
millennial kingdom would arise. The saving remnant consisted
primarily of the poor and dispossessed and was mainly black.

As Jones' denunciations of American society became increasingly vociferous he attracted more and more adverse

publicity. This in turn prompted an IRS investigation into the Temple's financial affairs. Expecting the world to go up any moment in a billowing mushroom cloud, Jones had been remiss in filling out his tax returns. In 1977 the net was closing in, prompting 'Dad' to put a radical contingency plan into operation. The whole congregation would relocate to a tract of land in Guyana, South America which the People's Temple had purchased three years earlier. There they would establish a new millennial colony, untainted by American capitalism.

Apocalyptic groups often react in predictable ways when government representatives, law enforcement agents and reporters come knocking on their door. They regard them not as legitimate figures who have a genuine reason to investigate but as figures from a hopelessly corrupt outside world intent on destroying their community. This was what was to happen with Jonestown – with catastrophic results. When concerned relatives of cult members contacted the government about what was happening, the Californian Congressman Leo Ryan was despatched to Guyana to investigate and interview its inhabitants. On the first day of his visit in November 1978, cult members threatened Ryan, prompting him to cut short his trip and return immediately to the US with those who wanted to leave. As they were about to depart, Ryan's party came under fire from Jones' guards. When the shooting stopped, Ryan and four other members lay dead; ten had also been wounded. Some of the party managed to escape. On hearing about the murders, Jones told his followers that it would now be impossible for them to continue. Rather than stand trial in America, however, members of the People's Temple would keep the integrity of their church intact by committing 'revolutionary suicide'. This is where the vat of Flavor-aid laced with cyanide came in.

As Catherine Wessinger has brilliantly shown, the millennium can often come violently for those prepared to defend their right to worship freely.[13] This was what happened when a gung-ho squad from the Bureau of Alcohol, Tobacco and Firearms attempted to serve a warrant to the Branch Davidians based at Waco, Texas in February 1993. Serving a warrant became a military-style assault. Their violence simply triggered off a corresponding violence in the Davidians. At the end of the initial fire-fight, four agents from the Bureau lay dead along with five members of the community. The tragedy was all played out on primetime American television, thanks to the Bureau who wanted some good publicity and so therefore arranged for the television cameras to be present.

Who shot first was hotly contested. The subsequent siege lasted fifty-one days and was finally lifted by the FBI with the help of tanks and vast quantities of CS gas. In the *mêlée* a fireball engulfed the Mount Carmel compound (who started it was another bone of contention). What is certain, however, is that on the final day of the siege eighty-five Branch Davidians perished, twenty-five of whom were children.

Like the People's Temple, the Branch Davidians of Waco were presented in the media as a sinister, aberrant 'cult'. The press did their best to demonize, dehumanize and trivialize them in equal measure. They were perceived as weird and 'wacko'. The leader of the church, David Koresh – a bearded and bespectacled individual – was labelled the 'Sinful Messiah'. It was claimed wrongly that this meant he believed he was Christ. Lurid stories about sexual deviancy emerged. Didn't he have numerous children by numerous 'wives'? Wasn't wife number one only fourteen years of age when he married her? Weren't allegations of child sex abuse made against him?

The media onslaught was remorseless. Phrases like 'barricaded religious cult', 'compound' and 'bunker' conjured up images of a war of attrition.[14] In such a scenario, the enemy

was a cult which represented everything that was anathema to
the Clinton administration – religiously inspired irrationality
and fanaticism. When Mount Carmel finally went up in flames
and all those men, women and children perished they had
ceased to be entirely human. They were cultists, 'wackos', the
'Other'. Their leader was mad and bad, a conman, a poly-
gamist, a man who had under-age sex with females. Finally, he
had persuaded the other cult members to make the ultimate
sacrifice and kill themselves.[15]

An important award-winning documentary about the
Waco tragedy redresses the balance.[16] According to James
Tabor, a religious scholar who appears in the documentary,
the key to the tragedy was the authorities' failure to understand the nature of the group's apocalyptic faith. Consistently
derided as 'bible-babble', their beliefs were never given ser-
ious consideration in determining how they would react in
the event of an armed assault. Instead, tactical issues came to
dominate discussion. In the end, the language of conciliation
gave way to confrontation and the apocalyptic ending to the
siege – a great ball of fire engulfed the compound when the
FBI stormed it – became a self-fulfilling prophecy. The Mount
Carmel centre became 'Ranch Apocalypse' just as Koresh had
predicted. Details of the kind of psychological warfare the
authorities waged on the community are truly shocking. They
include federal agents mooning at Davidian women, shining
bright lights into the compound at night, and playing Nancy
Sinatra's 'These Boots were Made for Walking' at full volume. For some reason, the Bureau even found fit to play the
sound of rabbits being slaughtered as part of their psychological warfare.

Such pressure tactics simply convinced Koresh that the forces
of Babylon had arrived. It was this apocalyptic script, and not

the FBI's one, that the Davidians were following. They cast themselves in the role of the martyrs besieged by the forces of evil. When God spoke to Koresh, telling him not to give himself and his followers up because he had to write down his predictions about the Seven Seals, then that was the authority he was compelled to follow. Only when he had fulfilled his divinely appointed task would he attend to the less important secular authorities.

James Tabor's description of Koresh's leading role in the apocalyptic drama is particularly noteworthy:

> What he essentially claimed was not to be God or not to be Jesus Christ. The Davidians believe that Jesus Christ is in heaven and they are Christian in the broad sense. But he claimed to be a final Christ figure, an anointed one, where Christ really doesn't refer just to Jesus but it means someone that is chosen, or sent or anointed, he claimed to be that final one that is mentioned in the *Book of Revelation*, the seventh messenger, the final messenger that is to come.[17]

For Tabor, Koresh's beliefs were not bunkum but actually theologically founded. One of the most notorious appellations applied to Koresh was that of the 'Sinful Messiah'. Lurid revelations about the sexual arrangements of the Branch Davidians filled the newspapers (allegations about sexual immorality and cult members go back to the time of Montanus). In 1984, Koresh had legally married Rachel Jones, who was fourteen at the time. Then in 1989, Koresh presented a 'New Light' teaching that all the male members of Mount Carmel, except himself, should be celibate. Women already married to other men were from now on to become his 'wives'. For the popular press such polygamous arrangements were simply a cover for Koresh to indulge his debased sexual appetites. Then there was the fact that he was having sex with female minors albeit with their parents' consent.

Koresh's actual theological beliefs were buried beneath a welter of lurid press headlines and stories. Community members handed over their wives and daughters to Koresh in the belief that he, the Lamb and the messiah, would implant his 'seed' in selected wives and produce a new lineage of twenty-four future rulers in God's kingdom after the End of the World. In contravening conventional sexual morality, therefore, the community members were doing God's work. In their eyes, this was not 'sinful' in the way in which the media used that word. What was sinful in their eyes was feeding children a diet of junk food and television. This was the world that was in thrall to Babylon. Koresh's children, on the other hand, would be pure and form the seedbed from which the new Eden would grow. This was the gift he was offering to a sinful and corrupted world. In the film, James Tabor claims that Koresh himself would have interpreted this notion of the Sinful Messiah in a similarly theological way. He reminds us that throughout the Hebrew Scriptures, but particularly in the *Book of Isaiah* and many of the *Psalms*, there are references to a Sinful Messiah.

If like Koresh you believe in the literal truth of such a prediction because it is in the Bible, then, it is an easy step to start looking around for such a figure. For Koresh, the point about the Sinful Messiah figure is that he will be recognizably human with easily identifiable frailties and the like. Koresh cast himself as this figure not because he was some latter-day antinominian. He did not go out to deliberately sin like the Ranters of seventeenth-century England because he thought he was in a state of grace. Instead, he believed that the final chosen one would be different from his messianic forebears because of his very humanness. Unlike the one-and-only Messiah, the embodiment of perfection, the messiah of the final days would be all too human. Like David Koresh, he might drink beer, succumb to sexual temptation, be semi-literate or wear dodgy spectacles. In fact, he might be so like the real-life David Koresh that it was only logical to assume that he *was* David Koresh. Paradoxically, Koresh's very imperfections equipped him to fulfil the role of this new type of messiah.

David Koresh's original name was Vernon Howell. How this former rock guitarist from a broken home came to re-invent himself as the Waco Messiah is a fascinating and convoluted story. It begins decades before his birth in 1959 when a splinter group from the Seventh-Day Adventists came into existence, splintered again and then mutated and developed into the Branch Davidians. Originally known as 'The Shepherd's Rod', the movement was founded in 1929 by Victor Houteff, a Bulgarian immigrant and a former Seventh-Day Adventist. Houteff believed that God had once again visited his people with a living prophet and he was that figure. He established the Mount Carmel centre at Waco in 1935 and moved his followers there from southern California. The *Book of Revelation* and its cryptic Seven Seals in Chapter 5 were their focus. Christians generally believe the Seals tell God's planned sequence of events leading to Judgement Day, and that their true meaning can be explained only by the Lamb of God, a Messiah who'll come during the Last Days.

When Victor Houteff died in 1955, he left behind a bitterly disappointed congregation. Here was someone they had come to regard as the new Elijah who would 'help usher in the reign of God'. He had died with his prophetic claims unfulfilled. Disconfirmation led to apostasy and splintering. What was needed was a new apocalyptic prophecy to galvanize support and cement group solidarity. Houteff's wife, Florence, assumed leadership of the movement and took up the prophetic mantle. She predicted that the End would come four years after the death of her husband. The date 22 April 1959 was set for Armageddon. With America in the grip of a Cold War psychosis, end-of-the-worldism was very much in the air. Florence's prophecy was based on reading the signs and interpreting the figures from *Revelation* 11. In mid-April, hundreds of followers began to assemble at Mount Carmel in preparation to move to the Holy Land. When the appointed day passed without incident, the disappointment was intense. This was the Davidian equivalent of the Millerite Great Disappointment. The Davidian Church almost disappeared after that. What kept it alive were Ben and Lois Roden who purchased Mount Carmel. Like Houteff, both saw themselves as prophets (Lois claimed she had received a message from God to say that the Holy Spirit was female).

After her husband died, Lois led the Davidians. It was she who was to tutor a young Vernon Howell as her understudy after he joined the group in 1981. It was rumoured that she and Koresh had an affair in spite of an age gap of more than forty years. Certainly it was the interloper Howell and not George her biological son who was to get her blessing as the group's next prophet. Not surprisingly, George had other ideas. Dubbed the 'Mad Man of Waco', George became embroiled in a violent leadership conflict between Howell and himself, claiming he was the next prophet. In 1984, he succeeded in chasing off Howell and his followers at gunpoint from Mount Carmel. At this point, Vernon Howell could simply have disappeared without trace and the world would never have heard of him or the person he was later to become – David Koresh. Instead, Howell took his splinter group off to Palestine, Texas, where they regrouped and lived in buses and tents like the Israelites in exile.

Howell bided his time and waited for an opportunity to re-enter the Promised Land. Late in 1987, he and seven of his male followers turned up at Mount Carmel in camouflage and heavily armed. The ensuing Gunfight at the OK Carmel left George Roden with chest and hand wounds. Howell and his followers were charged with attempted murder. At the trial, Howell testified that he went to Mount Carmel to uncover evidence that George Roden had been attempting to resurrect a dead body. They had gone armed, Howell claimed, because of the manner in which Roden had expelled him at gunpoint from Mount Carmel originally. Howell's followers were acquitted, and in Howell's case a mistrial was declared. When Roden was later committed to a mental institution in an unrelated murder conviction, Howell finally became undisputed leader of the Branch Davidians at Mount Carmel. The way was now clear for him to assume his prophetic mantle. In 1990, during a pilgrimage to Israel, Howell received a message from God proclaiming him to be the contemporary Cyrus, the ancient Persian king who had liberated the Israelites from the Babylonian yoke and had thus been proclaimed a messiah. (Koresh is the Hebrew equivalent for Cyrus.) The first name David was in honour of the Hebrew King David, another messiah figure. David Koresh's messianic pretensions were there for all to see. They were inscribed into his very name. Vernon Howell, the high school underachiever and drifter, was no more. In his place was David Koresh, the anointed one who would help usher in the final days.

The events leading up to the FBI attack on the compound are chronicled in great detail in *Waco: The Rules of Engagement*. They provide a fascinating case study of what happens when a powerful secular authority like the FBI and a religious group claiming divine authority go head to head. The combined effect is to suggest that the Branch Davidians were not a cult but a valid religious group practising under First Amendment freedoms. Koresh was busily at work writing his prediction about the Seven Seals when the FBI led its assault on the morning of 19

April. In the film, the Branch Davidians are very much seen as victims: firstly there was the utterly inept ATF raid, then a media campaign of vilification, followed by an unbelievably crass FBI campaign of psychological warfare. Finally, there was the tank and CS gas assault which caused the conflagration and the deaths of so many, followed by a cover-up.

But the tragedy did not just end with the fireball engulfing Mount Carmel. Two years later to the day, a clean-cut young man drove a Ryder rental truck up to a parking area outside the Alfred P. Murrah Building in Oklahoma City. It was packed with four thousand pounds of explosive. At 9:02, the deadly cargo blasted the government building with enough force to devastate one-third of the seven-storey building. One hundred and sixty-eight lives were snuffed out in an instant. A children's day centre was part of the government building, providing an iconic picture – the body of a little girl being held in the arms of a fireman. Just as at Waco, there had been a Massacre of the Innocents. For the bomber, Timothy McVeigh, this was pay-back day for Waco. For him, the earlier tragedy was not so much about religious freedom as the right to bear arms. It emerged that one of McVeigh's favourite books was *The Turner Diaries* written by former American Nazi Party leader William L. Pierce, under the pen name Andrew Macdonald. Its hero – Earl Turner – responds to gun control by making a truck bomb and blowing up the Washington FBI Building.

*

With the passing of the Cold War, the threat of a Soviet invasion of Israel has been replaced with a new fear. In the early 1990s, the Middle East was still at the centre of Arma-geddon theology due to the emergence of Saddam Hussein on the international stage. A great admirer of King Nebuchad-nezzar, his plans to rebuild the lost city of ancient Babylon stirred many prophecy believers into life (the Bible says Babylon will be rebuilt in the Last Days and live again as 'the seat of Satan'). It would then be destroyed as foretold in the *Book of Revelation*. Some interpreted Saddam's rebuilding of a New Babylon, therefore, as the fulfilment of Bible prophecy. But Saddam was not content with just being a brutal dictator at home, spending his people's money on grandiose monuments to himself and his ancient forebears. He also had expansionist ambitions. His invasion of Kuwait led to the first Persian Gulf War of 1991 and a welter of end-time prophecies. This brought him to the absolute forefront of the international stage and made him a household name around the world.

For prophecy believers, his advent was a godsend. Apocalyptic thought needs enemies in order to uphold its rigidly dualistic scheme of things. Saddam fitted the bill perfectly as America's Number One Enemy. He was cast as the 'Destroyer' spoken of in *Revelation* 9:11. The 1990–1 conflict represented a major paradigm shift in American prophecy. Rather than the Soviet Union being the leading force in the attempted annihilation of Israel, it was now a Saddam Hussein-led Iraq. The dramatic news coverage of the first Persian Gulf War – burning oil fields and seas of crude oil and the annihilation of Saddam's fleeing army on the road to Basra – rekindled the fires of apocalyptic speculation. Charles Dyer's 1991 book, *The Rise of Babylon: Signs of the End Times*, featured Saddam on the cover and sold several hundred thousand copies.

For Americans, it was not just the Scud missiles raining down on Tel Aviv that kept Israel at the forefront of apocalyptic speculation. Messianic Jews living in Jerusalem kept American Evangelicals in a frenzy of apocalyptic expectation. As the second millennium loomed ever closer, the Temple Mount in Jerusalem became the focus of intense apocalyptic speculation. The Babylonians had destroyed the First Temple, the Romans the second; with the building of the Third, messianic Jews in Israel and Christian Evangelicals in America believe that the last piece in God's apocalyptic scheme will fall into place. In May 1989, blueprints for building the Temple upon the site of the Dome of the Rock were completed. Short of bombing Mecca, it is hard to imagine a more inflammatory action for the 1.2 billion people that make up the world's Muslim population. Nevertheless, in the last decades of the twentieth century, organizations such as The Temple Institute in Jerusalem found allies in so-called Christian Zionists in America. For them, Israel occupies a central place in 'God's Time-piece'. The establishment of the state of Israel in 1948, the capture of Jerusalem in the Arab–Israeli war of 1967 and the building of the Third Temple is seen as the modern ingathering of the Jewish people. This is believed to be in accordance with biblical prophecy and is a precondition for the return of Jesus to reign on earth. In their reading of the *Book of Daniel* and *Revelation*, many Christian Evangelicals in America cast Antichrist as either being a Jew or a European gentile who will be a world leader. He will strike a peace deal with Israel, only then to make war on it and kill millions in the time of Tribulation. It is left up to Jesus to rescue the remnant. Those Jews who survive see the error of their ways, convert to Christianity and live happily ever after.

In the late 1990s, this convergence of Jewish and Christian apocalyptic traditions was given a tremendous boost by a publishing phenomenon – the tremendous success of the *Left Behind* series. There are twelve books in the series – the last one was published in 2002 – charting the adventures of the 'Tribulation Force' as they do battle with the forces of the Antichrist in the days after the Rapture (the 'left behind' refers to those not sufficiently blessed to be raptured). Co-authored by Timothy LaHaye and Jerry B. Jenkins, the sixth book in the series, *Assassins: Assignment: Jerusalem, Target: Antichrist*, fictionalizes the end-time scenario of Christian Zionists. In LaHaye's view the Antichrist will be of European gentile extraction. He is fictionalized as the Romanian Nicolae Carpathia, former secretary-general of the United Nations and now the self-appointed Global Community Potentate who resides in the GC palace, New Babylon. In *Assassins*, it is up to a small band of rebels, 'Tribulation Force', to expose this figure as Antichrist and dethrone him.

The phenomenal popularity of the *Left Behind* series is a reflection of the apocalyptic yearnings of many Americans. As the millennium clock started ticking down in the mid-1990s, their sales soared. The $3-billion-a-year Christian book industry shows that there is a profit to be made out of prophecy. Apocalyptic literature is the fastest growing part of this publishing sector. Number seven in the series, *The Indwelling Beast* (2001), was number one in the *New York Times'* bestseller list for four weeks. The way in which the seven-year period of the Tribulation is broken up guarantees repeat business. If you want to find out about the last year of the Tribulation, then you are going to have to buy *Armageddon: The Cosmic Battle of the Ages*, number eleven in the series. There you can read about how all the armies of the world gather in the Middle East to do final battle. If you then want to find out how Nicolae Carpathia is eventually defeated and how Jesus ushers in a new millennium of peace and righteousness, you'll need to buy the final instalment, *Glorious Appearing* (2004).

In this concluding novel to the series, the notion of the vengeful Messiah takes on a whole new meaning. The Lord only has to speak and the blood of the unbelievers – liberals, secularists, unconverted Jews and those that have not been born again – boils up and bursts through their skin and veins. Soon LaHaye's and Jenkins' Warrior King is laying low the vast armies of the Antichrist in a manner redolent of the goriest multiplex horror schlock: their internal organs ooze out, explosive geysers of blood from vast pools.[18] The blood of billions issues in a vast river, the antitype of the river of life in *Revelation*, and overflows the Holy Lands.

The success of the Christian Right has not only been in shifting vast amounts of apocalyptic novels. Since the 1970s, the Christian Right has enlisted the support of politicians in its cultural war with the secular world. Falwell's Moral Majority played an important role in electing Ronald Reagan president in 1980. In the mid-1980s LaHaye's American Coalition for Traditional Values helped to get him re-elected. Under George W. Bush another right-wing group, the Council for National Policy (CNP) has enjoyed access to the Oval Office. Indeed the Church Age has really come to fruition with the inauguration of the 43rd President of the United States. George W. Bush is the latest in a line of recent Republican presidents who routinely invoke God in a political context. What distinguishes him though from Reagan and his father is the openness with which he discusses his evangelical faith.

The incursion of faith-based concepts and language into the political sphere was particularly marked in the wake of 9/11. The whole discourse was imbued with a strong apocalyptic flavour. The administration echoed and amplified such sentiments. When the then Attorney-General, John Ashcroft, a devout Pentecostal Christian, addressed the National Association of Religious Broadcasters he spoke about the United States as God's chosen nation, engaged in an apocalyptic struggle with the forces of evil. In an interview with Barbara Victor in October 2003 he spoke of how America's suffering was the fulfilment of biblical prophecy. 'It says so right in the *Book of Revelation*', Ashcroft said, 'that the agony we endure is part of the birth pains of the coming Messiah.'[19] In such a catastrophic world-view, all social action to alleviate suffering becomes irrelevant. Believers cultivate an extreme passivism as they await a supernatural solution to the world's problems.

For many Evangelicals, America's domestic social, moral and ethical problems are part of an ongoing global battle between the forces of goodness and the forces of evil. Such a view was revealed in the wake of 9/11. Two days after the atrocity, the Rev. Jerry Falwell and Pat Robertson were in conversation on *The 700 Club*, a live television programme broadcast on Robertson's Christian Broadcasting Network. Falwell made the following statement in which he viewed the attacks as God's judgement on America:

> I really believe that the pagans, and the abortionists, and the feminists, and the gays and the lesbians who are actively trying to make that an alternative lifestyle, the ACLU, People For the American Way, all of them who have tried to secularize America. I point the finger in their face and say 'you helped this happen'.

Pat Robertson, host of the programme, seemed to agree with Falwell's earlier statements in a prayer during the programme. 'We have sinned against Almighty God, at the highest level of our government, we've stuck our finger in your eye', said Robertson. 'The Supreme Court has insulted you over and over again, Lord. They've taken your Bible away from the schools. They've forbidden little children to pray. They've taken the knowledge of God as best they can, and organizations have come into court to take the knowledge of God out of the public square of America.'[20]

The 1,776-feet-tall Freedom Tower, symbolizing the year of American independence, will replace the Twin Towers on the Manhattan skyline. When it is completed it will emit a beam of light from its spire. The symbolism is clear; this building will be another one of those beacons of light in a world enveloped in totalitarian darkness so beloved by American speech writers. Like Winthrop's City on the Hill, the Freedom Tower will become a symbolic locus, destined to bulk large in the speeches of future American presidents. At the present moment, however, American forces find themselves embroiled in a vicious guerrilla war in post-Saddam Iraq. The mission has most definitely not been fully accomplished. But this has not deterred Bush or clipped the wings of his apocalyptic rhetoric. He began his second presidential term on 20 January 2005 with an inauguration speech full of fiery metaphor as he made clear that the Afghan and Iraqi wars were part of a much broader mission. On the steps of the Capitol, he addressed thousands of the Republican faithful who had braved snow and severe wind chill to hear him. He whipped up a fire-storm of apocalyptic rhetoric designed to warm Republican spirits and put the rest of the world on notice: 'By our efforts, we have lit . . . a fire in the minds of men. It warms those who feel its power, it burns those who fight its progress, and one day this untamed fire of freedom will reach the darkest corners of our world.'

Bush portrayed a planet consumed by the struggle between liberty and tyranny in which the United States would not stand aside. Threats to the homeland could only be removed by striking at the source and promoting instead democratic movements and institutions. He also suggested that God had ordained the worldwide struggle against oppression. In exporting liberty, Americans would be upholding one of the key ideas enshrined in the United States constitution that all people have God-given rights. 'History', he said, 'has a visible direction set by liberty and the author of liberty.'[21] This was language familiar to latter day Evangelical Christians, as it would have been to the original Pilgrim Fathers of America. Just as Moses had been led to the Promised Land by a pillar of fire so too would their very own 'burning Bush' lead the American people, the chosen people, to their promised land. In such a scenario, America's national purpose reflected the divine purpose of God.

A good way of justifying America's mission abroad is to engender fear and paranoia at home. The 9/11 attacks demonstrated just how vulnerable the country was on the domestic front. To create a monstrous enemy abroad is a good way to bolster political support for governments at home. Under Reagan, the Soviet bloc served this purpose. It is a technique of course that has been used by religious leaders and sectarians to terrorize people into following their faith. 'Look at the evil forces ranged against you', our leaders warn, 'only we can save you.' During the Cold War, the politics of fear created a climate of collective paranoia. There were reds under every God-fearing American's bed. Now we are warned about sleeper cells, like malignant cancer cells, which threaten to break out in the body politic and do their worst. The only thing that can deliver us from such evil is an administration that is so closely in league with God. Fear therefore strengthens faith, both in God and in the Republican Party. After all, how can you possibly lose the war on terror when you have God or George on your side?

8

THE END OF THE WORLD
AS WE KNOW IT

The Judaeo-Christian notion of limited historical time, with a beginning, middle and an end, has been increasingly challenged by New Age beliefs. For New Agers, the world won't end with a climactic event like the one envisioned at the end of *Glorious Appearing*. They challenge such a diachronic notion of time and history in which events unfold along a lineal axis and travel towards an apocalyptic climax. In contrast, time is conceived in synchronic terms, as a vast cycle in which temporal categories such as past, present and future are dissolved. In the last decade or so, the battle between Christians and New Agers to win the hearts and minds of potential believers has been intense. Both sides have drawn up the battle lines in stark and uncompromising terms.

Whereas Christian Evangelicals seek to close the world in their prophetic system, New Agers battle completedness in order to keep the world open for new forms of becoming. In such a view, the new millennium is not the terminal phase of some divinely instituted time-line but the beginning of the Age of Aquarius in which the *illuminati* will achieve self-actualization and finally evolve towards a unity of consciousness. Instead of churches or mosques preaching dogmatic, monotheistic faith, New Agers see themselves as part of a vast global network, knitted together by a faith with many different strands to it but united by a common purpose – to prepare the world for a New World Order founded on peace, economic sharing and universal love. This will be accomplished primarily through the leadership of 'the Christ' (also known as 'Lord Maitreya'), who will supposedly come to teach us how to live in peace with each other. To enter the New Age, an individual has to take the 'Luciferic Initiation', a kind of pledge of allegiance to the Christ of the New Age and to the New World Order. For those who fail to evolve, to make the journey from self-centred to whole-centred being, 'their souls will begin again within a different planetary system which will serve as kindergarten for the transition'.[1]

For their part, Christian Evangelicals regard such notions about the New World Order as satanic in origin, equivalent in their eyes to the one-world government prophesied in *Revelation* and *Daniel*. The evangelical website, *www.armageddonbooks.com*, sells videos and books with such titles as *Megiddo 11: The New Age* and *FINAL WARNING: A History of the New World Order*. Global adherents of New Ageism, we are warned, claim to await a 'universal Christ' to lead the world. 'What happens to those who will not follow this world leader?' the blurb writer asks darkly.[2] In the past, Jews and communists were believed to be conspiring to take over the world. Now it is the turn of New Agers to be cast as the latest incarnation of absolute evil.

In contrast, secularists and scientists point to the destruction of the biosphere as the great catastrophe of our age. Since the publication of Rachel Carson's groundbreaking *Silent Spring* in 1962, it is customary to speak about the destruction of the environment and war on nature in apocalyptic terms. It is human actions, not God's, which are key in such a world-view. James Lovelock's famous Gaia hypothesis posited the existence of a planetary body that is in some way alive. In *Gaia: The Practical Science of Planetary Medicine* the earth is seen to be sufficiently like a living organism to be laid out on the doctor's couch and given a systematic mid-life health check. Lovelock, the planetary physician, gives an alarming diagnosis and prognosis. In Chapter 8, memorably entitled 'The People Plague', he compares swarming humanity to behaving in some ways like a 'pathogenic micro-organism, or like the cells of a tumour or neoplasm'.[3] Our presence on earth is likened to invading disease organisms that might just lead to the destruction of the host.

Chernobyl illustrates how readily a single environmental catastrophe can be converted into apocalyptic mythmaking. On 26 April 1986 a nuclear reactor exploded at Chernobyl in the former Soviet Union, releasing far more radiation than was unleashed on Hiroshima. Radionuclides contaminated the surrounding land for miles around. The subsequent evacuation of towns, villages and farms created 'dead zones' which will be uninhabitable for many centuries to come.

Around this modern man-made disaster an ancient apocalyptic tale has been spun. In the West, it was widely reported that 'Chernobyl' in the Ukrainian language is the name of a type of grass that was translated (controversially) as 'wormwood'. Apocalyptic groups were quick to point out that in *Revelation* 8:10–11, Wormwood is the star that was cast into the earth when the third trumpet was sounded, making the waters bitter and killing those that drank from them. For prophecy believers, the nuclear cloud produced by Chernobyl is equivalent to the star in *Revelation*, a source of global contamination and a harbinger for the end of the world. As the cloud drifted over the Soviet Union and Europe, an extraordinarily large amount of rain fell, showering down radioactivity on to soil, trees, crops and animals and into the rivers. Some saw such events as the unfolding of *Revelation*'s end-time scenario.[4]

Twenty years on, the blighted wastes of Belarus and the Ukraine still haunt the imagination. The medical, environmental and cultural legacy of the world's worst-ever nuclear accident will be with us for many years. New generations of sick children continue to be born. But it is not only the radioactivity that has penetrated deep inside. What happened at Chernobyl has also entered the modern psyche. 'Meltdown', denoting any cataclysmic event, has now become part of the lexicon.

The destruction of our biosphere is now a major concern of most secular-minded people, particularly the young. In his 'Earth Song' (1995) Michael Jackson reflected the popular zeitgeist with his futurological musings about the fate of the planet. 'What about Us?', he asked, speaking on behalf of all future generations as the present-day one ransacked and raped the earth. The best-selling song was accompanied by a video in which Michael the Messiah was the central figure in an apocalyptic montage for the MTV generation. Deforestation was reversed, the dead resurrected and a tank propelled backwards.

This synergy between popular culture and catastrophism was particularly evident in the multiplexes. In the 1990s, a host of apocalyptic scenarios hit the screens: annihilation through asteroid, nuclear war and invading alien armies. A recent Hollywood blockbuster dealt with the prospect of cataclysmic climate change. Rock stars too have tapped into this rich vein of apocalyptic foreboding. Teenagers have always barricaded themselves in their rooms, listening to rock and pop. In the 1990s, Marilyn Manson's Goth-shock music, makeup and clothes, were the ultimate in counter-culture cool and one of the best ways to seriously annoy the parents. Like all the best heretics, Manson was brought up a believer. In his autobiography, he recalls the pounding hell-and-brimstone apocalyptic rhetoric of his Bible teachers.[5] Manson's songs bear the imprimatur of this early saturation in apocalyptic language and imagery. The lyrics of 'Antichrist Superstar' invert traditional end-time beliefs into Manson's own satanic version.

For Middle America, the Manson persona – a Bible-ripping self-mutilator – has turned him into the polestar of human evil. It was widely reported that the two trench-coat wearing misfits who carried out the Columbine massacre were devotees of Manson's satanic cult (it later emerged that they did not actually like his music). But, hey, when's the truth ever got in the way of a good story?

Amidst all these new fears and forebodings about the future of the planet, the old nuclear one remains ever present. During the Cold War era, the world was transfixed with terror by the prospect of an all-out thermonuclear exchange between the superpowers. With the collapse of the old Soviet Union, the immediate threat is not from one nation state but from nuclear 'mega-terrorism' – the prospect of some al-Qaeda-type group obtaining a nuclear weapon and detonating it in some western major city. This was the scenario of Tom Clancy's thriller *The Sum of Their Fears* which portrayed a Muslim group destroying a crowded football stadium by a 'broken arrow' – a nuclear device that had been 'lost' during the Yom Kippur War.

The threat of twisted individuals, terrorists groups or death-cults launching their own chemical and biological attacks is also a very real one. Certainly, they have the capability. In 1995, Aum Shinrikyo, an obscure Japanese doomsday cult, made headlines round the world when members released the nerve gas sarin on the Tokyo underground, killing thirteen and injuring hundreds. A series of raids on the cult's centres around Japan yielded stockpiles of chemicals and AK47 automatic rifles. In America, there were anthrax attacks days after 9/11, announcing the arrival of the bioterrorist on American soil. In his doom-laden book, *The Final Century*, the Cambridge scientist, Martin Rees, raises the spectre of a bioterrorist, using his own body as a weapon of mass destruction, a 'suicidal zealot . . . becom[ing] intentionally infected with smallpox and trigger[ing] an epidemic'.[6]

The new communications technologies have empowered isolated terrorist cells, enabling them to do their worst. The 9/11 hijackers used the Internet to communicate with each other and plan their attacks. Mobile phones were used to detonate the bombs on the Madrid commuter trains in 2004. The July 2005 London bombings focused a great deal of media attention on how militant Islamist groups have created a Virtual School of Terrorism in cyberspace. The 1999 Y2K computer scare demonstrated just how fearful our reliance on the new technology made us. The media was awash with stories about this supposed ticking global time bomb. Survivalists stockpiled supplies of freeze-dried food and hunkered down in their bunkers, waiting for computer chip meltdown. Some fundamentalists claimed that Y2K was all part of God's divine plan; as global economic chaos engulfed the world, Antichrist would take the opportunity to seize power, precipitating the end of the world.

Even presidents were not immune to incipient panic. In his

State of the Union speech of 19 January 1999, President
Clinton enjoined the nation to pull together so that the
computer bug 'will be remembered as the last headache of
the twentieth century, not the first crisis of the twenty-first'.[7]
There were even rumours that the Russian nuclear weapons
system was non-Y2K compliant. The members of the media
seemed to be vying with each other to scare us most.[8] In the
event, of course, the millennium did not arrive in darkness or
chaos as the clock rolled over into the year 2000.

Threats, real and imaginary, crowd out our collective imaginations. Whether you are a Jew, a Christian or a Muslim,
whether you subscribe to secularism or to one of the many
alternative new faiths springing up, the world appears to be in
the middle of a particularly dark and threatening period. This
is the end of the world as know it.

*

In these new end-times, a terrifying and dark cult has arisen –
that of the suicide bomber. Although suicide is expressly
forbidden in the Koran, extreme Islamists term those who
carry out such operations as 'martyrs' who will win a special
place in paradise.[9] The use of suicide bombers in the 9/11
attacks and the 7/7 London attacks represent a new phase in
this cult of death. Previous to them, suicide missions were
always something that happened elsewhere – in the Lebanon
of the 1980s and in present-day Israel. Now it was the turn of
Londoners and New Yorkers to be on the receiving end of
them. Members of the Hamburg cell responsible for the 9/11
attacks had shaved their beards and discarded their traditional
robes and deviated from strict Muslim practices in order to
blend in and avoid detection. Under this cloak of subterfuge
these Saudi and Egyptian outsiders had successfully infiltrated
American society. They had become what are known as

Takfiris. The militant Islamist, hell-bent on waging war on western infidels, did not do so from some cave in Afghanistan dressed in traditional robes and hat. Now he was more likely to be the guy next door, going about his ordinary humdrum life just like you and me. Such radicalized European Muslims have been dubbed 'Generation *Jihad*'.[10]

Much of the discourse surrounding the 'war on terror' has an end-of-the-world feel to it. Bush has characterized the conflict as being between the forces of good and the forces of evil in a metaphysical sense. An article in *Time* magazine noted that sales of the *Left Behind* series increased 60 per cent after the 9/11 attacks.[11] Extreme Islamists have a similarly dualistic take on the war – except, of course, it is they who are the good guys and America and its allies who are the bad. For them the world can be divided up between the world of Islam (*dar al-Islam*) and the land of conflict or war (*dar al-harb*). Although they represent only a fraction of the 1.2 billion Muslims worldwide these extremists regard *jihad* in its violent and militaristic terms as part of a millennial mission. Men like bin Laden and his deputy Ayman al-Zawahiri, the former Egyptian doctor, wish to extend the frontiers of the Muslim world so that it resembles the Great Caliphate. At its height, this ranged across continents: from Europe to Africa, from the Middle East to India. For them, it is not enough for the Americans and other western infidels to simply get out of the Holy Lands of Islam and leave Iraq and its oil alone. They see the conflict as a Holy War between Muslims and non-Muslims, between the forces of absolute good (the house of Islam) and the forces of absolute evil (the house of war).

Through violence against the secular materialistic West, bin Laden and his al-Qaeda operatives want to establish an Islamic utopia on earth which will be ruled under one leader, the *caliph*. He will be the commander of the faithful, whose words will go forth and influence Muslims worldwide and help propagate the faith so that eventually all humanity will accept Allah as its God. The term currently being used by European academics to refer to these revolutionaries is Salafist *jihadists*.

The former Egyptian militant, Ayman al-Zawahiri, is now very much the ideologue of al-Qaeda. After the London bombings of July 2005, al-Zawahiri appeared on video to comment on the events and warn Britain that it could expect more of the same. The media image had been carefully orchestrated and choreographed. Whereas bin Laden wears camouflage jacket for his global television appearances, al-Zawahiri opted for long white robes and a black turban similar to the ones worn by the Taliban. A gun with a grenade launcher fixed to its barrel stood to his side. The iconography was precisely calculated. He was the warrior-cleric calling the faithful to Holy War. Wagging his finger at the camera, he delivered a chilling message as to what the 'people of the crusader coalition' could expect. Having failed to accept bin Laden's 'truce' – the withdrawal of their 'infidel armies' from Iraq and Muslim lands – they were now going to reap the apocalyptic whirlwind. In this media war such utterances become acts of violence. Words are verbal bombs detonated for their propaganda value:

> Instead [of accepting the truce], you spilled blood like rivers in our countries and we exploded the volcanoes of wrath in your countries.

> Our message is clear, strong, and final: there will be no salvation until you withdraw from our land, stop stealing our oil and resources, and end support for infidel [Arab] rulers.[12]

Previously it was the camera-loving bin Laden who was very much the face of al-Qaeda. It was his image that appeared on headscarves and T-shirts in Kuala Lumpur, the Gaza Strip and the *banlieues* of Paris. With the 7/7 video, Al-Zawahiri launched himself as a key player in this media war. After the Afghanistan war when al-Qaeda had its infrastructure and training camps destroyed, it no longer existed as a fully functioning operational entity. Instead, it exists primarily as an idea. In its place has come the 'new al-Qaeda', groups of radicalized Muslims scattered worldwide who answer to bin Laden's call for the global nation of Islam to rise up and wage war against the West.

In the different cyber-communities, bin Laden has been recast as both saviour and demon. The London-based Islamic website www.muhajiroun celebrates 9/11 and its perpetrators as an act of divinely inspired violence. In this apocalyptic Muslim view, bin Laden is taking the battle to the West and using its superior technology to destroy it. In contrast, the figure of Osama the Antichrist also looms large on the Internet. Tap in 'Osama bin Laden Antichrist' on *Google* and you get over 51,000 listings. One site notes that the 'Angel of the Bottomless' appears in Chapter 9 verse 11 of the *Book of Revelation*. The inference is clear: the terrorist mastermind is this 'dark angel . . . demon . . . who was responsible for the 9 11 2001 terrorist attacks on the US'. The writer goes on to note that the names in *Revelation* 9:11 translate as 'the destroyer'. There can be only one candidate for this satanic sobriquet: bin Laden had a degree in construction engineering but chose instead to go into the demolition business, becoming 'The Destroyer'.[13] For his supporters, bin Laden is a hero, redolent of Saladin who repelled the western crusaders all those centuries ago. Others cast him as the Mahdi, the rightly guided *caliph* who, it is predicted, will appear and bring about the last days of the world and the Muslim millennium – the 'Day of Islam' when the whole world, believers and non-believers alike, will bow down in front of the throne of Allah.

The Internet has proved an invaluable tool for both sides in this ideological war of words. It is a great progenitor of propagandist myths for those who want either to demonize bin Laden or hail him as the saviour of the Muslim world. One such cyber-myth involved 9/11 and Nostradamus. Within hours of the Twin Towers toppling, the first e-mail containing what purported to be one of Nostradamus' predictions was circulating:

> In the City of God there will be a great thunder,
> Two brothers torn apart by Chaos,
> While the fortress endures,
> The great leader will succumb.

Devotees of the famous prophet form cyber-communities dedicated to proving that every cryptic utterance he ever made was uniquely predictive of actual historical events such as the Great Fire of London, the rise of Hitler, the Iranian revolution in 1979 and the death of Princess Diana. So what was stopping this prophet of mass destruction from predicting what the American security forces had so signally failed to predict – the destruction of the World Trade Center? When more of what were supposed to be Nostradamus' prophecies appeared on the web there was a massive resurgence of interest in him. Sales of his books entered the bestseller list on the online retailer site Amazon.com.[14] His name entered the top fifty of the most popular search words on the Internet.

There was only one problem. The prophecy quoted above was not actually written by Nostradamus. In fact, the text originated on a web page with the title 'A Critical Analysis of Nostradamus', written several years earlier by a student named Neil Marshall.[15] Marshall made up the quatrain to demonstrate how Nostradamus' writings were so cryptic and impenetrable that they could be used to 'predict' almost anything. Marshall's debunking of Nostradamus proved supremely ironic. His own piece of cod Nostradamus ended up being used to convince people that the French soothsayer had predicted the events of 9/11.

Recent writers on Nostradamus have focused on the prophecies which suggest that an Islamic invasion of Europe is in the offing. Certainly there are many reasons why Nostradamus himself should have feared such a prospect. The spectacular advances of the Ottomans in the East engendered doom and gloom throughout Western Europe. Nostradamus' *Prophéties* are permeated with such a fear. Writing before 9/11, Peter Lemesurier argues that such an invasion scenario is particularly relevant to our times and that we should heed the French prophet before it is too late.[16]

Not that we need Nostradamus to fear al-Qaeda. From the very outset, when western journalists first started interviewing him, bin Laden's message has been brazenly apocalyptic. In May 1998, a little more than two months before the bombings in Tanzania and Kenya, bin Laden gave an interview to ABC's John Miller in which he revealed the Armageddon-style conflict he envisaged with the West:

> We are certain that we shall – with the grace of Allah – prevail over the Americans and over the Jews, as the Messenger of Allah promised us in an authentic prophetic tradition when He said the Hour of Resurrection shall not come before Muslims fight Jews and before Jews hide behind trees and behind rocks . . . We anticipate a black future for America. Instead of remaining United States, it shall end up separated

states and shall have to carry the bodies of its sons back to America.[17]

Some three years and four months later, bin Laden fulfilled his dire threat to America. Suicide terrorists crashed three hijacked American airliners into New York's Word Trade Center towers and the Pentagon in Washington, killing close to three thousand. It was the worst terrorist attack against the United States in its history. The iconography of the event had been precisely calculated for maximum propaganda effect. For Islamists like the architect Mohamed Atta, who piloted the first plane into the WTC, modernist architecture symbolized a satanic world order presided over by Uncle Sam. For him, the increasing number of high-rises in his native Cairo reflected encroaching western control. The source of that control was New York, a centre of architectural modernism and a global Jewish conspiracy designed to infiltrate and destroy Muslim society. Bin Laden had similar views. Three months after 9/11 he referred to them as 'the blessed strikes against world infidelity and the head of infidelity, namely America'.[18]

Global television coverage elided the gap between reality and representation as it became the greatest media event of the new century. When the first plane struck the world's media was taken unawares; when the second struck thousands of cameras were trained on the Twin Towers to capture the moment when a commercial airliner, used as a guided missile, impacted. The ensuing fireball seemed more cinematic fantasy than reality. In 1998, cinema audiences had seen New York been hit by a meteor shower in the asteroid-disaster movie, *Armageddon*, starring Bruce Willis. Along with the Chrysler Building, one of the Twin Towers is destroyed. The events of 9/11 lent an eerie prophetic quality to such scenes.

Political and cultural commentators were quick to inscribe 9/11 with metaphysical meaning. Edward Said saw the attack in explicitly apocalyptic terms; it was an act which 'transcended the political and moved into the metaphysical. There was a kind of cosmic, demonic quality of mind here . . . It was a leap into another realm'.[19] The devastated area was termed 'Ground Zero', a phrase which seems to have been first used at the start of the atomic age with Hiroshima.[20] There were images of shards of rectilinear steel frame, still standing defiantly, swathed in smoke. From ground level in New Jersey came stunning images of the iconic Lower Manhattan skyline ablaze. From above, images of fighter planes patrolling the Manhattan air space the day after the attack, smoke still ascending stratospherically. From outer space came weirdly beautiful geometric images of the Pentagon, blackened on one side.

In the days following the attacks, American news magazines rushed out special editions with unforgettable images on their covers. *Time* magazine's had the first of the great fireballs to engulf the Towers. *Newsweek*'s featured firefighters raising the Stars and Stripes amidst the rubble under the headline 'God Save America'.[21] It was an image which recalled Joe Rosenthal's iconic photograph, 'Flag Raising on Iwo Jima'. The image later appeared on commemorative wall posters or fine art prints ('Ground Zero', 'Home of the Brave'). Two weeks after the attacks major news magazines in the US switched the focus of their attention to the alleged perpetrator of them – Osama bin Laden. His face was on all the covers which included such headlines as 'Trail of Terror' (*Newsweek*), 'Terror Inc.' (*U.S. News*), 'Target: Bin Laden' (*Time*). From being an obscure Saudi dissident, bin Laden had become a global terrorist superstar, America's 'Most Wanted' with a bounty of $25 million on his head, the evil mastermind behind a global network of terror.

As noted earlier, a week after 9/11 came the anthrax attacks. Beginning on 18 September and carrying on for several weeks, bio-terrorists sifted anthrax spores into four envelopes and mailed them. After the trauma of 9/11, this terriorst outrage allowed President Bush to up the ante in the war on terror. In the midst of the Afghan war, Bush raised the bone-chilling prospect of bin Laden's arsenal: 'They're seeking chemical, biological and nuclear weapons,' he said. 'Given the means, our enemies would be a threat to every nation; and, eventually, to civilization itself. So, we're determined to fight this evil and fight until we are rid of it. We will not wait for more innocent deaths.'[22]

There's a great deal of talk now about how the 'new al-Qaeda' exists as a 'virtual' organization in cyberspace. The Internet is a fulcrum for the fomenting of a Holy War or *jihad* against the West. Home-grown *jihadists* in any major western city can read the official al-Qaeda training manual, discovered by British security forces in 2000, in which there are detailed and practical instructions about how to wage 'Holy War'. Written originally in Arabic, the manual has been translated into English and consists of eighteen chapters in which there is detailed and technical information and instruction about how to become a proficient terrorist. It's a kind of Open University-style correspondence course for terrorists. There is information about the use of timers and explosives, the mixing of poison, how to carry out urban killings and make a do-it-yourself suicide-bomber jacket. Mixed up with the technicalities of terror is the ideological material for anyone who aspires to join the exalted ranks of the *mujahideen* (holy warriors). The preface to the manual is a parade ground of rhetorical posturing:

> The confrontation that we are calling for . . . knows the dialogue of bullets, the ideals of assassination, bombing and destruction – the diplomacy of the cannon and machine gun.

Our main mission is the overthrow of the godless regimes and to force their replacement with an Islamic regime . . . The Al Qaeda member has to be willing to undergo martyrdom for the purpose of establishing the religion of majestic Allah on earth.[23]

Despite the best efforts of the security services in Britain and America to keep the document secret and close down any website that reveals its contents, this material has travelled the world through fibre optics. At the MI5 headquarters in London, special intelligence agents monitor Islamists' websites looking for the manual and other inflammatory material. The trans-national nature of the Internet, however, makes it virtually impossible to police. Material sent down the information superhighway travels at extraordinary speed. It can be copied, repackaged and launched into cyberspace in a matter of seconds. As one website with one particular name is closed down it simply re-appears somewhere else with another name. Information can be posted anonymously by webmasters hiding behind the anonymity the Internet affords them. In Britain, young Muslims can watch the latest execution or suicide-bombing video from Iraq in the privacy of their homes or catch up with the latest propaganda from militant Islamists in Algeria, Afghanistan, Egypt and Chechnya. Internet chatrooms can provide a way to recruit and radicalize them to the cause. For the new 'virtual' al-Qaeda, websites, email or instant messaging provides unparalleled communication and marketing opportunities.

But it is not only terrorists who are alive to the potential of the Internet to act as a recruiting sergeant. In the 1990s, hundreds of millennial cults started using the Net to propagate their beliefs and win new converts. Tap in 'Apocalypse' on *Google* and you get over two million entries; 'Armageddon' yields a similarly high number. The extent to which the Internet can be used to propagate an apocalyptic message was vividly illustrated in 1997 when thirty-nine members of a cult known as Heaven's Gate committed suicide in a San Diego mansion. The UFO cult was founded by Marshall Herff Applewhite (spiritual name 'Do') and Bonnie Lu Trusdale Nettles ('Ti'). Collectively they were known as 'The Two', a reference to the story in *Revelation* which describes how two witnesses who are killed, remained dead for three and a half days, and were then revived and taken up into the clouds. Blending such traditional apocalyptic material with alien-abduction lore and New Age mysticism, 'The Two' came up with their own truly bizarre blend of belief.

The cult captured news headlines around the world when they sensationally announced their group suicide on the Internet. 'Hale–Bopp brings closure to Heaven's Gate' was the simple message on their home page. Cult members believed that a flying saucer was flying behind the Hale–Bopp comet, populated by extraterrestrials from the 'Level Above Human'. In order to join them and thus find redemption, they 'exited' their bodies, which they referred to as 'vehicles', by downing a cocktail of drugs and alcohol and suffocating each other with plastic bags. Of course the home page did not quite put it like that. There the horror of what happened is shrouded in euphemisms and cult mumbo-jumbo: 'Our 22 years of classroom here on planet Earth', it chirpily announces, 'is finally coming to conclusion – "graduation" from the Human Evolutionary Level. We are happily prepared to leave "this world" and go with Ti's crew.' Even when they were announcing their deaths, cult members were still on the look-out for new recruits. Readers of the home page are given one last chance to be beamed up to the Starship Enterprise: 'You may even find your "boarding pass" to leave with us during this brief "window".'[24]

When further details about Heaven's Gate emerged in the press – cult members wore unisex garments; they were required to commit themselves to celibacy and be totally cut off from the outside world; some members voluntarily submitted to castration; they committed suicide in purple shrouds; they were obsessed by *Star Trek* – it seemed like everyone's worst nightmare about cults and cult members had been realized. The fact that such bizarre and disturbing behaviour was linked to the Internet made the new technology a source of suspicion and fear. A collective paranoia seized America about the dangers of surfing the net. Cult fanatics displaced pornographers as the most reviled figures in cyberspace.

*

The power of the media to shape and influence our perceptions of what happens was borne out in 1987, the year of the great AIDS scare. Like all deadly infectious diseases such as the bubonic plague, tuberculosis and SARS, AIDS is more than its biological components. The way in which we speak and write about such diseases reflects the way in which they are part of a larger social and cultural discourse. Mediated through language and the visual image, diseases reflect the prevailing concerns and pressures of the society in which they break out. The year 1987 was the one in which a terrifying new disease took on the character of a 'plague' which, it was feared, would lay low vast swathes of western society. In that year, Princess Diana shook the hand of an AIDS patient without wearing gloves, twenty-three million households in Britain received leaflets about AIDS and an advertising campaign with the slogan 'Don't Die of Ignorance' hit our television screens with exploding volcanoes and the like. On the other side of the globe, in Australia, a similarly apocalyptic note was struck. The Grim Reaper education campaign was launched. Graphic television images of Death mowing down a range of victims in a bowling alley were broadcast. It was also the year when stories about 'Patient Zero' – supposedly a French-Canadian flight attendant who had a played a key role in the early spread of AIDS in North America – were widely publicized by the media.

In America, it was left up to the doyenne of daytime television, Oprah Winfrey, to conjure up visions of a rapid spread similar to the Black Death. 'AIDS has both sexes running scared', she said. 'Research studies now project that one in five – listen to me, hard to believe – one in five heterosexuals could be dead from AIDS at the end of the next three years – believe me.' Madonna popped up on television to tell us that AIDS was not just confined to gays and intravenous drug users but was 'an equal opportunity killer' (when the disease first appeared in 1983 scientists called it GRID, an acronym for Gay-Related Immune Deficiency).

Meanwhile, some on the Christian Right wasted no time in renaming the disease the 'gay plague', seeing it as God's vengeance on homosexuals for their perceived moral laxity. The plague metaphor suggests that the disease is a punishment, a 'visitation' inflicted not only on the ill but also on society at large. Like medieval flagellants, who took it upon themselves to expiate the sin that they thought caused the Black Death, we create a correlation between literal sickness and moral and spiritual sickness. Because it was asymptomatic, infecting many thousands before anyone new what was happening, it felt as though some vicious deity, full of demonic cunning, had invented this terrible new disease. Before combination therapy, HIV-infection automatically spelled AIDS and a hideously protracted and painful death. Kaposi's sarcoma was the sign that HIV-infection had now mutated into full-blown AIDS,

making it the 1980s equivalent of the red spots of the oritinal
bubonic plague.

In sub-Saharan Africa, where the spread of the disease is not
associated with homosexuality and intravenous drug abuse,
'the plague' usage conveys the speed with which the viral
invasion spread and the apocalyptic scale of the catastrophe.
In November 2001 Stephen Lewis, the UN Special Envoy for
AIDS in Africa, gave a powerful address to a university
audience in which he attempted to convey the magnitude of
the pandemic. Every day in sub-Saharan Africa, he told his
audience, more than seven thousand people die of AIDS, more
than died in the 9/11 attacks. Two and a half million people die
from the disease every year, making this virus a 'modern
apocalypse'. Lewis compared the scene in parts of eastern
and southern Africa to 'standing in a graveyard'.[25] Almost 10
per cent of South Africa's forty-two million people are now
believed to be HIV positive.

Another biological disaster confronting our age is the destruction of the environment. Like the AIDS crisis, this is an
apocalypse without a millennium, a catastrophe pure and
simple. For environmentalists the world won't end in a cosmic
conflagration but will, instead, slowly simmer towards its
destruction. In this end-time scenario, scientific facts are the
new apocalyptic 'signs' that all is not well on planet earth. The
year 2003 saw the hottest European summer on record result-
ing in more than twenty thousand deaths. Some fifteen hundred people died in India in the extreme heat wave.

But it is at the earth's poles that the full impact of global
warming can be observed. When massive glaciers and sea ice
melts, there is less land reflecting sunlight and more open
water and bare ground absorbing it. This pushes up temperatures and accelerates sea-level rise. In Antarctica, the break-up
of the Larsen B ice shelf in 2002 led to a significant accelera-

tion of West Antarctic glaciers flowing into the Weddell Sea. On the other side of West Antarctica, glaciers flowing into the Amundsen Sea have also speeded up considerably since the 1990s. The complete collapse of the West Antarctic ice sheet would result in a massive rise in sea levels. In centuries to come, this would not just mean occasional flooding in coastal areas but the submergence of small island nations, low-lying countries and major cities.

With global warming come turbulent changes in weather conditions and a whole host of environmental ills. There is an increased risk of droughts – Western Europe in July 2005 sufferd a particularly severe one. Hurricanes, tornadoes, flash floods and freak weather conditions generally are all signs that the planet is hotting up. In 2003, the United States was battered and bruised by a series of violent natural disasters which led to loss of life and huge economic disruption. In one month alone, an average of sixteen tornadoes a day were reported. On 28 July 2005, a 130-mph tornado ripped the roofs off thirty houses and left a three-mile trail of destruction – not in classic 'twister' country like Texas but in a Birmingham suburb!

Things aren't looking too good either in the great blue yonder. Levels of ozone fell to record lows. Beginning over Antarctica, the ozone hole has spread rapidly across parts of Australia and New Zealand. Atmospheric depletion means dangerous levels of ultraviolet light which can cause malignant melanomas, a virulent and often fatal skin cancer. A depleted ozone layer also means an increase in the outbreaks of infectious disease because normal immune systems become less effective when they have been exposed to ultraviolet 'B' radiation. What and who has caused this environmental meltdown? Carbon dioxide emissions from cars, industries and heating are responsible for the greenhouse effect. CFCs are responsible for punching a hole in the ozone layer. As the greatest consumer of coal and oil, the two fossil fuels that contribute the greatest carbon dioxide to the atmosphere, the United States bears the heaviest responsibility for global warming.

Collapsing glaciers, rising sea levels, the highest world temperatures ever measured, new records for storms, floods and drought: the omens of environmental doom are everywhere. The United States government's response to this cataclysmic crisis has been less than impressive. During the 2000 election campaign, George W. Bush made promises to regulate carbon dioxide as a pollutant. Once in power, he pulled the US out of the Kyoto accords in order to safeguard American jobs. Under his presidency, the White House has even questioned the validity of the science behind global warming. Bush's avowed intent to spread democratic freedom globally presupposes there is a globe left to spread it to.

Often the discourse surrounding the environmental movement takes on an apocalyptic colouration. Writers and commentators invoke biblical images of the Gadarene swine's headlong rush to mass extinction. Eco-warriors often see themselves as Last Day Warriors in an Armageddon-style showdown with the demonic powers that be – global brands like Nike and McDonald's, great financial centres like the City of London or Wall Street, and western governments. In this scenario, environmentalists and scientists are the new Jeremiahs. They have taken it upon themselves to issue dire warnings and prophecies about the state of the planet. The natural historian David Attenborough was at first sceptical about climate change but was recently converted to the cause and now proclaims the bad news with evangelical zeal.

One of the most stunning pieces of environmental literature is *The Gaia Atlas of Planet Management*, the definitive guide to the crisis of the planet and humanity. It reads like the *Book of Revelation*, rewritten by scientists and environmentalists. There's an origin myth – earth as the goddess Gaia, beautiful and resplendent in all her primal innocence. Then there's the environmental equivalent of the Fall, our banishment from paradise due to industrialization, the arms race, powerful commercial interests etc. Prophecies abound about the coming end occasioned not by a wrathful deity but our own dear selves through carbon emissions, CFCs and nuclear waste. The 'signs' in nature that all is not well are glaringly obvious. As in all good apocalyptic narratives a final showdown is predicted. The great Babylon/Satan is the greatest consumer and polluter of them all – the United States of America. Salvation comes in the form of educating our children (and our leaders) about alternative sustainable energy sources. We can join the elect through recycling, cycling, and generally treating a Gaia with tender loving care.

The famous author and zoologist, Gerald Durrell, has written a powerful foreword to *The Gaia Atlas*. Like an Old Testament prophet, he balances excoriation and exhortation. He condemns the sins of the past while offering hope for the future; it is not too late because 'nature . . . is a resource that is ever renewing itself which, if managed correctly, offers us a "never-ending largesse" '. But we must act before it is too late, he warns, or we will end up in an environmental hell in which 'we find ourselves breeding like a mass of greenfly on a cinder'.[26] As in the Christian end-time myth, the difference between damnation and salvation is starkly drawn. But unlike Christian Evangelicals and fundamentalists, green activists do not want to see the world destroyed and replaced by a superior heavenly one. For them, it is the present-day earth we must save. There will be no Noah's ark to save us from rising sea levels, no pre-tribulation Rapture which will spare us the worst of the environmental catastrophe, no divine intervention to replace the old earth with a new one. For the science community, it is governments and ordinary people who must act and act now. Only then can disaster be averted and the planet saved.

This emphasis on human instrumentality in the fate of our planet sharply distinguishes secularists from believers. James Watt is not a name that perhaps rings too many bells today. But in his day Watt was a very powerful man – Secretary of the Interior in the first Reagan administration in fact. He was also a devout Pentecostalist. On 5 February 1981, he stood up in the United States Congress and proclaimed that protecting natural resources was unimportant because Christ was about to return. Could it be that President Bush's recalcitrance on environmental issues also has something to do with his evangelical beliefs? Those who hold extreme millenarian views often regard reform as the metaphoric equivalent of polishing the brass on the *Titanic*. Why not simply let the ship go down – hook, line and sinker?

Fears about the dangerous depletion of the planet haunt today's cinema screens. The Korean epic anime, *Sky Blue*, went on release in the United Kingdom in the summer of 2005. Its story is worth analysing in detail because it is an excellent indicator of the kind of fears that arise in a society that has undergone an industrial revolution over the last forty years and transformed itself from being one of the poorest countries in the world to one of the most rapidly developing. During this time, South Korea has gone from being one of the great polluters of the planet to actively putting its own house in order when it comes to environmental issues.

In the year 2140, all the environmentalists' grim prognostications and worse have been realized. A global environmental catastrophe has resulted in the sun being obscured from view and all but ended human civilization on earth. Amidst these scenes of desolation, stands the city of Ecoban, built by an elite who had the technological know-how to create an organic city powered by turning carbon compounds into usable energy. Not surprisingly, those condemned to live outside Ecoban want to enjoy its benefits – which is where Jay, a nineteen-year-old female trooper, comes in. It is her job to guard the city against the incursions of outsiders. Refugees seeking asylum in the city are refused entry and condemned to squat in the surrounding Wasteland where they become Diggers whose job it is to mine the Wasteland for the carbonite needed to power Ecoban.

When she encounters her childhood sweetheart, Shua, leading a rebellion against Ecoban her loyalty is put to the test. She joins the forces of rebellion, fighting alongside Shua for the chance that the clouds may clear and the people of earth might see the blue sky for the first time in their lives. What makes this compelling drama is the reshuffling of the apocalyptic types. There is a dystopian vision of a corrupted world, crying out to be saved. The forces of goodness and the forces of evil are clearly delineated. Earth's destiny hangs in the balance as they do combat, the possibility of a heavenly salvation being symbolized by the azure blue of an unpolluted sky.

The 2004 Hollywood blockbuster, *The Day After Tomorrow*, also caught the zeitgeist of impending ecological doom. Stunning computer-generated special effects conjure up images of multiple hurricanes, tornadoes, earthquakes, tidal waves, floods, and the beginning of the next Ice Age. Such is the visual appeal of the movie that it easily plasters over the inadequacies of the script. The scriptwriters' attempts to strike a suitably apocalyptic note involve the repeated use of the word 'cataclysmic'. Salvation comes in the form a climatologist (Dennis

Quaid). It's his job to figure out a way to save the world from abrupt global warming and rescue his son holed up in an ice-bound New York.

As we saw earlier, movies have always been excellent indicators of the apocalyptic fears of a particular age. In the wake of Hiroshima and Nagasaki came a whole series of monster-mutation movies: cinema screens were awash with giant women and spiders, tearing down cities and terrorizing the inhabitants. In the 1990s, a new monster appeared on western cinema screens. Since the middle of the decade, the old-style Soviet adversary has given way to the figure of the Islamist seeking world domination. As John Esposito puts it, the Red Menace has been replaced by the Green one.[27] For Edward Said, Muslims and Arabs 'are essentially covered, discussed, apprehended, either as oil suppliers or as potential terrorists'. Such crude caricaturing, Said contends, serves a political purpose: Hollywood's Islamophobia bolsters Israel and stereotypes Palestinians as 'the mad Islamic zealot, the gratuitously violent killer of innocents, the desperately irrational and savage primitive'.[28]

The 1996 movie *Executive Decision* demonstrates that the Arab = terrorist equation was established long before 9/11. When a group of Arab terrorists hijack a plane flying from Athens to Dallas it appears to be a straightforward attempt to get the notorious terrorist leader, Jaffa, released from jail (the film begins with him being arrested in Nicosia). In fact, the sinister and crazed leader of the hijackers, Nagi Hassan (David Suchet) has something far more spectacular in mind; the plane is packed full of chemicals and bombs capable of wiping out the east coast of America. It is not just the airborne terrorist attack on American soil which is reminiscent of 9/11. When Hassan speaks to the newly released Jaffa on the radio and discloses what his true intentions are, he uses the kind of apocalyptic rhetoric used by Mohamed Atta and the other 9/11 terrorists:

> Allah has blessed us. A great destiny awaits us both. In a few hours you will see I have achieved a glorious victory on your behalf. All the people of Islam will embrace you as its chosen leader. I am your friend, the sword of Allah, and with it I will strike deep into the heart of the infidel.[29]

Unlike what really happened on 9/11, however, help is at hand. The job of saving America and the 406 passengers on board falls to the Kurt Russell character, a National Security officer, aided and abetted by a crack team of commandos and a beautiful and resourceful flight attendant (Halle Berry). He leads the assault on the terrorists, overpowers them and then gets to land the Jumbo.

In recent years, Hollywood has become more circumspect in its portrayal of Muslims on film. As noted earlier, Tom Clancy's thriller *The Sum of All Fears* depicted the threat of nuclear mega-terrorism. In the original book the centre of the conflict is the Middle East, where a nuclear weapon falls into the hands of Muslim terrorists. Their plan is to blow up a football stadium on American soil and have it look as though the Russians were responsible, thereby plunging the world into a new Cold War era and so preventing reconciliation between the Israelis and the Palestinians. Such complicated geopolitical manoeuvrings are ditched in the 2002 film. From being Middle-Eastern Muslim terrorists, the villains are changed into European neo-Nazis. Moreover, the film never mentions the conflict between Israelis and Palestinians.

The interplay between Hollywood apocalyptic fantasizing and modern American politics still persists to this day, according to Michelle Ciarrocca and William D. Hartung. In their 2002 essay 'Bush's Nuclear Plan: Dr. Strangelove Revisited', they compare Bush's current nuclear strategy to the worship of nuclear weapons in Kubrick's film. They fear that Bush's handling of the nuclear arsenal would change its usage 'from a tool of deterrence and a weapon of last resort' to a central, usable component of the US "anti-terror" arsenal'. If terrorist groups got their hands on a nuclear weapon and used it they could expect an all-out nuclear response from the United States:

> By increasing the kinds of situations in which the United States might employ nuclear weapons, from launching them 'against targets able to withstand non-nuclear attack' to retaliation for the use of nuclear, biological or chemical weapons, the Bush nuclear posture dramatically lowers the threshold for using these weapons.[30]

*

The first five years of the new century has abounded with predictions about the End of the World. There is no reason to suspect that the second half of the decade will be any different. Much New Age speculation has focused recently on the end of the ancient Mayan 'Long Count' calendar on 22 December 2012. The world will end according to this ancient calendaric system on this date. Apparently, the ancient Mayans believed that the sun, which they had assiduously fuelled with their human sacrifices, would no longer sends its life force and thus bring to an end the last age of man.

Many fear that a massive asteroid will do to humans what one did to the dinosaurs sixty-five million or so years ago. Perhaps this is why we are so fascinated by the dinosaurs. For millions of years they ruled the planet only to disappear in the blink of an eye – well, a few million years. An asteroid, catalogued as 2004 MN4, was discovered in June 2004. It reappeared again in December of that year and for a brief time had scientists worried: it had the highest odds of hitting earth ever given to a 'Near Earth Object'. Fortunately, subsequent observations refined the future path and scientists expect it to fly past earth in 2029 when it will be visible to the naked eye. This will be the closest encounter the earth has had with a good-sized asteroid – it's about 300 metres (1,000 feet) wide.

If collision with an asteroid is not going to bring about the end, at least in the foreseeable future, then there are always the new technologies to get worried about. Scientific commentators are full of dire warnings about the dangers of robotics, genetic engineering and nano-technology and the threat they pose to human civilization as we know it. They maintain that the current pace of technological innovation poses a very real threat to the future of the human race as Frankenstein-type scientists become blind to the ramifications of even their own technologies. Take computers for example. In the next few decades, fully conscious computers with superhuman levels of intelligence will be built, raising fears that a scenario straight out of the science fiction fantasy, *Terminator*, might come true – the prospect of robots 'taking over'.[31]

The vexed issue of genetic engineering will increasingly exercise doom-mongers and ethicists in the next few years. Cults like the Raelians have made sure of that, combining as they do 'scientific creationism' with UFO alien abduction lore and New Age and apocalyptic beliefs. At the end of 2002, this Canadian-based cult claimed to have produced the first cloned human baby through their genetic engineering company Clonaid. The founder of the movement, Claude Vorilhon, a former sports car journalist now known as 'Raël', claims to be a direct descendant of extraterrestrials, the Elohim, who came down to earth 25,000 years ago in their flying saucers and created human life on earth through their knowledge of DNA.[32] Because Raelians believe that the soul dies along with the original body, the ultimate goal is to re-create human beings through cloning and thus confer immortality. Young female members of the 55,000 worldwide following are eager to donate their eggs and womb for the chance of Raelian-style immortality. The prospect of achieving 'cyber immortality' is also eagerly anticipated in the next few decades – when Raelians will be able to download their brains in a computer and then have them transferred into new cloned bodies. Meanwhile our extraterrestrial creators are expected back in 2035. Much effort has been expended on finding them suitable accommodation. Originally, Raël wanted to rebuild the Third Temple in Jerusalem in the form of a government-sanctioned embassy but the plans foundered. Apparently, matters were not helped by the original Raelian symbol which combined the Star of David and the swastika.

For those with more traditional religious beliefs, there is always 2033, the estimated two-thousandth anniversary of Jesus' crucifixion and resurrection. For many Christians, disappointed that the Rapture did not take place in 2000, this is the next big date in the apocalyptic calendar. For their part, Muslims were equally exercised about the year 2000. There was much speculation that this would be the year when Jews would rebuild the Temple in Jerusalem, which they assumed would involve pulling down the Dome of the Rock and Al-Aqsa Mosque.

Whether Sunni or Shiite, Islamic apocalypticism is an important factor in today's Middle East. The apocalyptic mentality of 'let's do away with it all' appeals particularly to powerless and angry young Muslims who see little hope that there will be positive changes that will benefit Islam in the immediate future except through divine intervention. For them, the koranic term *jihad* is not an internal struggle to live a good Muslim life; rather it is a 'holy war' to be waged against the West with suicide bombers and the like. For such radicalized Muslims these are the end-times prophesied in their holy book. Radical clerics and other Islamists add fuel to the apocalyptic fire by recasting figures such as George W. Bush and Ariel Sharon as the Antichrist.

Apocalyptic scenarios featuring a Mahdi are particularly popular in Palestine and Iraq. The charismatic Shiite cleric, Muqtada al-Sadr, emerged as an important leader after the fall of Saddam. His stronghold is the holy Shiite city of Al-Najaf. Like most other Shiite clerics, he wants US troops to leave as soon as possible and believes that Iraqis should be given the opportunity to create an Islamic state. What distinguishes him, however, from the other Shiite clerics is the radically eschatological nature of his beliefs. For al-Sadr has claimed that the Mahdi's coming is imminent and that he will return to Iraq. He claims that the Americans were aware of the imminent reappearance which was why they invaded Iraq in order to seize and kill him. For his part, al-Sadr has achieved messianic status among some Shiites. His supporters chant his name at rallies, implying that he is the 'son of Mahdi'.

Iran's new hardline president, Mahmoud Ahmadinejad, frequently refers to the Mahdi and even managed to get him into his speech to the UN General Assembly in September 2005.[33] Some are worried that the president's religiosity has taken an apocalyptic turn. His declaration that Israel should be 'wiped off the face of the earth' is proof positive for many commentators that he regards international turmoil as the sign that we are living in the end-times which herald the return of the Mahdi.

In today's world, ultra-orthodox Third Temple Jews, Christian fundamentalists and Muslim apocalyptists like al-Sadr and

Ahmadinejad are all helping to fan the flames of the apocalypse like never before. Their beliefs are ancient and rooted in the apocalyptic traditions of the three great monotheistic faiths, once regarded as members of the Abrahamic family, now polarized and alienated from each other. The rising tide of Muslim anti-Semitism is a deeply worrying trend, one which fills commentators on the Middle East with a profound sense of foreboding as they contemplate the foreseeable future. Some Muslim clerics currently preaching on the Palestinian Authority television combine traditional apocalyptic beliefs with the most virulent anti-American and Jewish attitudes. Sheik Ibrahim Mudeiris gave a sermon on Palestinian Authority TV entitled 'Muslims Will Rule America and Britain, Jews are a Virus Resembling AIDS'. PA TV aired this on 13 May 2005. Mudeiris uses the kind of disease rhetoric Hitler employed in his genocidal war against the Jews. Like Hitler, Mudeiris harbours genocidal fantasies about Jews because they are deemed to be demonic exponents of a global conspiracy who have harmed every civilization they have ever come into contact with. For Mudeiris, when Muslims finally achieve world domination, there can be no place for the Jews in this new global order: 'the day will come when everything will be relieved of the Jews – even the stones and trees which were harmed by them . . . will want the Muslims to finish off every Jew'.[34]

The dire situation of many Muslims worldwide means that Mudeiris's hate-filled message falls on receptive ears. You can both view and hear him on the Internet. In the global era, such cataclysmic millennialism can reach many angry young Muslim men around the world, who want something to happen very urgently. Rather than wait, they are prepared to stoke the apocalyptic fires themselves; the suicide bomber is increasingly taking on the configurations of an eschatological figure. For *jihadists*, Muslims stand on the brink of a glorious global victory for Islam. By blowing themselves up and killing innocent civilians, the suicide bomber is doing his (and her) bit in the cosmic battle between good and evil. In such a hate-filled atmosphere many Hadiths, which envisage a genocidal slaughter of Jews, are being revived.

The extraordinary resurgence of Christian and Muslim apocalyptic belief over the last few decades will keep the End of the World in the forefront of our consciousness for decades to come. Our children's children will be living with the fallout of 9/11 – the great apocalyptic act of our times. Like Christian Zionists and messianic Jews, radical Muslims place Jerusalem at the centre of their apocalyptic drama; it is the site of the Last Judgement. In one Hadith, the Kaaba stone will come from Mecca to Jerusalem. Such a prophecy places Israel at the centre of the global apocalyptic battle. There is therefore a curious circularity about our story of the End of the World. Having begun with Jerusalem, we end there.

NOTES

Introduction

1 See 'The Bible and Apocalypse', *Time*, 1 July 2002.
2 See Norman Cohn, *Cosmos, Chaos and the World to Come: The Ancient Roots of Apocalyptic Faith*, second edition (New Haven: Yale University Press, 2001), p.77.
3 Richard Dawkins, 'Religion's Misguided Missiles', *The Guardian*, 15 September 2001.
4 *Genesis* 1:2.
5 C.G. Jung, *Answer to Job*, trans. R.C. Hull (London: Routledge & Kegan Paul, 1979). For an extensive Jungian reading of the *Book of Revelation*, see Edward F. Edinger's *Archetype of the Apocalypse: Divine Vengeance, Terrorism and the End of the World*, ed. George R. Elder (Chicago and La Salle: Open Court, 2000).
6 Frank Kermode, *The Sense of an Ending: Studies in the Theory of Fiction* (New York: Oxford University Press, 1967).
7 Northrop Frye, *The Great Code: The Bible and Literature* (London: Routledge & Kegan Paul, 1982) xi–xxiii.
8 James Hall, 'Jake and Dinos Chapman: Collaborating with Catastrophe', from *Apocalypse: Beauty and Horror in Contemporary Art* (Royal Academy of Arts: London, 2000), pp.214–15.
9 Israel News from Jerusalem Newswire, http://www.jnewswire.com/library/article.php?articleid=699

10 See Chapter 3, Rachel Carson, *Silent Spring* (London: Penguin Classics, 2000).
11 *Daniel* 12:10.
12 For those who claim to have prophetic powers Jesus has a warning: no one knows when he will return but God (*Matthew*: 24:36).
13 Leon Festinger, Henry W. Reicken and Stanley Schachter, *When Prophecy Fails* (Minneapolis: University of Minnesota Press, 1956), p.3.

Chapter I – The Origins of Apocalyptic Faith

1 See Mary Boyce, *A History of Zoroastrianism: The Early Period, Volume 1* (Leiden: E.J. Brill, 1975), pp.229–31. For a succinct analysis of Zoroastrian doctrines to which I am indebted, see Mary Boyce, *Zoroastrians: Their Religious Beliefs and Practices*, (London: Routledge and Kegan Paul, 1979)
2 Ibid., p.232.
3 Ibid., p.242.
4 Cohn, *Cosmos, Chaos*, pp.220ff.
5 Herodotus, *The Histories*, Book 1 (London: Penguin, 1972), p.113.
6 *Isaiah* 44–45:28–1.
7 *Ezekiel* 36:25.
8 *Ezekiel* 34:25–27.
9 *Ezekiel* 37:24.
10 *Revelation* 20:13.
11 *Isaiah* 65:17–25.
12 *Daniel* 7–12.
13 *Daniel* 2:35.
14 *Daniel* 2:44.
15 *Daniel* 7:23.
16 *Daniel* 7:9–10.
17 *Daniel* 7:13–14.
18 *Daniel* 12:7.
19 *Daniel* 12:2.
20 *Daniel* 12:3, 4.
21 Matthew Black, *The Book of Enoch or I Enoch: A New English Edition with Commentary and Notes* (Leiden: E.J. Brill, 1985), pp.25–6. All subsequent references are to this edition.
22 *1 Enoch* 5:4, p.27.
23 *Genesis* 6:4.
24 *Genesis* 6:5.
25 *1 Enoch* 7:5, p.28.
26 *1 Enoch* 8:1, p.28.
27 Black, *The Book of Enoch*, p.8.
28 *1 Enoch* 10:12, p.30.
29 *1 Enoch* 10:13, p.31.
30 *1 Enoch* 15:11–12, p.34.
31 *1 Enoch* 18:11–12, p.36.

Chapter 2 – The Birth of Apocalyptic Faith

1 *Luke* 40:3.
2 Biblical scholars refer to it by the acronym 1QM (1 = Cave, Q = Qumran and M = *milchamah*, war).
3 *The Dead Sea Scrolls: A New Translation* by Michael Wise, Martin Abegg and Edward Cook (San Francisco: HarperCollins, 1996), p.166.
4 See John Meier, *A Marginal Jew: Rethinking the Historical Jesus, Volume 2: Mentor, Message and Miracles* (London: Doubleday, 1991).
5 *Mark* 1:15, 1:34.
6 *Matthew* 16:28; *Luke* 9:27.
7 *Luke* 9:26; *Luke* 13:28; *Matthew* 13:41–42; *Matthew* 25:31–32.
8 *Mark* 12:25; *Matthew* 13:43.
9 *Matthew* 10:23.
10 *Mark* 13:22.
11 *Mark* 13:24–27.
12 *Jeremiah* 8:13: 'When I wanted to gather them, says the Lord, there are no grapes on the vine, nor figs on the fig tree; even the leaves are withered, and what I gave them has passed away from them.'
13 *Matthew* 16:28.
14 *Matthew* 16:27.
15 *Romans* 13:11–12.
16 *2 Peter* 3:8.
17 Bart D. Ehrman, *Jesus: Apocalyptic Prophet of the New Millennium* (New York: Oxford University Press, 1999), p.3.
18 Cohn, *Cosmos, Chaos*, p.212
19 *Revelation* 1:10–11.
20 *Revelation* 1:10–18.
21 *Revelation* 2:26–27.
22 *Revelation* 22:10.
23 This Greek word has been variously translated as 'advocate', 'teacher', 'helper', 'comforter'. See *Gospel According to St John*: 14:16, 26; 15:26; 16:7.
24 For an in-depth analysis of the position of women in the movement see Christine Trevett, *Montanism: Gender, Authority and the New Prophecy* (Cambridge: Cambridge University Press, 1996).
25 For Montanism's influence on Tertullian and vice versa see Jaroslav Pelikan, *The Christian Tradition: A History of the Development of Doctrine, Volume 1: The Emergence of the Catholic Tradition (100–600)* (Chicago: Chicago University Press, 1975), pp.101–5.
26 All references are to *The Koran Interpreted* translated by Arthur J. Arberry (Oxford: Oxford University Press, 1982), p.632.
27 Koran, p.559.
28 Koran, p.527.
29 Richard Dawkins, 'Religion's Misguided Missiles'.

30 Koran, *surah* 16:77, p.267.
31 See Sunan Abu-Dawud, Book 37 at http:www.usc.edu/dept/MSA/
    fundamentals/hadithsunah/abudawud/037.sat.html

Chapter 3 – Visions of the End in Europe: Part One

1   Richard Landes, 'On Owls, Roosters, and Apocalyptic Time: A Historical
    Method for Reading a Refractory Documentation', *Union Seminary Quar-
    terly Review*, 49 (1996): 165–85.
2   2 Peter 3:8.
3   See Stephen Jay Gould, *Questioning the Millennium: A Rationalist's Guide to
    a Precisely Arbitrary Countdown* (London: Jonathan Cape, 1997), p.81.
4   See Norman Cohn, *The Pursuit of the Millennium: Revolutionary Millenar-
    ians and Mystical Anarchists of the Middle Ages*, revised edition (London:
    Pimlico, 1993), pp.30–5.
5   St Augustine, *Concerning the City of God Against the Pagans* (London:
    Penguin, 2003), p.908.
6   *The City of God* 20:ff.; 22:30.
7   *The City of God*, 20:7, p.907.
8   See Harold Bloom, *Omens of the Millennium: The Gnosis of Angels, Dreams
    and Resurrection* (New York: Riverhead Books, 1996), p.222.
9   For the latest in modern prophecy beliefs go to www.armageddonbooks.com
    which styles itself 'the world's largest Bible prophecy bookstore'.
10 Quoted in Jane Lampman, 'Apocalyptic – and Atop the Bestseller Lists',
    Christian Science Monitor, 29 August 2002, p.14.
11 Quoted from *Apocalyptic Spirituality: Treatises and Letters of Lactantius,
    Adso of Montier-En-Der, Joachim of Fiore, the Franciscan Spirituals, Savo-
    narola*, edited by Bernard McGinn (New York: Paulist Press, 1979), p.90.
12 Ibid., p.96.
13 *The Song of Roland*, trans. Glyn Burgess (London: Penguin 1990), p.146.
14 Ibid., p.84.
15 Ibid., pp.106–7.
16 Hillel Schwartz, *Century's End: An Orientation Manual Toward the Year
    2000*, revised and abridged edition (New York: Doubleday, 1996), pp.4–5.
17 See Nicholas Campion, *The Great Year: Astrology, Millenarianism and
    History in the Western Tradition* (London: Penguin 1994) provides a good
    introduction to the vast number of specific numerical theories about the End.
18 See *The Prose Edda of Snorri Sturluson: Tales from Norse Mythology*,
    translated by Jean I. Young (Berkeley: University of California Press, 1964).
19 Ibid., p.87.
20 Ibid., p.88.
21 See August C. Krey, ed. and trans., *The First Crusade: The Accounts of Eye-
    witnesses and Participants* (Princeton: Princeton University Press, 1921)
    pp.24–40.
22 Ibid., p.31.
23 Ibid., p.63.

24 Norman Cohn, *The Pursuit of the Millennium*, p.69.

25 See Barbara Victor, *The Last Crusade: Religion and the Politics of Misdirection* (London: Constable & Robinson, 2005).

26 For further reading on Joachim's system and its influence see Marjorie Reeves, *Joachim of Fiore and the Prophetic Future* (London: SPCK, 1976); M.W. Bloomfield, 'Recent Scholarship on Joachim of Fiore and his Influence', in *Prophecy and Millenarianism: Essays in Honour of Marjorie Reeves*, ed. Anne Williams (London: Longman, 1980), pp.23–39.

27 See Bernard McGinn, *Apocalyptic Spirituality*, pp.136ff.

28 For European images of Islam see John L. Esposito, *The Islamic Threat: Myth or Reality* (Oxford: Oxford University Press, 1992), pp.42–6.

29 See Bill McGuire, *Apocalypse: A Natural History of Global Disasters* (London: Cassell, 1999).

30 Johan Huizinga, *The Waning of the Middle Ages: A Study of the Forms of Life, Thought and Art in France and the Netherlands in the Fourteenth and Fifteenth Centuries* (New York: Doubleday Anchor, 1954), p.138.

31 Quoted from Paul Boyer, *When Time Shall Be No More: Prophecy Belief in Modern American Culture* (Cambridge, Mass.: The Belknap Press, Harvard University, 1992), p.225.

32 For the historical setting of the frescoes see Jonathan B. Reiss, *The Renaissance Antichrist: Luca Signorelli's Orvieto Frescoes* (New Jersey: Princeton University Press, 1995).

Chapter 4 – Visions of the End in Europe: Part Two

1 See Norman Cohn, *The Pursuit of the Millennium*), p.236.

2 *Revelation* 6:13.

3 Quoted from Norman Cohn, *The Pursuit of the Millennium*, p.239.

4 John Milton, *Areopagitica and Of Education*, ed. Michael Davis (London: Macmillan, 1963), p.53.

5 *A Collection of Ranter Writings from the 17th Century*, ed. Nigel Smith (London: Junction Books, 1983), p.80.

6 Ibid., p.82.

7 Ibid., p.83.

8 Ibid., p.87.

9 Ibid., p.90.

10 See John Carey's Foreword to *A Collection of Ranter Writings from the 17th Century*, p.3.

11 *The Shorter Pepys*, ed. Robert Latham (London: Penguin Classics, 1993), p.662.

12 I am indebted here to the excellent website 'A Brief History of the Apocalypse' section 1701–1970 at www.abhota.info/endb.htm

13 David V. Erdman, *Blake: Prophet Against Empire: A Poet's Interpretation of the History of His Own Times*, revised edition (New Jersey: Princeton University Press, 1969), p.165.

14 From 'A Vision of the Last Judgement' in *Blake's Poetry and Designs*, ed.

Mary Lynn Johnson and John E. Grant, Norton Critical Edition (New York and London: W.W. Norton, 1979), p.416.

15 A.L. Morton, *The Everlasting Gospel: A Study in the Sources of William Blake* (London: Lawrence and Wishart, 1958).

16 Robert Southey, *The Correspondence of Robert Southey with Caroline Bowles*, ed. Edward Dowden (Dublin: Hodges, Figgis and Co., 1881), p.52.

17 William Wordsworth, *The Prelude: A Parallel Text*, Book VI, ed. J.C. Maxwell (London: Penguin, 1986), p.224. For an excellent analysis of apocalyptic expectations during the French Revolution era, and to which I am indebted, see Norton Topics online at www.wwnorton.com/nto/romantic/topic_3/welcome.htm

18 Thomas Carlyle, *On Heroes, Hero-worship and the Heroic in History* (New York: Frederick A. Stokes & Brother, 1888), p.223.

19 Thomas Carlyle, *The French Revolution* (Oxford: Oxford University Press), p.331.

20 Samuel Taylor Coleridge, *Selected Poetry*, ed. William Empson and David Pirie (Manchester: Carcanet Press, 1989), pp.108–9.

21 Karl Marx and Friedrich Engels, *The Communist Manifesto*, Penguin classics edition (London: Penguin, 2002), pp.225–6.

22 See *Exodus 25*.

23 John Wesley, *Explanatory Notes upon the New Testament* (London: Epworth Press, 1929), p.997.

24 William Booth, *In Darkest England and the Way Out* (London: International Headquarters, 1890).

25 H.G. Wells, *Anticipations of the Mechanical and Scientific Progress upon Human Life and Thought* (London: Chapman and Hall, 1902), pp.298–300.

Chapter 5 – War and Apocalypse in the Twentieth Century

1 Paul Fussell, *The Great War and Modern Memory* (London: Oxford University Press, 1975).

2 See Jeremy Black, *War and the World: Military Power and the Fate of Continents 1450–2000* (New Haven: Yale University Press, 1998), p.239.

3 D.H. Lawrence, *Lady Chatterley's Lover*, second edition (Harmondsworth: Penguin, 1961), p.1.

4 Wilfred Owen, *Collected Letters*, ed. Harold Owen and John Bell (London: Oxford University Press, 1967), p.282.

5 Fussell, *The Great War*, p.131.

6 Quoted from Fussell, *The Great War*, p.136.

7 John Buchan, *The Battle of the Somme* (New York: George H. Doran, 1917), pp.42–3.

8 Quoted from *The Faber Book of Reportage*, ed. John Carey (London: Faber, 1996), p.463.

9 Roland Dorgelès, *Wooden Crosses* (London: William Heineman, 1920), p.180.

10 D.H. Lawrence, *Apocalypse and the Writings on Revelation*, ed. Mara Kalnins (Cambridge: Cambridge University Press, 1980), p.59.

11 D.H. Lawrence, *The Letters of D.H. Lawrence*, Volume 2, eds. James T. Boulton and George J. Zytarut (Cambridge: Cambridge University Press, 1981), p.669.

12 J.M. Murray, *Love, Freedom and Society* (London: Jonathan Cape, 1957), p.30.

13 J.M. Murray, *Reminiscences of D.H. Lawrence* (London: Jonathan Cape, 1933), pp. 61, 63.

14 *Letters*, Volume 2, p.263.

15 Ibid., p.634.

16 *The Rainbow*, ed. Mark Kinkead-Weekes (Cambridge: Cambridge University Press, 1989), pp.458–9.

17 *Letters*, Volume 2, p.229.

18 D.H. Lawrence, *The Lettes of D.H. Lawrence*, Volume 3, eds. James T. Boulton and Andrew Robertson (Cambridge: Cambridge University Press, 1984), pp.25–6.

19 Ibid., pp.142–3.

20 *Letters*, Volume 2, pp.389–90.

21 *Letters*, Volume 3, pp.97, 125.

22 See Patrick Wright, *Tank: The Progress of a Monstrous War Machine* (London: Faber, 2000).

23 Quoted from Patrick Wright, *Tank: The Progress of a Monstrous War Machine*, p.59.

24 T.S. Eliot, 'The Wasteland', *Complete Poems and Plays of T.S. Eliot* (London: Faber, 1969), p.62.

25 W.B. Yeats, *The Collected Poems of W.B. Yeats* (London: Macmillan, 1978), pp.210–11.

26 Adolf Hitler, *Mein Kampf*, introduction by D.C. Watt, trans. Ralph Manheim (London: Pimlico, 1998), p.263.

27 Ibid., p.269.

28 See Norman Cohn, *Warrant for Genocide* (New York: Harper and Row, 1967).

29 Quoted from *Nazism 1919–1945, Volume 3, Foreign Policy, War and Racial Extermination: A Documentary Reader*, ed. J. Noakes and G. Pridham (Exeter: Exeter University Publications, 1988), p.1049.

30 Mark Roseman, *The Villa, the Lake, the Meeting: Wannsee and the Final Solution* (London: Penguin, 2002), p.70.

31 Antony Beevor, *Stalingrad* (London: Penguin, 1999), p.26.

32 Jonathan Schell, *The Fate of the Earth* (London: Jonathan Cape, 1982), p.37.

33 See Eric Hobsbawm, *The Age of Extremes: A Short Twentieth Century 1914–1991* (London: Michael Joseph, 1994).

Chapter 6 – Apocalypse in America: Part One

1 Alexis de Tocqueville, *Democracy in America*, Volume 2, ed. J.P. Mayer (New York: Garden City, 1969), p.432.

2 Bernard McGinn, *Antichrist: Two Thousand Years of the Human Fascination with Evil* (San Francisco: HarperSan Francisco, 1994), p.16.

3 Richard Calef, *More Wonders of the Invisible World*, reprinted 1976 (Ann Arbor: University Microfilms International, c.1700).

4 Quoted from Andrew G. Gardner, 'A Mysterious Darkness: The Day the Sun Went Out in New England', *The Colonial Williamsburg Journal*, Summer 2005, p. 29.

5 See *Free Love in Utopia: John Humphrey Noyes and the Origin of the Oneida Community*, compiled by George Wallingford Noyes, ed. Lawrence Forster (Urbana: University of Illinois Press, 2001), pp.322–8.

6 For a succint overview of Miller's system see L. Michael White, 'Frontline: Apocalypse' at www.pbs.org/wgbh/pages/frontline/shows/apocalypse/explanation/amprophesy.html

7 Festinger, *When Prophecy Fails*, p.13.

8 Quoted from Festinger, *When Prophecy Fails*, p.20.

9 Steve Jones, *In the Blood: God, Genes and Destiny*, (London: Flamingo, 1997), p.58.

10 *The Time is at Hand*, 1888; see pp.77 and 78.

11 Charles T. Russell, 'Foreword' to *Studies in the Scriptures Series 11: The Time is at Hand* (New York: International Bible Students Association, 1924), p.III.

12 'Studying God's Word, we have measured the 2520 years, the seven symbolic times, from that year 606 B.C. and have found that it reached down to October 1914, as nearly as we were able to reckon. We did not say positively that this would be the year.' *The Watchtower*, 1 November 1914, p.325. The next month things got even more desperate: 'Even if the time of our change should not come within ten years, what more should we ask? Are we not a blessed, happy people? . . . If any of you ever find anything better, we hope you will tell us.' *The Watchtower*, 15 December, p.376.

13 Joseph Rutherford, *Millions Now Living Will Never Die* (New York: Watch Tower Bible and Tract Society of New York, 1920), p.88.

14 Quoted from *The Lincoln Reader*, ed. Paul M. Angle (New Brunswick: Rutgers University Press, 1947), pp.492–3.

15 See Kirkpatrick Sale, *The Conquest of Paradise: Christopher Columbus and the Columbian Legacy*, Papermac edition (London: Macmillan, 1992).

16 In the *United States Magazine and Democratic Review* (July–August 1845) John L. O'Sullivan prophesied 'the fulfilment of our manifest destiny to overspread the continent allotted by Providence'.

17 See Dee Brown *Bury My Heart at Wounded Knee: An Indian History of the American West* (New York: Henry Holt, 1970), p.444.

Chapter 7 – Apocalypse in America: Part Two

1 D.L. Moody, *Notes from My Bible and One Thousand and One Thoughts from My Library* (Grand Rapid: Baker Book House, 1979), p.326.

2 Boyer, *When Time Shall Be No More*, p.100.

3 Ibid., p.106.

4 Albert Speer, *Spandau: The Secret Diaries* (London: Phoenix Press, 2000), p.80.
5 See Jason S. Bauer's excellent essay on Hollywood's fascination with nuclear war, 'First Strike to Fallout: American Culture, Nuclear War and the Movies: 1949–1999, at www.jmn.edn/writeon/documents/2001/bauer.pdf
6 Bob Dylan, *Chronicles: Volume 1* (London: Simon & Schuster, 2004), pp.270–1.
7 Quoted from Simon Callow, *Orson Welles: The Road to Xanadu* (London: Jonathan Cape, 1995), p.403.
8 Ronald Reagan, First Inaugural Address. It can be read online at www. bartleby.com/124/pres61.html
9 Hal Lindsey, *There's a New World Coming: 'A Prophetic Odyssey'* (London: Coverdale House Publications, 1974), p.97.
10 See 'the official site of Pat Robertson' at www.patrobertson.com
11 *Revelation* 14:20.
12 Michael Barkun, *Religion and the Racist Right: The Origins of the Christian Identity Movement* (Chapel Hill: University of North Carolina Press, 1994), p.110.
13 See Catherine Wessinger, *How the Millennium Comes Violently: From Jonestown to Heaven's Gate* (New York: Seven Bridges Press, 2000).
14 See *The Dallas Morning News*, 13 March 1993.
15 A poll by CNN/Gallup found that 73 per cent of Americans believed that the decision to use CS gas on the residents of Mount Carmel was 'responsible', and that 93 per cent of Americans blamed David Koresh for the deaths of the Branch Davidians.
16 *Waco: The Rules of Engagement*, directed by William Gazecki, USA, 1997.
17 Quoted from *Waco: The Rules of Engagement*.
18 For an informative and entertaining overview of the attitudes, influence and beliefs of LaHaye, see 'American Rapture' by Craig Unger, *Vanity Fair*, December 2005.
19 Quoted from Barbara Victor, *The Last Crusade*, p.35.
20 Quoted from *CNN.com*, 14 September 2001.
21 See *The Guardian* 21 January 2005 which carried a full analysis of his speech on its front page.

Chapter 8 – The End of the World as We Know It

1 Barbara Marx Hubbard, *Happy Birthday, Planet Earth: The Instant of Co-operation* (New Mexico, Ocean Tree Books, 1986), p.17.
2 www.armageddonbooks.com
3 James Lovelock, *Gaia: The Practical Science of Planetary Medicine* (London: Gaia Books Ltd, 1991), p.153.
4 See Irvin Baxter, 'Chernobyl Shuts Down – Prophecy Comes to Light', *Endtime Magazine*, Jan/Feb 2001 at www.endtime.com
5 Marilyn Manson, *The Long Road out of Hell* (New York: HarperCollins, 1998).

6 Martin Rees, *Our Final Century: Will Civilisation Survive the Twenty-first Century?* (London: Arrow Books, 2003), p.42.

7 www.cnn.com/allpolitics/ stories/1999/01/19/sotu.transcript/index.html

8 See Robert Sam Anson, 'The Y2K Nightmare', *Vanity Fair*, January 1999.

9 Koran, *sura* 2:195, 'And spend of your substance in the cause of Allah, and make not your own hands contribute to (your) destruction; but do good; for Allah loveth those who do good'.

10 Bill Powell, 'The Enemy Within', *Time*, 31 October 2005, pp.30–9.

11 Nancy Gibbs, 'Apocalypse Now', *Time*, 1 July 2002, p.43.

12 Quoted from Jason Burke, 'Al-Qaida is now an idea, not an organization', *Guardian*, 5 August 2005.

13 'Revelation13.net' at http://www.revelation13.net/

14 See *BBC News*, Friday 14 September 2001.

15 http://www.quatrocantos.com/lendas/imags/nostradamus_imag/neil_marshall.htm

16 See Peter Lemesurier, *Nostradamus in the 21st Century and the Coming Invasion of Europe*, revised edition (London: Judy Piatkus, 2000), pp.80–2.

17 John Miller's interview for ABC with Osama bin Laden, www.pbs.org/wgbh/pages/frontline/shows/binladen/who/interview.html

18 Al-Jazeera TV broadcast from Dubai on 27 December 2001.

19 Edward Said interview, *Global Policy Forum*, November 2001, http://www.globalpolicy.org/wtc/analysis/1101said.htm

20 See *New York Times*, 7 July 1946 about a year after Hiroshima: 'The intense heat of the blast started fires as far as 3,500 feet from "ground zero" (the point on the ground directly under the bomb's explosion in the air)'.

21 *Time*, 14 September 2001; *Newsweek*, 15 September 2001.

22 Matthew Engel, 'Nuclear Threat Is Real – Bush. President Says All Nations Must Join Fight', *The Guardian*, 7 November 2001.

23 Quoted from Sue Reid, 'Manual for Murder', *Daily Mail*, 16 July 2005, pp.6–7.

24 www.trancenet.org/heavensgate

25 Hilary Spilberg, 'African AIDS Horror Hits Home: More Than 7,000 Die Daily; Most Can't Afford Medicine', *The Varsity*, 1 November 2001.

26 Foreword to *The Gaia Atlas of Planet Management*, fully revised and extended (London: Gaia Books Ltd, 1994).

27 Esposito, *The Islamic Threat*, p.35.

28 Edward Said, *Covering Islam: How the Media and the Experts Determine How We See the Rest of the World* (New York: Pantheon, 1981) p.26.

29 Quoted from Daniel Mandel, 'Muslims on the Silver Screen', *Middle Eastern Quarterly*, Spring 2001. I am indebted to this excellent discussion of how Hollywood action films portray Muslims.

30 Michelle Ciarrocca and William D. Hartung, 'Bush's nuclear plan: Dr Strangelove Revisited', www.lightmillennium.org/summer_02

31 Rees, *Only Final Century*, p.17.

32 For the first in-depth look at the Raelian movement, see Susan J. Palmer's, *Aliens Adored: Raël's UFO Religion* (New Brunswick: Rutgers University Press, 2004).

33 See Lindsey Hilsum, 'Preparing for Judgement Day', *New Statesman*, 5 December 2005.

34 *The Middle East Media Research Institute*, http://memritv.org/Transcript.asp?P1=669

INDEX